# STORY MEDICINE

# STORY MEDICINE
## MULTICULTURAL TALES OF HEALING AND TRANSFORMATION

*Norma J. Livo*

2001
Libraries Unlimited
Teacher Ideas Press
A Division of Greenwood Publishing Group, Inc.
Englewood, Colorado

*To Andrea and Brooke*

Libraries Unlimited
Teacher Ideas Press
A Division of Greenwood Publishing Group, Inc.
P.O. Box 6633
Englewood, CO 80155-6633
1-800-237-6124
www.lu.com


ISBN 1-56308-894-0

# CONTENTS

## STORIES AND HEALING

# THE STORIES

# ACKNOWLEDGMENTS

I am thankful for all the healers who have given of themselves throughout history. Also, I am indebted to Barbara Ittner of Libraries Unlimited for her perceptiveness and her caring for and encouraging of this book.

# FOREWORD

Upon learning that Norma Livo intended to write a book about medicine and healers, a smile came quickly to my face. Stories, cultures, traditions, legends, and even some myths are to be found in abundance when exploring the colorful history of the healing arts. Who better to explore them than Norma!

Storytelling provides a timeless thread that tethers us to both the past and to our current experience; it enriches a legacy we will pass to the future. This is just how the profession of medicine impressed me from my first day of medical school. Every lesson was a story, a discovery passed on by earlier healers, some stories traced to antiquity. Above all, medicine, then and now, has proven to be a study in humanity, in the very nature of persons and their brethren, and inevitably a revelation of spirituality as both patient and healer grow into the inescapable realization of their own mortality. Along the way, various elements of storytelling prove just as integral to the healing arts as they are to folk arts and legend. Norma Livo recalls "healing rituals," and a day in my practice reveals many. An examination is itself something of a "story" evolving. From the prologue as a patient and I exchange pleasantries, to the introduction as I explain how to dress in one of my (always the wrong size) examination gowns, and then the flow of the story itself.

Each system examined unfolds a new chapter, as my battery of questions leads to the genuine ritual of the physical examination, often colored by anecdotes derived through the lessons of my mentors (who each had a story to tell). The completed evaluation will flow logically and coherently as a whole, yet each individual chapter holds great significance—both alone and as part of the whole. The practitioner then places this experience into a mental catalog of similar exams, similar stories, and incorporates the teachings of other storytellers. In this manner an individual patient encounter becomes a rich part of a doctor's own tradition—and a part of medical "folklore."

As a story is told, it by necessity demands listening. As healers, we must be expert listeners. We are granted a passport into people's lives, a sacred bestowal of trust that derives from the traditions of our predecessors, and, ultimately, from the Hippocratic oath. I was touched that Norma included this most important instrument of my profession in this book. For this, I offer true thanks. Not infrequently all doctors should revisit this profound document, study it slowly, and realize anew the marvelous and solemn tradition it entrusts to us.

A smile and a cure are perhaps the most gratifying reward for a healer's toils. This is what the shaman seeks, what the medic risks all for on the battlefield, what the nun and priest, during medieval times, contracted the plague trying to attain. Trudging through a snowstorm to reach a bedridden grandmother, the general practitioner in Nebraska brings hope in a "little black bag." Yes, indeed, I agree with Norma when she recognizes stories worth telling hidden in the timeless chronicles of the healing arts.

*James R. Regan, M.D.*
President of the Denver Medical Society

# A SHORT HISTORY OF MEDICINE

**I have an earache—**

| | |
|---|---|
| 2000 B.C. | Here, eat this root |
| 1000 B.C. | That root is heathen. Here, say this prayer. |
| A.D. 1850 | That prayer is superstitious. Here, drink this potion. |
| A.D. 1940 | That potion is snake oil. Here, swallow this pill. |
| A.D. 1985 | That pill is ineffective. Here, take this antibiotic. |
| A.D. 2000 | That antibiotic is artificial. Here, eat this root. |

*Anonymous*

# INTRODUCTION

## How This Book Came About

It all started in the waiting room at the doctor's office one day. I was eavesdropping on the conversations of other waiting patients. There were remarks such as, "Dr. R. is a really good doctor, he listens." "Dr. R. is a really bright young doctor." "I went to another doctor who was too brusque with me." "Dr. R. tells me the truth every time." And so it went in quiet murmurs. As I listened, I thought of all the stories these people (strangers) were telling each other.

When it was my turn to see Dr. R. I told him that he had passed the waiting room test and told him some of the remarks. He laughed and told me a story about his elder, elegant, partner. It hit me! Here was the stuff of stories and a book about stories from the doctor's little black bag. I told Dr. R. what I had just decided and again he laughed and replied, "I'd like to read that one!"

I was subsequently sent to the lab to have some blood drawn for tests. I told Dr. R.'s nurse what brainstorm I had just had, and she started to tell me stories from the nurses' perspective as blood flowed from my body into glass tubes. Later that afternoon, I was picking up my new glasses at the optical office, and the same thing happened. The fellow adjusting my glasses, after he heard my comments about "I bet you hear a lot of stories as you do your work," told me the story of a great grandfather who got a thorn in his eye. Now this was back in the old frontier days and the man was left in the care of Yaki Indians. (Unfortunately, even with their herbs and salves, the eye got infected and had to eventually be removed and replaced by a glass eye.) There were stories everywhere!

I wondered what folk stories had to say about doctors, healing, and cures. Thus I began my research into this fascinating topic.

Actually, doctors are storytellers for their patients. We expect them to tell us the stories about our particular maladies, to predict the future and to know the endings for these—the prognosis. Research in medicine is story, too. It is a working out of a universal story from particular stories. What are the stories behind the development of vaccinations? The discovery of medicines? How did they figure out what works for what ailments?

In this time of so-called insurance reform, malpractice litigation, herbal and holistic treatment, health shops, wellness centers, doctors/shamans/*curanderos*, scientific advances, and new pharmaceutical discoveries, do the old stories of medicine, healing, and cures hold meaning? References to medical interests are everywhere in the news. You'll find them in cartoons, science reports, lifestyle sections, financial and business columns, sport stories, and religions. Media entertainment has given us *Dr. Kildaire, ER, Chicago Hope* and other medical programs.

How much has medical practice (do you love the word "practice?"), and our respect and reverence for healers in various cultures, changed or stayed the same? What is important? What is lasting? These are some of the questions I hope to analyze from folk stories. Just what does a doctor keep in his little black bag?

It is not only the medical profession that heals, our stories provide us vaccinations, preventatives, and cures, conferring some degree of immunity against social, emotional, and physical pressures. How is this so?

## Purpose, Scope, and Organization

My intent is to explore folk stories and show how they can relate and contribute to the healing professions. Together we will examine how stories can be part of the doctor's little black bag.

Another purpose of the book is to provide stories as examples of healing and invite readers to see general and metaphorical similarities to their own lives and other stories. This book is designed to be used by readers and listeners of all ages. You may discover that stories have been part of your own healing, although you never recognized what was happening.

This book is divided into theme-based sections. After a brief discussion of the healing power of stories, what healing is, and how stories heal, I present stories with healing themes. These are grouped into sections on healing the self, healing relationships, healing the community, and healing the Earth. In the appendixes we explore some of the multicultural views of healing, including folk medicine and the roots of Western medicine (the Hippocratic oath and the history of the Caduceus).

I have selected stories from around the world to exemplify the different themes of the book. These tales illustrate physical, emotional, spiritual, and philosophical aspects of healing from a broad multicultural perspective.

# How to Use This Book

How can this book be used? That depends on who is using it. Certainly parents, teachers, and people in healing professions or organizations devoted to furthering the wholesome development of individuals will apply their own specific points of view. Storytellers may want to select tales to share and discuss with specific groups they work with. For example, "Iron Logic" could provide a humorous springboard to a discussion on the topic of aging. Or a more serious approach to the same topic might be taken with "Abandonment Canyon" or "The Golden Cup," in which the contributions of the elderly are clearly conveyed.

Of course, educators looking for tales to complement social studies or environmental curricula can also use this collection. Students will also find this a rich resource for term papers and school reports on subjects ranging from history to science. For instance, the legend "Constantine, Emperor of Rome" is a natural for those teaching or learning about the Roman Empire, just as "Silver Heels" and "The Legend of Hackberry Hill" fit in well with the study of westward expansion in U.S. history. Tales in the "Healing the Earth" section are appropriate for environmental studies. They can be cited in reports, used for oral presentations, or simply read as a means of piquing student interest.

Psychologists, therapists, school counselors, and clergy can share such tales as "The Ugly Duckling" to broach the topic of alienation or "The Tiger's Whisker" to demonstrate the importance of patience and understanding in getting through tough times and relationship challenges. Many of these stories also can be used effectively as tools for "character" or "values" education. Consider the tale "The Wonder Doctor," which promotes an enlightened vision of the true healer and shows the effects of greed and dishonesty.

Finally, parents will find many tales to share and discuss with their children; general readers with an interest in folklore and healing will also enjoy and learn from this collection.

With each story, I offer a brief comment based on my own impressions and interpretations of the tales. These are meant to stimulate thoughts and discussion, not to restrict the story's meaning or use in any way. As you read and enjoy, I hope you will find other meanings and applications for the tales.

Each reader and listener is unique, and each reader or listener will develop his or her own thoughts as each story is read. This book is intended as a guidepost for the long journey that is the human enterprise.

In this era, when we sorely need healing on all levels—individual, interpersonal, social, and environmental—we also have the opportunity to draw on not only the wisdom of the past, but the wisdom of other cultures and peoples. The stories and comments in this collection are here for your enjoyment, nourishment, and education. Throughout history, people from around the world have known that understanding is the first step to healing. It is my sincere hope that these stories plant the seeds of understanding in the reader and stimulate further exploration and sharing of the wisdom and healing power of stories.

# Part I

# Stories
# and
# Healing

# THE HEALING POWER OF STORIES

## Personal Stories

I became a believer in the healing powers of stories ten years ago at a storytelling conference I had organized. For two days, 350 people participated in the event, held by the University of Colorado at Denver. At the end of the conference, a sweet-faced, older woman thanked me. I asked her why she was thanking me so profusely. She replied, "I am the mother of the grocery store clerk who was killed by a robber at his store two years ago." She mentioned her son's name, and I remembered the murder.

"This conference has helped me more than anything else I have done since his death. That is why I thank you," she said. "The stories I have heard in the last two days have made me cry, laugh, and find that I am once again able to feel more than just deep depression."

If that isn't healing, what is? Stories, especially those told by a human storyteller, have the rich ability to touch people. What more can we do to heal than touch people and share our imaginations?

Another time, I had an opportunity to witness the healing power of stories within my own family. Some years ago, my brother Howard, who was two years older than I, was diagnosed with brain cancer. The medical profession could not do anything to help him. They tried several procedures, but his cancer progressed at a horrific pace. Howard's wife, Maxine, telephoned from Pennsylvania to tell me what was happening. She said they were keeping him in the hospital to document events because they really couldn't do anything for him. I flew back to Pennsylvania, and Maxine and I decided that between us we would get him back to his beloved home and farm and out of the hospital.

3

Maxine couldn't take any more time off of work because their health and medical insurance depended on her job. I went to the hospital and was directed to Howard's room. I found him sitting by a window, head on his hand, staring out. Our reunion was so touching. I told Howdy that I was going to take him home, and he cried. I went to the nurses' station and told them that I had come to take him back home. "But the doctor needs to sign off on that," I was told.

"Don't worry, I am a doctor, and I am signing him off," I told her. I proceeded to pack his things, and as we were leaving his room, a nurse came in with some releases for me to sign. I did, and we left hand-in-hand.

Back at the farm, Howard became animated. It was obvious he needed his family, his birds singing outside, and the comfort of his beloved farm.

Howard had married when he was 50, and he and Maxine became parents of a son, Daniel, the next year. Dan was now a teenager in a desperate home. It was summer, so he was out of school.

The stories started on the front porch swing. I told stories of the mischievous things we had done growing up. Howard's disease had damaged his speech, so he could only respond with facial and body movements. As I spoke, I could see that I had hit pay dirt. His spirits became livelier. He smiled and motioned for more stories. Dan was hearing family stories he never heard before. He was grinning now, too—no longer in panic and scared as he had been when we began. I told stories for a week. In the evening, Howard was able to build a bonfire in the spot where our whole family for years had held wiener roasts, told stories, and sung songs. Our four children considered these magic events. At this particular night's bonfire, Howdy indicated he wanted to hear some folk stories like we used to tell our kids around the fire. His responses on that night were so special for us all.

So the stories went for a week. Then I had to leave for Colorado, and I was aware that this might be the last time I would see my brother alive. Indeed, that was true, for very shortly after I left, he quietly died. The doctor and visiting nurse said they had never seen such a peaceful, gentle giant as Howard was at the end.

The stories had helped Howdy, me, Maxine, and Dan. Through our stories, Dan had heard so many different sides of his father that he had never known. I am convinced it was these stories and Howard's being home with his family that were the best medicine at this point of his life.

Storytelling has power. When you tell a story, the listener becomes an active part of the telling. Stories connect people. Storytelling transforms and transmits information to the listener and validates the teller's truth. It transcends time and orders events to make existence more sensible and meaningful. Storytelling brings a higher level of comprehensibility to the things we know and are learning. One of the most important aspects of storytelling is the sharing of imagination—not only that of the storyteller but also anyone who is listening.

Albert Einstein said, "Imagination is more important than knowledge." He was, of course, right. The word *imagination* is related to *mage* (which means magician or wise man), magic, image. It is a special ability to see reality, fantasy, and possibilities. Stories help us to develop and share our imaginations. From my personal experience I know how effective stories and storytelling are to sharing, transforming, and making existence more meaningful. Today storytelling is being used in senior centers, with troubled youths, and in addiction programs. Therapists and psychologists have used storytelling as paths to wholeness for decades.

There is one more story I'd like to share to demonstrate the healing power of story. It is a personal story of how an experience combined with story helped me more than anything the medical profession had done up to then.

I had read and heard many stories related to blindness and accepted them easily. My favorite such story is "Jumping Mouse" found in *Seven Arrows* by Hyemeyohsts Storm (Ballantine, 1972), which is a story of the Plains Indian people.

In 1986 I woke one morning to horror—I was blind in my right eye! Absolutely and totally blind. Of course, I went to the doctor, who told me that I had a central retinal vein occlusion; the vein had burst and covered my retina with blood. (Subsequently, I received 2,000 laser shots to seal off the bleeding—it was that or physically lose the eye.)

The glorious fall weather was inviting to me after the initial blindness. I decided to take my Jeep and spend a day in the Colorado mountains. I had two purposes: I wanted to see how one-eyed driving went, and I wanted to take some photographs. Photography had been a pleasurable hobby of mine, and I was concerned because I had always used my right eye to focus my 35-millimeter camera. I realized I had several new habits to develop that my new vision limitations dictated.

I successfully (and with some growing confidence) drove up to the mountains. I took the steep, narrow shelf road to our cabin, a challenge even with both eyes working. After opening the cabin, I hiked up the road with my camera. The following story is an article I wrote about my amazing experience with nature and blindness. Aesop could have added to it with another fable, I am sure.

# Getting Ready for Winter*

Harvest time is coming and the animals of the wild prepare carefully. The squirrels collect pinecones and other available goodies. The stellar jays raucously demand the crumbs and peanuts we place on the boulder outside our mountain cabin. We sit on the deck and watch them gather the treats and stash them away. The jays glide in, pick up their good gifts, and wing away to the trees by a nearby stream. They deposit their loot in the crotch of branches or under the tree bark and swoop back for more.

Late fall trips to Mount Evans find the mountain goats shedding their old coats for new winter ones. Their shaggy covering resembles that of some bag lady from downtown Denver.

The aspen trees get their leaves ready for their glorious seasonal binge of color and light. The leaves start turning nearest the trunk, and then the change spreads out to the tips of the branches. The golden offerings dance in the crisp breeze and are enriched by the deep blue of the sky. In these resplendent forests the elk bugle announces the coming of winter. They are advertising their territory, and their calls are another signal for us humans of the passing of the seasons.

Up above the 9,000-foot level, the marmots, or whistle pigs, are taking their last sunbaths of the season. When approached, they whistle a shrill warning to each other.

If you observe and are patient, many of these mountain creatures can be caught in the act of preparing for winter. During a recent October, I was treated to the food-gathering actions of a new, to me, small critter. I was hiking in the woods above Eldora, crunching leaves underfoot and absorbing the peace. I spied movement near a large boulder and went over to check it out. Hiding on the other side of the rock was a reddish brown weasel. He peeked out at me and then quickly ducked back. We skirmished around the rock and then he dashed up the hill. I hung around the rock and was pleased to see him returning down the hillside with a large vole (a small tailless rodent that averages from four to six inches in length) in his mouth. When he again noticed me, he dropped his banquet and disappeared farther downhill. Now I had him. I had his vole, so I waited. Sure enough, he scampered back up to me but surprised me by continuing past me and the dropped vole. When I saw him again, he was heading downhill with a second vole in his mouth.

He returned shortly and headed up the hill again. And then raced down with yet a third vole. I was beginning to wonder how many voles he had stashed away. I felt certain that he would eventually be back for the vole I was guarding. Sure enough, this time he edged near to the rock and the abandoned vole. He stopped, stared at me with his pussycat face and prepared to battle this monster for the vole. He jumped behind the vole, and assumed an attack stance. When no attack came from me, he grabbed our vole and tore off with it.

Maybe somewhere this winter, up above 9,000 feet and under the snow, the weasel has again filled his larder and is surviving the winter by crunching on delicious vole bones and flesh. I'll also rationalize the fact that there are at least three voles that won't have to worry about where their food is coming from.

> ∾ "Getting Ready for Winter" by Norma J. Livo. *Colorado Outdoors.* September/October, 1987, 23.

---

*This article makes no mention of my blindness and the need for this trip. However, this incident was an absolute gift to me. I shot pictures of the various events with the weasel and our vole. Awkwardly using my left eye to focus, I fumbled, but I shot pictures.

Yes, the pictures turned out less than sharp, but the weasel was distinguishable. I had these images blown up to twelve-by-sixteen inches and framed. This day, this trip, and this event gave me more therapy and courage than I could ever have dreamed of. I knew life would go on—it would not be perfect, but exciting surprises waited around every corner and rock. Aesop would have liked that!

Since the story was symbolic for me in my new blindness, isn't it a coincidence that my weasel was stashing away voles? Voles have notoriously bad eyesight because they live underground! Experiencing the event and writing about it were definitely therapeutic for me.

My own experiences have shown me the healing power of story—of sharing stories. Perhaps you have similar stories of your own. I hope this work encourages you to share those stories and the story medicine of others, for in the words of a wonderful author and storyteller,

> The stories people tell have a way of taking care of them. If stories come to you, care for them. And learn to give them away where needed. Sometimes a person needs a story more than food to stay alive. That is why we put these stories in each other's memories. That is how people care for themselves.
>
> —*Barry Lopez*

# WHAT IS HEALING?

**I**n the tradition of folklore, healing is usually seen as a transformation or making whole. Think of all the folk stories you have heard that involve transformations. The ugly duckling becomes a swan and the fool becomes the hero in a variety of ways in diverse stories from around the world.

Health and healing are also natural subject matter in religious stories. In Holy Scriptures, healing by the laying on of hands, for example, creates miracles such as the raising of Lazarus from the dead. In every religious and cultural tradition there are many healing rituals and practices.

For Westerners, these healing rituals may be medicines, doctors, hospitals, clinics, and research. But religions from other cultures use music, chanting, herbs, spices, unguents, and aromatics as well.

Today, our medical professionals use puppets, tours, and make-believe to educate children before a hospital stay. We refer to doctors in the operating "theater" and its spectacular setting; their activities therein can be compared to shamans and their special rituals.

Folklore also shares the healing traditions and medical lore from our past, including herbal cures, food, leeches, and wine. For example, in "The Cure for Ax Wounds in the Knee," we learn that tar was used to treat lesions. Some of the natural and folk remedies we find in stories are being used again today as alternatives to Western medicine's sometimes harsh and invasive procedures.

Storytelling is the oldest and still the best teacher. It has healing and therapeutic powers too seldom recognized in today's sophisticated society. According to Clarissa Pinkola Estes (*Women Who Run with the Wolves*), "Stories that instruct, renew, and heal provide a vital nourishment to the psyche that cannot be obtained in any other way. Stories reveal over and over again the precious and peculiar knack that humans have for triumph over travail. They provide all the vital instructions we need to live a useful, necessary, and unbounded life—a life of meaning, a life worth remembering."

Recently storytellers have been asked to participate in corporate stress management seminars and to tell stories in nursing homes and at seniors' centers. The therapeutic value of stories also is beginning to be recognized as a valuable tool in helping both children and adults deal with illness.

## The Healing Traditions of the Past

Where can we find references to healing in stories? Nearly everywhere. Consider some of our popular nursery rhymes.

## Ring Around the Roses

Ring around the roses,
A pocket full of posies;
A-tishoo! A-tishoo!
We all fall down.

Many scholars explain the old nursery game of Ring around the Roses as a reference to the Great Plague. These scholars say that roses (rosy) refers to the rash of the plague, the posies were herbs and spices carried to sweeten the air, and "a-tishoo" represents the sneezing that was a common symptom of the plague. Of course, "we all fall down" signified the death of the person with the plague. Interesting as this theory is, dates of when this rhyme was first published and the time of great plagues do not correspond. Regardless, would-be origin finders still put forth this theory, which appears in scholarly articles.

Mother Goose rhymes also include references to health, safety, and healing. Among them is Jack and Jill, with its clever use of folk medicine.

## Jack and Jill

Jack and Jill
Went up the hill,
To fetch a pail of water;
Jack fell down
And broke his crown,
And Jill came tumbling after.

Up Jack got, and home did trot,
As fast as he could caper,
To old Dame Dob,
Who patched his nob,
With vinegar and brown paper.
When Jill came in, how she did grin,
To see Jack's paper plaster;
Dame Dob, vexed, did whip her next
For causing Jack's disaster.

Astringent vinegar was known for its cleansing power and was used widely by the folk. Another cure common in past times is curiously making a comeback today—leeches.

## Leeches

If there's anything in the world I hate, it's leeches.
The filthy little devils!

*Humphrey Bogart's character,
Charlie Alnutt, in* The African Queen

Most people fear leeches with righteous revulsion. Maybe they have heard stories of giant leeches that enter a sleeping person's nose where, feeding on blood, it becomes so fat that it can't get out again and suffocates its victim!

But in medical folklore, other stories of leeches abound. Hippocrates dominates modern accounts of Greek medicine, but that good doctor shared the stage in antiquity with Asclepius, who was elevated to the status of a god. The cult of Asclepius spread throughout the Greek world and established itself in Rome. Temples to Asclepius were places for hopeful pilgrimages and miraculous cures. One of the cures attributed to Asclepius was of a man who claimed to have swallowed leeches. Asclepius cut the patient open and removed the infestation and stitched up the incision. Leeches go back even further—to Egyptian medicine. There is a painting on an Egyptian tomb wall from the Eighteenth Dynasty (1567–1308 B.C.), which depicts the use of medicinal leeches.

Reprinted with special permission of North American Syndicate.

Early doctors were called leeches from an old English word meaning to heal. By the late eighteenth century, the word *leech* began to acquire a darker meaning, referring to unpleasant people who "drain others dry" by their clinging and acquisitive behavior. People doing this are said "to stick to someone like a leech."

Today leeches are standard treatment in microsurgery. When a vein clogs in reattachment surgery, blood backs up and causes the body part to swell and turn blue. To solve this problem, the medical staff may apply leeches. The insects' saliva numbs the patient's skin, widens the veins, and ensures the blood won't clot again for several hours. Once the leeches are bloated from gorging themselves on blood, they drop off the patient.

The following true story shows how effective this folk medicine can be.

## Leech to the Rescue

A freckled face, seven year old boy named Jim was playing with his best friend while visiting his house. As boys will do, they were roughhousing, wrestling, thumbing, and bumping. The friend's large dog was joining them in their rambunctious action.

"Let's push your dog upstairs," Jim said and started trying to push the dog. The dog turned around, and its flashing teeth bit the youngster and almost tore Jim's ear off.

The boy was transported to a hospital with sirens and flashing lights to have his ear reattached. The team of surgeons reattached his ear, but within twelve hours they were apprehensive. The ear was turning blue and swelling. That meant the red blood bringing oxygen to the ear couldn't do its job. The oxygen-spent blue blood wasn't draining and the wound was clogged.

The doctors telephoned Leeches U.S.A. in New York and asked for a rush delivery of fourteen sterile leeches. They needed only six. The doctor made tiny incisions in Jim's ear and brought the leeches mouths to the cuts. The four-inch-long squirmers sucked the blood for forty-five minutes before getting their fill and falling off. The nurse placed the leeches in a jar of alcohol.

After the leeches fell off Jim's ear, the ear continued to drain for eighteen more hours. When told about what the doctors had done, young Jim said the "leeches didn't scare me."

After returning home, Jim's ear healed perfectly. Friends and family in his small town lovingly call Jim "the leech."

In addition to tapping into the animal world, the ancients also used their plants for healing, and many of these healing herbs took on legendary proportions. Take, for example, the South American plant, Mate.

Mate, or erva mate (pronounced AIR-vah MAH-chee), is a bitter concoction brewed from tree leaves and sprigs. Some say it looks like finely milled grass clippings with a sprig or two dropped in. The shoots and leaves are from a tree named *Ilex paraguariensis*, which is a relative of holly. In Brazil, devotees say it can cure baldness, ward off obesity and pimples, as well as add years to one's life. Extremely popular with millions across the southern cone of South America, mate is an important herb to both Indian and Spanish colonial people.

## Legends of Mate (South America)

The Guarani Indians imbibed mate long before European explorers arrived at the Paraguayan and Brazilian panhandle in the sixteenth century. The herb was one of their great gifts to the settlers. There are three Indian legends that explain the origin of the bitter green brew.

The first legend has it that Tupa (pronounced Too-PAH), a Guarani spirit of goodness, was on a journey across the Earth when he arrived at the adobe of a very poor, solitary old man.

The old man did not know who Tupa was, but he gave him food and drink and allowed the spirit to stay the night in his hut. To thank the old man, Tupa left him the magical herb to cure him in times of illness.

According to the second legend, Yasi, the moon spirit, and Arai (pronounced a-rah-EEE), the cloud spirit, were in a forest when a jaguar attacked them. A hunter appeared and chased off the giant cat, and for his efforts, the gods rewarded him with mate to protect him from evil.

In the third legend, an old man welcomed two lost spirits to stay at his meager hut. As a sign of gratitude, the spirits transformed the old man's daughter into a mate tree, so that she would be immortal.

Alcoholic beverages, too, were put to good use by the folk. This tale demonstrates the positive attributes of wine.

# Wine As Doctor (Germany)

For more than five hundred years the wine of Bernkastel was called Doctor. In the middle of the four-teenth century, Bishop Bohemund lay ill of a very violent fever at Bernkastel. He had to swallow many bitter pills and many sour drinks, but none of them had any effect on his fever. The bishop began to fear the worst.

He ordered a proclamation throughout the length and breadth of his diocese: Whoever should cure him of his terrible fever would receive his highest blessing and a rich reward as well.

A brave old warrior who lived at Treves heard about the suffering of the bishop and took pity on him in his hour of need. Many years before, Bohemund, who was then a general, had saved the gray-haired champion from the hands of the enemy in a battle near Sponheim. Therefore, the noble old soldier was quite distressed to hear that the holy man was now suffering so intensely. He also remem-bered that he once had been attacked by violent fever and had himself fought hard against death. His friends had offered him pills and bitter drinks, but he sent them all away. He called his servant and asked him to bring him a good bowl of fiery Bernkastler wine.

When the soldier had taken a hearty drink, which was no small matter for a knight so ill with fever, he slept a deep sleep for twelve hours. When he awoke, the fever had completely disappeared. "Maybe this same Bernkastler cure might have effect on the leader of the church," the old warrior mused. He considered this for a short time and then set out from his castle in the forest of Soon to visit the bishop. He took only a little cask with him on his trip.

Bohemund the bishop was lying on his sick bed when the warrior arrived. The churchman gave him a very suspicious look when the warrior stated he could cure him. "What is your remedy?" the bishop asked. "All I see is that you have a little cask on your shoulder. Are all of your medicines and mixtures in that cask?"

The knight made a signal to the servants and attendants to leave the room. He then told the bishop what he was about to do. With a cool hand, he took the plug out of the cask and gave the sick man a drink of sparkling wine.

The bishop swallowed the wine willingly in one long swig. Then another was administered to him. Soon the prelate fell into a deep sleep.

The next day the people of Treves heard with great joy that the clergyman's fever was gone.

When he awoke from his long sleep the bishop took another stout draught and sang out from the depths of his grateful heart, "This wine, this wine restored my health. This is a marvelous Doctor."

As you can see, every part of our ancestors' world was used for healing—plants, animals, food, drink, and more. Perhaps that is why so many of the old cultures value the natural world and have developed traditions to honor and protect resources. But beyond folk remedies, stories have also traditionally helped with mental, emotional, and spiritual healing. Let's turn to the topic of how stories heal to explore this amazing story medicine.

# HOW STORIES HEAL

**S**tories make us laugh and cry; they teach us the power of honesty, generosity, hard work, and keeping one's word; they show the value of trust, generosity, and obedience to and respect for the wise ones; and they also teach us about the power of imagination. They show us the way to happy endings and sometimes the way to not-so-happy endings. Stories teach us what behaviors will be rewarded and what behaviors will be punished. In stories all the layers of the individual—including relationships with others, with the community, as well as with the natural world—relate to each other.

## Stories As Connectors

First and foremost, stories provide a way for people to connect with others. They allow the storyteller to speak the truth and to be heard. And they allow the listener to learn from the experience of another person. This sharing builds bridges between people. Stories are not unlike the dancing rituals of the Kung people of the Kalahari Desert. The Kung credit healing through their dance with sharing, reaffirming the group's spiritual cohesion, managing the release of hostility, and enhancing consciousness. These are all components of healing through narrative as well.

At a recent gathering of The Mountain and Plains Chapter of the American Horticulture Therapy Association, participants shared their beliefs that gardening possesses healing powers. They refer to ancient prescriptions for healing by Egyptians in which the remedy was to walk in gardens to soothe nerves.

One therapist developed a program that involves diabetic patients in growing vegetables and learning more about their illness and healthier diets. This is a story of healing through reflection and doing!

## Humor As a Preventative and Cure

Many stories also heal by helping us laugh. Health professionals have begun to accept the value of mirth as a vital force in care and recovery. Clowns, humor carts, funny books and videos, and humor rooms are available in hospitals for the patients.

Members of the American Association for Therapeutic Humor believe that humor changes our emotional state, our perspective on life, and, through laughter, our physiological state. That is not new information; a passage in the Judeo-Christian Bible says, "A merry heart doeth good like a medicine." Witness the lists of jokes available on the Internet. People are seeking, reading, and transmitting humor daily.

Thirty years ago writer Norman Cousins published *Anatomy of an Illness,* in which he tells how he fought intense pain and beat a deadly disease by getting himself discharged from the hospital and checked into a hotel room. There he deliberately dosed himself with humorous books and reruns of *Candid Camera.* This was the beginning of the medical profession looking at humor and disease and how humor aids in recovery. Patch Adams, a Virginia doctor who defied medical "gravity" for three decades by making patients laugh, was recently the subject of a popular movie starring Robin Williams.

Some doctors suggest that mirthful laughter does provide physical therapy. Among the benefits are providing exercise by increasing the heart rate, stimulating blood circulation and breathing, and improving muscle tone. (Laurel and Hardy movies are excellent material for this.) It is calculated that one hundred laughs equal ten minutes of working on a rowing machine. Norman Cousins refers to laughter as "inner jogging." Several studies show that laughing lessens the need for medication and shortens recuperation time. It reduces pain, probably by firing the release of endorphins, the body's natural painkillers.

Humor also serves to reduce stress by lowering levels of cortisol, a stress hormone that can weaken the immune system; laughing also stimulates the immune system. Some researchers found significant increases of interferon-gamma, a hormone that fights viruses and regulates cell growth, in a group of healthy men while they watched a humorous sixty-minute video. Those levels remained higher than normal twelve hours later.

Applying humor also stimulates mental functions such as alertness and memory. This is perhaps due to raising levels of adrenaline and other chemicals that prepare the body for action. One study recorded a wave of electricity sweeping through the entire brain half a second after the punch line of a joke.

Clinical applications of humor have also grown in recent years. Judy Goldblum, a humor therapist and staff member of the University of Maryland Medical Center, works with children hospitalized for cancer. She believes that once children can make fun of what they are most afraid of, they feel more in control.

Such therapists believe that physicians treat what is wrong with patients and they, as therapists, treat what is right. Doctors who use humor soon discover that it also builds a closer relationship with their patients.

Clifford Kuhn, M.D., clinical professor of psychiatry at the University of Louisville School of Medicine in Kentucky, believes that as we sharpen our capacity for laughter and use it, it can serve as a preventive medicine. This serves as a reservoir on which to draw in times of crisis. He states, "a sense of humor just happens to be one of the most powerful healing resources. It is a gold mine."

Brian Crane has dealt with this topic in a *Pickles* cartoon in which a man and woman—grandparent-type folks—are sitting in rocking chairs. As the man reads, he tells his wife, "According to this, laughter has been proven to be good for your health." He then continues, "I guess we should try to laugh more often." His wife, with folded hands in her lap asks, "About what?" to which he replies "I don't know." Then the wife has an idea. She says, "Why don't you go put on those plaid Bermuda shorts of yours?" Two other strips on the subject are featured on page 20.

One of the three *Hägar the Horrible* comics featured on page 21 shows Hägar seeking a cure from a wise man who tells Hägar to "Go and stand in the moonlight and turn around three times and say, 'Malady begone' while holding this magic weed in your hand."

The next panel has Hägar on the path home, holding a twig, saying, "And to think, for years I've wasted my time going to quacks!"

Humor can be invented or real concerning visits to the doctor.

Norm Clarke, in his *Rocky Mountain News* column, ran an item marked, "The Punch Line." True story: A local socialite went to her OB/GYN for her annual checkup and told the doctor, "While I'm here, maybe I should have a prostate exam, too."

© 2000, The Washington Post Writers Group. Reprinted with permission.

**Reprinted with special permission of North American Syndicate.**

# Healing the Spirit, the Family, and Society

The values presented in stories have come down to us from ancient times. Stories have always provided models of behavior that show what to do and what not to do. We see what behaviors will be rewarded or punished. The Grimm brothers initially began their collection of folk stories as materials they intended to analyze to develop a code of German law. Today, we hear a loud call for values education and character education. Stories can help.

The power of family is everywhere in stories. Some historians say that no culture survives without family at the center of society. Folktales demonstrate the rights and wrongs within families. Respect for the elders, being good parents, developing trust, nurturing the children, and positive sibling relationships are essential parts of family experience in folktales. Sharing with family is shown to be a solution to problems.

Stories such as "The Tiger's Whisker" teach us the value of patience and caring between husband and wife, while resourcefulness and family loyalty are seen in "The Lute Player."

Stories also teach us the value of community, the importance of sharing, and the rewards of kindness to strangers. We can clearly see the effect of our actions on the entire community in such tales as "Story of the Owl" in which a practical joke ends in loss of life.

# Aging and Death

In stories aging and death are natural. Folktales endorse respect for elders as evidenced in such stories "Grandfather's Corner," "Abandonment Canyon," and "The Golden Cup."

These three stories establish the theme that with age comes power and understanding. As we live, we experience more and are able to solve problems through wisdom rather than through the strength of the youth.

Of course, along with aging comes the subsequent fact of death. Many cultures honor death in their sayings such as, "No one is dead until people stop saying their name." The concept of death as a natural part of life can be found in stories and proverbs around the world—from Japan to Africa. Scientists have said, "We are all getting closer to death from the moment we are born," meaning that every life is on its own timetable and schedule to die. Stories show us how to use the time as we age for a richer life.

Readers interested in learning more about how stories can be used as a resource for healing children, celebrating our Earth, or learning from other cultures are encouraged to use resources by the authors listed in the bibliography at the end of this book.

## Process of Healing Through Narrative

Finally, by demonstrating how life unfolds, how one thing leads to another, how the child grows to be an adult, stories give us the blueprint for transformation and for becoming whole.

The balance of this book covers some of the themes of healing in stories—cures, diseases, and the healers themselves. Many cures hearken back to the earth (healing waters, herbs, food, and potions). Sometimes they also invoke the magic of words and understanding the knowledge of the wounds and resulting in the appropriate cure. Some stories (e.g., "The Cure for Axe Wounds") refer to healing practices of times past.

As you read through the following stories, you may find some of them that speak to you directly. One caution, though: Stories are not bandages applied as emergency cures for wounds. The use of story in healing is a much more subtle and thoughtful procedure. Happy reading.

# Part II

# The Stories

# HEALING THE SELF

**S**tories from the folk, folklore, pass on many themes of healing the self. The search for meaning is universal. Stories deal with universals and help us see how we are connected to the past and to each other. Stories teach us the importance of self-respect, and they show us the path of human development from child to sage.

Included in this section are stories of fools or "noodleheads" who are either totally foolish or who eventually succeed in their lives. We also have hero stories in which the hero or heroine has a problem, must leave home on a journey to solve it, and returns home transformed. These are stories of the universal event—coming of age. Other stories explore loss of the senses (such as sight or hearing), loss of body parts, overcoming hunger, and the miracle of coming back to life.

Illness in folklore reflects past beliefs and health conditions, and, in addition, may take on symbolic proportion.

For example, blindness has often been the result of physical and public health conditions. There is a deep fear, and the attendant stigma, of blindness. In Egypt, children often curse each other by saying, "I hope God makes you blind!" Blind people are sometimes seen as being worthless, weak, unkind, passive, dirty, and slow. For eons, blindness has been viewed as a form of punishment. In stories blindness is often used as a symbol of ignorance. Loss of hands may symbolize passivity or inability to act. Also, in some tales characters are paralyzed—"turned to stone" or changed to animal forms.

The Judeo-Christian Bible says, "And if any mischief follow then thou shalt give life for life, eye for eye, tooth for tooth, hand for hand, burning for burning, wound for wound, stripe for stripe. And if a man smite the eye of his servant, or the eye of his maid, that it perish; he shall let him go free for his eye's sake."

27

Even today blindness as punishment is still a threat. A child caught reading in bed under the blankets with a flashlight, might be threatened, "You'll go blind." There are numerous negative connotations concerning blindness, and stories can help counter these fears with a less-threatening aspect.

Stories instill values—self-esteem, honesty, responsibility, accountability—and many tales show the characters coping with such character flaws as pride and dishonesty. Overcoming depression has been a challenge of the human condition ever since the world began, and we find many stories about maidens and kings who do not smile or laugh. There are also many scenes of great feasts that were probably directed to folks who were hungry throughout their lives. Stories show us how the weak and disadvantaged, such as orphans or poor folk, achieve success through wisdom.

Let's explore stories that contain some of the universals of healing the self in body, mind, and spirit.

Humor is the antidote for sadness in
this tale—and the key to love.

## The Princess Who Would Not Laugh
(Norway)

Once upon a time there was a king, who had a
daughter, and she was so lovely that the reports of her
beauty went far and wide; but she was also so melancholy
that she never smiled or laughed. Besides she was so grand
and proud that she said, "No" to all who came to woo her.
She would not have any of them, were they ever so fine,
whether they were princes or noblemen.

The king grew tired of her attitude and decided his
daughter ought to get married like other people. There was
nothing she needed to wait for—she was old enough and she
would not be any richer either, for she was to have half the
kingdom, which she would inherit after her mother's demise.

So the king made known every Sunday after the
service, from the steps outside the church, that he who could
make his daughter laugh should have both her and half the
kingdom. But if there was anyone who tried and could not
make her laugh, he would have three red stripes cut out of
his back and salt rubbed into them. It is very sad to relate
that there were many sore backs in that kingdom.

Would-be lovers from south and from north, from
east and from west, came to try their luck—they thought it
was an easy thing to make a princess laugh. One man jug-
gled, and another made strange faces. Yet another told jokes
and funny stories. They were a queer lot altogether, but for
all their cleverness and for all the tricks and pranks they
played, the princess was as serious and immovable as ever.

Now close to the palace lived a man who had three sons,
and they eventually heard about the king's proclamation—
he who could make the princess laugh should have her and
half the kingdom.

The eldest of the brothers wanted to try first, and
away he went. When he came to the palace, he told the king
he wanted to try and make the princess laugh.

"Yes, yes! That's all very well," said the king, "but I am afraid it's of very little use, my man. There have been many here to try their luck, but my daughter is just as sad as ever. It's no good trying. I do not want to see any more suffer on my daughter's account."

But the lad decided he would try anyway. It couldn't be such a difficult thing to make a princess laugh at him. Had not everybody, both grand and simple, laughed so many times at him when he served as soldier and went through his drill under Sergeant Nils?

So he went out on the terrace outside the princess's windows and began drilling just as if Sergeant Nils himself were there. Oh, but it was all in vain! The princess sat as serious and immovable as before. So the king's men took him out and cut three broad, red stripes out of his back and sent him home.

The oldest son had no sooner arrived home than his younger brother wanted to set out and try his luck. The second son was a schoolmaster, and an altogether funny figure he was. He had one leg shorter than the other and limped terribly when he walked. One moment he was no bigger than a boy, but the next moment, when he raised himself up on his long leg, he was as big and tall as a giant. Besides all that, he was great at preaching.

When he came to the palace and said that he wanted to make the princess laugh, the king thought it not so unlikely that he might. "But I pity you if you don't succeed," said the king, "for we cut the stripes broader and broader for every one that tries."

The schoolmaster went out on the terrace and took his place outside the princess's window. He began preaching and chanting, imitating seven of the parsons, and at the same time he was reading and singing just like seven of the clerks whom they had had in the parish.

The king laughed at the schoolmaster till he was obliged to hold on to the doorpost, and the princess was just on the point of smiling. But suddenly she was as sad and immovable as ever. So, it fared no better with Paul the schoolmaster than with Peter the soldier—for Peter and Paul were their names, you must know!

The king's men took Paul and cut three red stripes out of his back, put salt into them, and sent him home.

Well, the youngest brother, John, thought he would have a try next. John's older brothers laughed and made fun of him and showed him their sore backs. Besides, the father would not let him go—he said it was no use his trying. "You have so little sense," the father told John. "All you can do is sit in a corner on the hearth like a cat, rooting about in the ashes and cutting chips." But John would not give in. He begged, he prayed, he begged some more, then he prayed even more until they got sick and tired of his whimpering. Finally his father granted him leave to go to the king's palace and try his luck.

When he arrived at the palace, John did not say he had come to try to make the princess laugh, but asked if he could get a job there. No, they had no work for him. John was not so easily put off. "You might want someone to carry wood and water for the kitchen maid in such a big palace as that," he said. Yes, the king finally agreed. To get rid of the lad, he gave him permission to remain there and carry wood and water for the kitchen maid.

One day when he was going to fetch water from the brook John saw a big fish in the water just under an old root of a fir tree from which the current had carried all the soil away. He put his bucket quietly under the fish and caught it. As he was going home to the palace, he met an old woman leading a golden goose.

"Good day, grandmother!" said John. "That is a fine bird you have there. It has such splendid feathers, too! I could see him shining from a long way off. If one had such feathers, one needn't be chopping firewood."

The woman thought just as much of the fish that John had in the bucket and said, "If you give me the fish you may have the golden goose. But let me warn you that this goose is such that if any one touches it, he will stick fast to it. You only need to say, 'If you'll come along, then hang on.'"

Yes, John would willingly exchange on those terms. "A bird is as good as a fish any day," he said to himself. "If it is as you say, I might use it instead of a fish hook." he told the woman. He was greatly pleased with owning the goose.

John had not gone far before he met another old woman. When she saw the splendid golden goose, she just had to go up to it and stroke it. She made herself so friendly and spoke so nicely to John. "May I stroke that lovely golden goose of yours?" she asked.

"Oh, yes!" said John, "but you must not pluck off any of its feathers!"

Just as she stroked the bird, John said, "If you'll come along, then hang on!"

The woman pulled and tore, but she had to hang on whether she liked it or not. John walked on as if he only had the goose with him.

When he had gone some distance, he met a man who had a spite against the woman for a trick she had played upon him. When he saw that she fought so hard to get free and seemed to hang on so fast, he thought he might safely venture to pay her off for the grudge he owed her. He gave the woman a kick!

"If you'll come along, then hang on!" said John, and the man was stuck. He had to limp along on one leg whether he liked it or not. When he tried to tear himself loose, he made it still worse for himself for he was very nearly falling on his back whenever he struggled to get free.

So on they went until they came in the neighborhood of the palace. There they met the king's smith. He was on his way to the smithy and had a large pair of tongs in his hand. This smith was a merry fellow and was always full of mad pranks and tricks. When he saw this procession coming jumping and limping along, he began laughing till he was bent in two. Suddenly he said, "This must be a new flock of geese for the princess. Who can tell which is goose and which is gander? I suppose it must be the gander toddling on in front. Goosey, goosey!" he called and pretended to be strewing corn out of his hands as when feeding geese.

But the procession did not stop. The woman and the man only glared furiously at the smith for making fun of them. The smith said, "It would be great fun to see if I could stop the whole flock, many as they are!" Now, he was a very strong man and he seized the old man with his tongs from behind in his trousers.

The man shouted and struggled hard, but John said, "If you'll come along, then hang on!"

With that, the smith was stuck, too. He bent his back and stuck his heels in the ground when they went up a hill and tried to get away but it was of no use. He hung on to the others as if he had been screwed fast in the great vise in the smithy. Whether he liked or not, he had to dance along with the others.

When the group came near the palace, the farm dog ran against them and barked at them as if they were a gang of tramps. The princess came to look out of her window to see that was the matter and saw the strange procession. She burst out laughing. John was not satisfied with that. "Just wait a bit. She will laugh still louder very soon," he said and made a tour around the palace with his followers.

When they came past the kitchen, the door was open and the cook was just boiling porridge. When she saw John and his train after him, she rushed out the door with the porridge spoon in one hand and a big ladle full of boiling porridge in the other. She laughed till her sides shook. When she saw the smith there as well, she thought she could have burst with laughter. After she had had a regular good laugh, she looked at the golden goose again and thought it was so lovely that she must stroke it.

"John, John!" she cried and ran after him with the ladle in her hand. "Just let me stroke that lovely bird of yours."

"Rather let her stroke me!" said the smith.

"Very well," said John.

But when the cook heard this, she got very angry. "What is it you say?" she cried. As she said this, she gave the smith a smack with the ladle.

"If you'll come along, then hang on!" said John and so she stuck fast to the others too. For all her scolding and all her tearing and pulling, she had to limp along with all the others.

The group stumbled past the princess's window again, and she was still there waiting for them. When she saw that they had got hold of the cook too, with the ladle and porridge spoon, she laughed till the king had to hold her up.

So, that's how John got the princess and half of the kingdom. They had a wedding that was heard of far and wide. Even his arrogant older brothers, who had once treated John with such disrespect, came to the wedding!

Our mistaken view of old age as a sickness is exposed in this humorous eye-opener.

## Iron Logic
### (Traditional Jewish Folktale)

An old Jewish woman, just turned ninety, became ill and called the doctor. He examined her carefully and looked doubtful.

"Can you cure me, doctor?" the old woman asked, hopefully.

"Dear Granny," said the doctor, soothingly, "you know what happens when one gets older. All sorts of ailments begin to happen. After all, a doctor is not a miracle man. He cannot make an old woman younger."

"Who's asking you to make me younger, doctor?" protested the old woman irritably. "What I want is to grow older!"

From *Gray Heroes: Elder Tales from Around the World*, edited by Jane Yolen (Penguin Books, 1999). This story originally appeared in *Treasury of Jewish Folklore* by Nathan Ausubell, published in 1948.

"I'm going to examine your eyes, ears, nose and throat, plus your blood pressure, breathing and reflexes, all for the amazingly low price of $75—a $225 value if purchased separately."

Reprinted with permission from *Parade Magazine* (April 4, 1999, p. 8).

A rascal of a doctor claims to have healed an old woman's malady, but she cleverly proves that she is not cured at all. Sometimes true healing lies in speaking the truth.

## The Old Woman and the Physician
## (Greece)

An old woman, who had become blind, called in a physician and promised him, before witnesses, that if he would restore her eyesight, she would give him a most handsome reward, but that if he did not cure her, and her malady remained, he would receive nothing. The agreement being concluded, the physician tampered from time to time with the old lady's eyes, and meanwhile, bit by bit, carried off all of her worldly belongings.

After a time he set about the task in earnest and cured her and thereupon asked for the stipulated fee. But the old woman, on recovering her sight, saw none of her belongings left in the house.

When the physician importuned her for payment, she continually put him off with excuses. Finally, he summoned her before the judges. Being now called upon for her defense, she said, "What this man says is true enough; I promised to give him his fee if my sight were restored, and nothing if my eyes continued bad. Now he says that I am cured; but I say just the contrary. When my malady first came on, I could see all sorts of furniture and goods in my house; but now, when he says he has restored my sight, I cannot see one jot of either."

As people of ancient times have warned, be careful what you wish for—your wish might come true. In this tall tale an unlikely hero beats the devil.

## The Greedy Youngster
## (Norway)

Once upon a time, a long, long time ago, when mice ran after cats and lions were chased by rats, there were five women who were in a field reaping corn. None of them had any children, but they were all wishing for a child. All at once they found a big goose egg, almost as big as a man's head.

"I saw it first," said one.

"I saw it just as soon as you did," shouted another.

"But I'll have it," screamed the third. "I saw it first of all."

They just kept on quarreling and fighting about the egg and they were very near tearing each other's hair out by the roots. At last they agreed that it should belong to them all and that they should sit on it as the geese do and hatch a gosling.

The first woman sat on it for eight days, taking it very comfortably and doing nothing at all while the others had to work hard both for their own and her living. One of the women began to make some sniping remarks to her about this.

"Well, I suppose you didn't come out of the egg either before you could chirp," said the woman who was on the egg. "But I think there is something in this egg, for I think I can hear someone inside grumbling every other moment, 'Herring and soup! Porridge and milk!' You can come and sit for eight days now and then we will sit and work in turn, all of us."

So when the fifth in turn had sat for eight days, she plainly heard someone inside the egg screeching for "Herring and soup! Porridge and milk!" And so she made a hole in it. Instead of a gosling out came a baby, but it was awfully ugly. It had a big head and a tiny little body. The first thing it screamed out as soon as it put its head outside the egg was "Herring and soup! Porridge and milk!" And so, they decided to call it "the greedy youngster."

Ugly as he was, they were fond of him at first. Before long, he became so greedy that he ate up all the meat they had. When they boiled a dish of soup or a pot of porridge that they thought would be sufficient for all six, he finished it all by himself. So they decided not to keep him any longer.

"I have not had a decent meal since this changeling crept out of the eggshell," said one of them. When the youngster heard that they were all of the same opinion, he said he was quite willing to go his own way.

"If they do not want me, I am sure I do not want them," and with that he left the place.

After a long time he came to a farm where the fields were full of stones, and he went in and asked for work. They wanted a laborer on the farm so the farmer put him to pick up stones from the field.

Yes, the youngster went to work and picked up the stones, some of which were so big that they would make many cartloads. Whether they were big or small, he put them all into his pocket. It did not take him long to finish that job. "What should I do next," he asked.

"You were to get all the stones out of the field," said the farmer. "I suppose you can't be ready before you have begun."

The youngster emptied his pockets and threw all the stones in a heap. Then the farmer saw that he had finished the work. "I ought to take good care of this one who is so strong," thought the farmer.

"You must come in and get something to eat," the farmer told the youngster. The youngster thought so, too. He, all by himself, ate what was prepared for the master and servants and still he was only half satisfied.

"He is the right sort of man for a laborer, but he is a terrible eater, to be sure," thought the farmer. "A man like him would eat a poor farmer out of house and home before anybody knew anything about it," he said. He had no more work for the youngster. "It is best for you to go to the king's palace for work," he told the youngster.

The youngster set out for the palace where he got a place at once. There was plenty of food and plenty of work. He was to be the errand boy and help the girls carry wood and water and do other odd jobs. So, the youngster asked, "What should I do first?"

"You had better chop some wood in the mean time," they said. He commenced to chop and cut wood till the splinters flew about him. It was not long before he had chopped up everything in the place, both firewood and timber, both rafters and beams.

And when he was ready with it, he came in and asked, "What should I do now?"

"You can finish chopping the wood," they said.

"There is no more to chop," he answered.

"That could not be possible," thought the overseer and he went to the woodshed for a look. But yes, the youngster had chopped up everything. He had even cut up the timber and planks in the place. "This is a vexation," the overseer said. Then he told the youngster that, "you should not have any food to eat until you have gone into the forest and cut just as much timber as you have chopped up for firewood."

The youngster went to the smithy and got the blacksmith to help him to make an axe of five hundredweight of iron. Then he set out for the forest and began to make a regular clearance, not only of the pine and the lofty fir trees, but of everything else which was to be found in the king's forests, and in the neighbors' as well.

He did not stop to cut the branches or the tops off but he left them lying there as if a hurricane had blown them down. He put a proper load on the sledge and put all the horses to pull it, but they could not even move it. He took the horses by the heads to give the sledge a start, but he pulled so hard that the horses' heads came off. He unharnessed the horses and drew the load himself.

When he came to the palace, the king and his overseer were standing in the hall to give him a scolding for having destroyed the forest. The overseer had gone there and seen what the youngster had done. When the king saw the youngster dragging half the forest behind him, he grew both angry and afraid. "It is better to be a little careful with him since he is so strong," he thought.

"Well, you are a wonderful workman, to be sure," said the king. "But how much do you eat at a time because I suppose you are hungry now?"

"Oh, when I have a proper meal of porridge, it takes twelve barrels of meal to make it," said the youngster. "When I eat all of that I can wait a while for my next meal," he thought.

It took some time to boil such a dish of porridge and in the meantime he was to bring in a little firewood for the cook. He put a lot of wood on a sledge, but when he was coming through the door with it he was a little rough and careless again. The house got almost pushed out of shape and all the joists creaked. He was very near dragging down the whole palace.

When the porridge was nearly ready, they sent him out to call the workers home from the fields. He shouted so that the mountains and hills around rang with echoes but the workers did not come quickly enough for him. He came to blows with them and killed twelve of them.

"You have killed twelve men," said the king. "You eat as much as many times twelve people. How many do you work for?"

"For many times twelve as well," answered the youngster.

When he had finished his porridge he was to go into the barn to thrash the grain. He took one of the rafters from the roof and made a flail out to it. When the roof was about to fall in, he took a big pine tree with branches and all and put it up instead of the rafter. He went on thrashing the grain and the straw and the hay all together. This of course, was doing more damage than good for the corn and the chaff flew about together, and a cloud of dust rose over the whole palace.

When he had nearly finished thrashing, enemies came into the country. A war was coming. The king told the youngster, "Take men with you and go and meet the enemy and fight them." The king thought that the enemy would surely kill him.

"No, I will not take any men with me to be cut to pieces. I will fight by myself," the youngster told the king.

"So much the better," thought the king. "The sooner I get rid of him the better, but he must have a proper club."

They sent for the blacksmith. He forged a club that weighed a hundredweight. "A very nice thing to crack nuts with," said the youngster. So the smith made one of three hundred weight. "It would be very well for hammering nails into boots," was the answer.

Well the smith could not make a bigger one with the men he had. So the youngster set out for the smithy himself and made a club that weighed five tons and it took a hundred men to turn it on the anvil.

"That one should do for lack of a better club," thought the youngster. Next, he wanted a bag with some provisions. They had to make one out of fifteen ox hides and they filled it with food. He went away down the hill with the bag on his back and the club on his shoulder.

When he came so far that the enemy saw him, they sent a soldier to ask him if he was going to fight them.

"Yes, but wait a little till I have had something to eat," said the youngster. He threw himself down on the grass and began to eat with the big bag of food in front of him.

The enemy decided not to wait but to fire at him at once. It rained and hailed bullets around him.

"I don't mind these crowberries a bit," said the youngster and went on eating and stuffing himself faster than ever. Neither lead nor iron took any effect on him, and his bag with food in front of him guarded him against the bullets as if it were a protective barrier.

The enemy commenced throwing bombshells and firing cannons at him. He only grinned a little every time he felt them. "They don't hurt me a bit," he said. But just then he got a bombshell right down his windpipe.

"Fy!" he shouted and spat it out again. Then a chain shot made its way into his butter can, and another carried away the piece of food he held between his fingers.

That made him angry. He got up and took his big club and struck the ground with it. "Do you want to take the food out of my mouth?" he yelled. "What do you mean by blowing crowberries at me with your peashooters?" He then struck the ground again till the hills and rocks rattled and shook and sent the enemy flying in the air like chaff. This finished the war.

When he got back to the king's palace, he asked for more work. The king was shocked because he thought he had rid himself of the youngster in the war. He knew of nothing else but to send a message to the devil.

"Your next job is to go to the devil and ask him for the rent for my land," he said. The youngster took his bag on his back and started at once. He was not long in getting there but the devil was gone to court. There was no one at home but his mother, and she said that she had never heard anything of any rent.

"You better come back again another time," the devil's mother told the youngster.

"Yes, call again tomorrow is always what is said," the youngster told her. "You are not going to make a fool of me. I am here now and I am going to remain here till I get the rent. I have plenty of time to wait."

When he had finished all the food in his bag, the time hung heavy on his hands and then he demanded the rent for the land again. "You had better pay it now," he said.

"No, I am not going to do anything of the sort," she replied. Her words were as firm as the old fir tree just outside the gates, which was so big that fifteen men could scarcely span it.

The youngster climbed right up in the top of it and twisted and turned the gates as if it were a willow. "Are you going to pay the rent now?" the youngster repeated.

She dared not do anything else so she scraped together as much money as she thought he could carry in his bag. The youngster then set out for home with the rent. As soon as he had gone, the devil arrived home. When he heard that the youngster had gone off with his bag full of money, he first gave his mother a tongue-lashing. Then, the devil started after the youngster thinking he would soon overtake him.

The devil soon came up to the youngster. He could travel faster since he had nothing to carry and of course, now and then he used his wings. Meanwhile, the youngster had to keep to the ground with his heavy bag. Just as the devil was at his heels, he began to jump and run as fast as he could. He kept his club behind him to keep the devil off, and in that way they traveled with the youngster holding the handle and the devil trying to catch hold of the other end of it. They came to a deep valley. The youngster made a jump across from the top of one hill to the other. The devil was in such a hurry to follow him that he ran his head against the club and fell down into the valley and broke his leg. There he lay.

"There is your rent," said the youngster when he returned to the palace. He threw the bag with the money to the king with such a crash that you could hear it all over the hall.

The king thanked him and appeared to be well pleased and promised the youngster good pay as well as a leave of absence if he wished it. The youngster only wanted more work.

"What shall I do now?" he asked.

As soon as the king had time to consider, he told the youngster, "You must go to the hill troll who took my grandfather's sword." The troll had a castle by the sea, and no one dared to go there.

The youngster put some cartloads of food into his bag and set out again. He traveled both long and far, over woods and hills and wild moors, until he came to the big mountains where the troll lived.

The troll seldom came out in the open air, and the mountain was well closed, so the youngster was not man enough to get inside. He joined a gang of quarrymen who were living at a farm on top of the hill. They were quarrying stones in the hill. They had never had such help before, for the youngster broke and hammered away at the rocks until the mountain cracked. Big stones the size of a house rolled down the hill. When he rested to get his dinner he found that all the cartloads of food in his bag were eaten up.

"I generally have a good appetite myself," said the youngster, "but the one who has been here can do a trifle more than I. He has eaten all the bones as well."

The first day passed. The second day was no better. On the third day, the youngster set out to break stones again. He took with him a load of food, but he lay down behind the bag and pretended to be asleep. All of a sudden a troll with seven heads came out of the mountain and began to eat his food.

"It is all ready here for me and I will eat," said the troll.

"We will see about that," said the youngster, and he hit the troll with his club so the head rolled down the hill. He went into the mountain and found a horse eating out of a barrel of glowing cinders. Behind it stood a barrel of oats.

"Why don't you eat out of the barrel of oats?" asked the youngster.

"Because I cannot turn around," said the horse.

"I will soon turn you round," said the youngster.

"Rather cut my head off," said the horse.

The youngster cut its head off and the horse turned into a fine handsome fellow. "I have been bewitched and taken into the mountain and turned into a horse by the troll."

The handsome fellow helped the youngster find the sword that the troll had hidden at the bottom of the bed. In the bed lay the old mother of the troll, asleep and snoring hard.

So they set out for home by water, but when they had got some distance out to sea, the old mother came after them. As she could not overtake them, she lay down and began to drink the sea. She drank till the water fell but she could not drink the sea dry. She burst!

When they came to land, the youngster sent word that the king must come and fetch the sword. He sent four horses but they could not move it. The sword remained where it was. The king's men were not able to move it from the spot. The youngster shrugged his shoulders, picked up the sword, and carried it to the palace alone.

The king could not believe his eyes when he saw the youngster back again. He pretended to be pleased to see him and promised him land and great riches. When the youngster wanted more work, the king said, "I want you to set out for an enchanted castle where no one dares to live. You will have to stop there until you build a bridge over the sound so that people can get across to the castle. If you are able to do this, I will reward you handsomely. Indeed, I will even give you my daughter in marriage."

"Well I think I can do it," said the youngster.

No one had ever got away alive. Those who had got as far as the castle lay there killed and torn to pieces as small as barley. The king thought that this time he would never see the youngster again.

The youngster started on his expedition. He took with him a bag of food, a crooked, twisted block of a fir tree, an axe, a wedge, some chips of the fir root, and the small beggar from the palace.

When he came to the sound, he found the river full of ice. The current ran as strong as in a waterfall. He stuck his legs to the bottom of the river and waded until he was safely across.

When he had warmed himself and had something to eat, he wanted to go to sleep. Before long he heard a terrible noise—as if someone were turning the castle upside down. The door burst wide open, and he saw nothing but a gaping jaw extending from the threshold up to the lintel.

"There is a mouthful for you," said the youngster. He threw the beggar boy into the swallow. "Taste that! But let me see who you are! Perhaps you are an old acquaintance?"

Indeed it was. In fact, it was the devil again. They began to play cards, for the devil wanted to try and win back some of the rent that the youngster had taken. The youngster was always the fortunate one, for he put a cross on the back of all the good cards. When he had won all the money the devil had, the devil had to pay him out of the gold and silver that was in the castle.

Suddenly, the fire went out, so they could not tell one card from another. "We must chop some wood now," said the youngster, who drove the axe into the fir block. He forced the wedge in, but the twisted knotty block would not split. The youngster worked as hard as he could with the axe.

"They say you are strong," the youngster said to the devil. "Just spit on your hands, stick your claws in and tear away. Let me see what you are made of."

The devil did so and put both his fists into the split, pulling as hard as he could. The youngster suddenly struck the wedge out, and the devil stuck fast in the block. The youngster let him also have a taste of the butt end of his axe on his back. The devil begged nicely to be let loose, but the youngster would not listen to anything of the kind unless he promised that he would never come there again and create a disturbance. "You must also promise that you will build a bridge over the sound so that people can pass over it at all times of the year. This bridge must be ready when the ice is gone," the youngster demanded.

"Those are very hard conditions," said the devil. There was no way out of it. If the devil wanted to be set free he would have to promise. He bargained, however, that he should have the first soul that went across the bridge. That was to be the toll.

"Yes, you can have that," said the youngster.

The devil was set loose and started home. The youngster lay down to sleep and slept till far into the day.

When the king came to see if he was cut and chopped into small pieces, he had to wade through all the money before he came to the sleeping youngster. There was money in heaps and in bags that reached far up the wall. The youngster lay there, snoring.

"Lord help me and my daughter," said the king when he saw that the youngster was alive. He had done everything asked of him. No one could deny that. The king decided that there was no hurry talking of the wedding before the bridge was ready.

Then, there it was. One day the bridge stood ready, and the devil was there waiting for the toll he had bargained for.

The youngster wanted the king to go with him and try the bridge, but the king declined. The youngster mounted a horse himself and put the fat dairymaid from the palace on the pommel in front of him. She looked almost like a big fir block. He rode over the bridge. The horse's hoofs thundered as it crossed the bridge.

"Where is the toll? Where have you got the soul?" cried the devil.

"Why, inside this fir block," said the youngster. "If you want it you will have to spit in your hands and take it."

"No, thank you! If she does not come to me, I am sure I can't take her," said the devil. "You got me once into a pinch and you won't do that again." With that, the devil flew straight home to his old mother. Since that time he has never been heard or seen thereabouts.

The youngster went home to the palace and asked for the reward the king had promised him. The king tried to get out of what he had promised. "It would be best if you got a good bag of food ready for him. I will take my reward myself," the youngster told the king.

"I will do that," said the king. When the bag was ready, the youngster asked the king to come outside the door. The youngster then gave the king such a kick, it sent him flying up into the air. The youngster threw the bag after him so he wouldn't be without food. If the king has not come down again by this time, he is floating about with his bag between heaven and Earth to this very day.

Consider this hero's journey. A young man gives in to temptation and loses his beloved. Only through persistence and sacrifice does he win her back and become whole. The story also contains a cure for magic. See if you can find it.

## The Princess and the Soldiers (Scotland)

A sergeant, a corporal, and a private had just been released from the army. They agreed to travel to the ends of the Earth and seek their fortune. They traveled from here to there and back again but never found their fortunes. "Let's part company and seek our fortunes and meet back here when we do," one of them said. The three of them agreed, and off they went.

The sergeant started walking and traveled for three days. He came to a huge palace and realized that he was hungry and quite tired. "The people in here would probably give me some food and a place to sleep for the night," he said to himself. So he went up to the ornate doors of the palace where a lovely lady greeted him.

"I am seeking food and a place to sleep," he told the lady.

"Come in then. I will have food brought to you," she answered. "In return I only ask you to share some stories with us."

He agreed and followed her into a grand room. There was a huge table that had places set on it. Candles danced on the polished wood of the table.

Servants brought in food and wine, and the sergeant's eyes took it all in hungrily while his empty stomach growled for food.

The lady told him, "Take whatever you want. Forgive me as I blow the candles out as that is our custom here."

47

"Of course, if that is your custom, I agree," he said. "The food you have had brought to me is like nothing I have seen in years."

The lovely lady blew out the candles, and the smoke from them floated towards the ceiling. The sergeant started to eat. He restrained himself from grabbing the food and gobbling it. To his surprise, the lady tapped her foot on the floor and two servants immediately came in.

"Yes, my lady," one of them said. "What are your wishes?"

She commanded, "Take this man and lock him up. Feed him only bread and water."

The sergeant was escorted out of the room and locked up in darkness.

As luck would have it, the corporal arrived the next day at the same palace, and he also asked for food and lodging. The same lady greeted him and welcomed him into the room with the table and the dancing candles on it.

"I suppose you are quite hungry so I will have food brought for you." She clapped her hands twice and servants brought in fragrant smelling food and sparkling wines. "Choose any of the food you want," the lady graciously said. "Oh, one other thing, it is the custom here to blow out the candles," she said and proceeded to blow the candles out.

"The hungry corporal agreed, "If that is your custom, so be it." He took some food on his plate and had only eaten one mouthful when the lady tapped her foot on the floor and in came the servants.

"Take him away," she ordered the servants. "Be sure to feed him only bread and water." With that, the corporal was led away to a dungeon.

The private arrived at the same palace the next night. Since he had been walking longer and farther than the others, he was especially tired and hungry. He, too, went to the great palace doors and asked for food and a place to sleep. The same beautiful lady greeted him and took him into the room with the table and glowing candles. She clapped her hands twice, "Bring some food and wine," she ordered the servants when they appeared.

The hungry private actually drooled when he saw the fine food that was brought to the table. Again, "It is our custom to blow out the candles," the lady said.

As soon as she blew out the candles, the private grabbed her around her waist and kissed her. "It is a wonderful meal you have provided but you are tastier than any food and more satisfying than any wine," he chortled.

The lady didn't just tap her foot but instead stamped her foot on the floor. The servants came but this time she told them, "Bring more candles and serve us our meal."

As the private and the lady feasted on the food, he told her many good stories that she enjoyed. "Have you been to school?" the lady asked him.

"Oh, yes," he replied.

"How is your handwriting?" she asked him.

The private never said anything but instead wrote his name clearly and with flair.

The lady admired his writing and went straight to the point, "Will you marry me?" she asked.

"With great pleasure. Of course I will," he answered.

"I am a princess," she told him. "I am the only daughter of the king of this land. Of course I am rich and own gold, silver, and jewels. It would be easy for me to marry a prince or even a king but I would rather marry someone like you. I prefer a handsome man of common birth with good sense, manners, and education like you."

The private flushed and told the princess, "That pleases me very much."

"I presume you are tired," she said and then personally showed him to a fine bedroom. The private slept soundly through the night.

In the morning, he followed his nose to where breakfast was being served. "Let us make the plans for our wedding," the lady said. "Take this bag of gold and go to the town tailor and have him make you a fine suit of clothes. Come back to me when they are finished."

The private went into the town and found the tailor. "I want you to make me the finest suit of clothes you can," he asked the tailor.

The tailor set to work. He measured the soldier and sewed clothes that fit him perfectly. "Here is payment for what you have done. It pleases me very much," the soldier told the tailor.

The princess was to meet him in her coach at a particular part of the road. The private prepared to leave the tailor shop. "Go with him." The tailor's mother told her son. She was a crafty old woman, just one step above being a witch. "Talk to the soldier, and keep him engaged with talk. When he sits down to rest, ask him if he is hungry, of course he will be, then give him this apple."

The tailor obeyed his mother, and it all happened just as she had said. "I am tired and thirsty," said the soldier after they had gone down the road with the hot sun beating down on them.

"Here, have this rosy apple," offered the tailor. He took it out of his pocket.

"Well, thank you for your kindness," said the soldier. He took the apple and polished it on his jacket, ate it, and immediately fell asleep.

The princess came driving up in her coach just at this very moment. "Is he asleep?" she asked the tailor. "Would you please wake him."

The tailor shouted in the private's ear, shook him, and even gave him a pinch but nothing happened. The soldier didn't seem to feel or hear anything. He gently snored as he slept.

"Ah, well," the lady signed. "Take him home with you tonight," she told the tailor. "When he wakes up, give him this ring and tell him to meet me here tomorrow."

"Yes, madam, I will do just as you say," the tailor promised.

The lady drove away. The tailor sat with the young man until it was almost dark. The soldier woke up and agreed to go home with the tailor. The next morning, the tailor gave the soldier the ring and the message from the lady. The soldier set off down the road again.

"Go with him," the tailor's mother told her son. "Just as before, he will become tired and thirsty again and this time you can give him this pear to eat. The princess might notice you, and there is a chance that you can win her for yourself."

Again, just before they reached the place where he was to meet the lady, the soldier sat down to rest. "I am thirsty," he complained.

"Here, have this pear," offered the tailor.

"Yesterday I fell asleep and did not wake up until after the princess had gone. That must not happen again," thought the soldier.

"Here, have this pear," again the tailor offered. "It will please you with the juices."

The soldier couldn't resist and ate the juicy pear. Of course, he fell asleep again.

The princess drove up again in her coach a short time later. "Is he asleep again?" she asked the tailor.

"I am afraid that he is," the tailor answered. "I will wake him up for you."

"I would appreciate that," she answered.

Again, the tailor shouted, shook, and pinched the soldier but nothing worked. The lady drove away quite sadly. She had left a knife with the tailor this time to give to the soldier when he woke. "Have him meet me here at the same time tomorrow," she told the tailor.

The soldier again spent the night with the tailor and his mother. In the morning the tailor gave him the knife and the message.

"Goodbye," the soldier said and he set out once more to meet the princess on the road.

The tailor's mother instructed her son again, "Go with him only don't offer him anything to eat. He won't accept anything this time. Instead, stick this pin into the back of his coat when he sits down to rest. He will fall asleep and this time will sleep for a very long time."

"I'll travel with you to make sure you meet the princess," the tailor told the soldier.

They walked in silence until they came near to where the soldier planned to meet the princess. Again, the soldier sat down to rest and the tailor took the moment to stick the pin into the back of his coat. The soldier fell into a deep sleep just as the princess drove up.

The exasperated princess asked the tailor, "Is he asleep again?"

"I am afraid that he is," answered the tailor. "Shall I try to wake him up?"

"Yes indeed," the princess told him.

Again the tailor roared, shook, and pinched the soldier, and the soldier just kept on sleeping as before.

"Give him this gold pin," the princess told the tailor. "This time, though, there will be no message for I will not come again."

She sadly drove away and turned the corner in the road. The tailor took the pin from the soldier's coat and he woke up.

The soldier was quite anxious, "Has the princess come yet?"

"Yes, she has come and gone. You probably won't see her again. She left no message this time," the tailor told him. "She gave me this pin to give you. I guess you have nothing to do but come home with me."

The soldier stood up and looked at the gold pin, "I will not," he stated. "I have gone home with you too many times and how I wish I had not done so!" He started off down the road, "I'll be off by myself on my own way. Goodbye to you!"

The soldier traveled on down the road and asked everyone where he might find the princess, but no one was able to tell him. No one had ever heard of such a palace and princess.

One day, the soldier came to a house where an old man was thatching the roof with sods of turf. He greeted the old man courteously, "Are you not too old to be doing such work?" he asked.

"I am old, but my father is older yet," answered the old man.

"Is he alive and well?" asked the soldier.

"He is. Where are you going you curious fellow?" asked the old man.

"I am looking for a grand palace and a lovely princess that lives in it," the soldier said with sadness in his voice.

"I have never heard of such a place. Maybe my father might know of it," mused the old man.

"I would like to ask him about it. Where can I find him?" asked the soldier.

"He will be here in a short time. He is out collecting the divots of turf for me. Ask him when he comes back," said the old man as he patted another piece of turf in place on the roof.

Sure enough, in a short time the old man's father came up with a cartload of turf. He was quite old indeed.

"Mercy," said the soldier in an amazed voice, "you are old."

"I agree with you," said the old man's father, "but my father is even older than I am."

The soldier's eyes opened wide as he asked, "Is he still living?"

"Why not? Of course he lives," was the answer.

The soldier asked him about the palace and the princess.

"Where can I find your father?" the soldier inquired.

"He is over there, cutting the turf. Go and ask him," was the answer. They found the third old man who truly seemed ancient.

"My goodness but you are old," blurted the soldier.

"Aye, old I am but my father is older yet," was the answer.

The soldier asked him about the palace and the beautiful princess but this third old man didn't know anything about the place. "My father might know," he told the soldier.

The soldier gulped and asked, "Where can I find your father?"

"He is out hunting birds. He will be home soon and you can ask him then," was the answer.

The fourth old man came back with some birds dangling. The soldier asked him about the palace and the princess but he didn't know any more than his son, his grandson, or his great-grandson. "I think my father might know," he offered kindly.

The soldier was beyond being amazed and again asked, "Where might I find your father?"

"He is inside the house. Come in with me and ask him yourself," said the oldest man. They went inside and there by the fire was an old, old, old man. This man was so old, he was lying in a cradle.

The soldier went to him quite respectfully. "You are the oldest person I could possibly imagine."

"You are right. I have certainly reached a ripe old age," the man in the cradle said.

The soldier asked him about the palace and princess. Surely a man as old as this man would know everything. "I don't know the place and lady of which you have asked about."

The old men felt really sorry for the soldier who seemed deep in despair by this time. "Come with me to the hill tomorrow," said the old man who had been hunting birds. "I will blow my whistle and all the birds will come flying to me from every corner of the world. We will find out where the palace and princess might be."

The next morning, just as the hunter had promised, they went to the hill. The hunter blew his whistle and a dark cloud of birds came from every direction. The last bird of all to come was a great eagle.

The hunter asked the eagle, "Why are you so late?"

"I had to fly much farther than the others," was the answer.

The old man asked the eagle, "Where did you fly from?"

"From the land of a magnificent palace," was the reply.

"That is good news. This young man wants to go there. Could you carry him on your mighty back to this palace?"

The eagle answered, "That would be no problem but I need enough meat to build my strength for such a trip."

The hunter promised the eagle all the food she wanted. "All the rest of you birds can go," the hunter told them and they all flew off. Together the hunter, the eagle and the soldier returned to the cottage. They all ate a good supper and then in the morning a good breakfast.

The eagle took the soldier up on her back, and the hunter handed the soldier a bundle of meat to take along with them. The eagle flew off and went high. They ate the meat as they flew.

"I am hungry and getting weak," the eagle announced to the soldier. "All the meat is gone. I must set you down."

The soldier begged the eagle "I have most of my share of the meat left. You may have it. Just keep on flying."

They continued to fly for a long distance but again the eagle grew hungry. "I am weak. I must set you down before we crash," the eagle said.

"Is it possible for you to at least take me to the borders of the land of the palace and princess?" pleaded the soldier.

"I need more meat," the eagle panted.

"I don't have any more. If I did I would gladly let you have it," moaned the soldier.

The eagle observed, "There is meat on your own thigh. I could eat some of that."

The soldier stretched out his thigh until it was under her beak. She ate and praised him for having such sweet meat. "In fact, that is the best meat I have ever tasted," she told him and she kept on flying.

"I can carry you no farther. I am weak from hunger. Give me your other thigh and I will be able to go on," said the bird.

The soldier didn't like this idea too much but he had no other choice. He put his other thigh beneath her beak. She ate her fill and flew on. "This time I think I can reach the place you want," she said as she flew on.

After a while, the eagle swooped down and left him near the palace. Then she flew away. The poor soldier thanked her profusely. However, he was lame, starving with hunger, and he felt weak from the loss of flesh and blood. His heart was brave, though, and he limped on. He came to the home of the gardener and begged for food and drink. The gardener's wife nursed his wounds, bathed him, fed him and let him sleep. Her knowledge of medicine and her kindness healed him.

When he was well and strong again, he worked with the gardener. One day the gardener came home with the news that the princess was to be married. "They are going to have a wedding feast."

The soldier was filled with sadness. "If I could only see the princess," he pondered.

"I will arrange that for you," the gardener's wife told him. She gave him a good suit and a basket of apples. "Take that to the princess. Give it only to her. Don't let the servants take it from you."

The polite soldier thanked her and set off for the palace. "I have a basket of apples from the gardener's wife for the princess," he told the guard at the gate. One servant after another tried to take it from him, but he refused to give the basket to them. "I have been told to give it to the princess's own hands," he told them. "Please take me to her."

He finally was led to the princess's room. Bowing low, the soldier handed the princess the basket of apples.

"Thank the woman who sent this," said the princess. "And thanks to you for bringing it. Will you take the time to drink a glass of wine?"

"Only if you drink a glass first," said the soldier. The princess laughed and drank a glass of wine. She filled the glass again for him.

The soldier bowed and accepted the wine. He drank it and gave the glass back, but not before he had slipped the ring into the glass. He had taken care of the ring all this time.

She took the glass, saw the ring, and asked the soldier, "Where did you find this ring?"

"Dear lady, do you remember the soldier you sent to a tailor to have a fine suit of clothes made?"

"Maybe I do," she answered. "Do you have further proof?"

With that, the soldier took out the knife and handed it to her. "I have this."

She looked at the knife, then looked into the soldier's eyes, "Is that all?"

He handed her the gold pin. "There is this besides."

"I rejoice to see you. Is it really true?" whispered the princess.

Before, the soldier had put his arms around her, but this time it was she who put her arms around him with great love. "This is the husband I have chosen," she told everyone. "I will wed no other!"

Everything was arranged. The princess thought of everything. In fact she even found a fine lady of the court for the man she had intended to marry before the soldier came back. Everyone agreed to everything. The soldier went back to tell the gardener and his wife the good news. "You may be sure," he told them, "that you will never lack for anything. You are my true friends and have helped me win back my bride."

The feast followed the wedding. There was great joy in the court. Everyone was so pleased to see the radiant bride and her groom. They went to the palace where they had first met. Somehow in their conversation, she mentioned the two men who had come to the palace before her husband. She told him that she had punished them because they had displeased her.

The soldier asked her for a wedding gift. "Will you release them?"

The soldier greeted his comrades when they were set free. He found good work for them and they remained friends forever. He was delighted with his beloved wife, his old comrades, and his benefactors the gardener and his wife. And so, everyone lived with joy and happiness in the palace of the princess and her devoted husband.

This story gives good examples of keeping your word, as well as speaking up for yourself—both necessary for development and growth.

## Intelligence and Luck
## (Slavonia)

In a time when the world was young and strange and there was magic in almost everything, Luck and Intelligence met on a garden seat.

"Make room for me!" shouted Luck. Intelligence was then as yet inexperienced and didn't know who ought to make room for whom.

"Why should I make room for you?" Intelligence asked. "You are no better than I."

"He's the better man who performs most," answered Luck. "See you the peasant's son who is ploughing in the field? Enter into him, and if he gets on better through you than through me, I'll always submissively make way for you whenever and wherever we meet."

Intelligence agreed and entered at once into the ploughboy's head. As soon as the ploughboy felt that he had intelligence in his head, he began to think, "Why must I follow the plough to the day of my death? I can go somewhere else and make my fortune more easily."

He left off ploughing, put up his plough, and drove home. "Father," he said, "I don't like this peasant's life. I would rather learn to be a gardener."

His father looked surprised at him and asked, "What ails you Vanek? Have you lost your wits?" Then the father had a change of mind and added, "Well, if you will, learn and prosper. Your brother will be heir to the cottage after me."

Vanek lost the cottage but he didn't care. He went and apprenticed himself to the king's gardener. For every little thing that the gardener showed him, Vanek comprehended ever so much more. Before long he didn't even obey the gardener's orders as to how he ought to do anything but did everything his own way. At first the gardener was angry, but seeing everything was getting on better, he was content.

"I see that you've more intelligence than I," said the king's gardener. From that point on he let Vanek garden as he thought fit. In no long space of time Vanek made the garden so beautiful that the king took great delight in it and frequently walked in it with the queen and with his only daughter.

The princess was a very beautiful maiden, but had ceased to speak when she was twelve years old. Since that time, no one had ever heard a single word from her.

This grieved the king, and he created a proclamation which said that whoever should cure his daughter and get her to speak again should be her husband.

Many young kings, princes, and other great lords announced their intention to heal her. One after the other they all went away just as they had come. No one succeeded in curing the princess and getting her to speak.

"Why shouldn't I try my luck?" thought Vanek. "Who knows whether I will succeed in bringing her to answer when I ask her a question?"

He at once had himself announced at the palace, and the king and his councilors conducted him into the room where the princess was. The king's daughter had a pretty little dog and was very fond of him because he was so clever, understanding everything she wanted.

When Vanek went into the room with the king and his councilors, he made as if he didn't even see the princess, but turned to the dog and said, "I have heard, doggie, that you are very clever and I come to you for advice. We are three companions in travel—a sculptor, a tailor, and myself. Once upon a time we were going through a forest and were forced to pass the night in it. To be safe from wolves, we made a fire and agreed to keep watch one after the other. The sculptor kept watch first, and for amusement to kill time took a log and carved a maiden out of it.

"When it was finished, he woke the tailor to keep watch in his turn. The tailor seeing the wooden maiden asked what it meant. 'As you see,' said the sculptor, 'I was weary and didn't know what to do with myself, so I carved a maiden out of a log. If you find time hanging heavy on your hands, you can dress her.'

"The tailor at once took out his scissors, needle, and thread, cut out the clothes, stitched away, and when they were ready dressed the maiden in them.

"He then called me to come and keep watch. I, too, asked him what the meaning of all of this was. 'As you see,' said the tailor, 'the sculptor found time hanging heavy on his hands and carved a maiden out of a log and I for the same reason, clothed her. If you find time hanging heavy on your hands, you can teach her to speak.'

"By the morning dawn I had actually taught her to speak. But in the morning when my companions woke up, each wanted the maiden for himself. The sculptor said, 'I made her," the tailor, 'I clothed her.' I also argued my right.

"Tell me therefore, doggie, to which of us the maiden belongs."

The dog said nothing but instead of the dog the princess replied, "To whom can she belong but to yourself? What's the good of the sculptor's damsel without life? What's the good of the tailor's dressing without speech? You gave her the best gift, life and speech, and therefore she by right belongs to you."

"You have passed your own sentence," said Vanek. "I have given you speech again and a new life, and you therefore by right belong to me!"

One of the king's councilors said, "His Royal Grace will give you a plenteous reward for succeeding in unloosing his daughter's tongue. You cannot have her as your wife as you are just a peasant."

The king said, "You are just a peasant. I will give you riches as a reward, but not my daughter."

Vanek wouldn't hear of any other reward and said, "The king promised without any exception that whoever caused his daughter to speak again should be her husband. A king's word is law. If the king wants others to respect his laws, he must first respect them himself. Therefore, the king must give me his daughter."

"Seize and bind him!" shouted the councilor. "Whoever says the king must do anything, offers an insult to his majesty and is worthy of death. May it please your majesty to order this peasant to be executed with the sword?"

The king stroked his beard, thought, and then said, "Let him be executed."

Vanek was immediately bound and led to his execution. When they came to the place of the execution, Luck was there waiting for him. Luck said secretly to Intelligence, "See how this man has got on through you. Now he will lose his head! Make way, and let me take your place."

As soon as Luck entered Vanek, the executioner's sword broke against the scaffold, just as if some one had snapped it. Before they brought up another sword, up rode a trumpeter on horseback from the city galloping as swift as a bird, trumpeted merrily and waved a white flag. After him came the royal carriage for Vanek.

This is what had happened. The princess told her father at home that Vanek had but spoken the truth, and the king's word ought not to be broken. If Vanek were just a peasant, the king could easily make him a prince.

The king said, "You're right. Let him be a prince!"

The royal carriage was immediately sent for Vanek, and the councilor who had argued against Vanek to the king was executed in his stead.

Afterward, when Vanek and the princess were going together in a carriage from the wedding, Intelligence happened to be somewhere on the road, and seeing that he couldn't help meeting Luck, bent his head and slipped on one side. It was just as if cold water had been thrown upon him.

From that time forth it is said that Intelligence has always given a wide berth to Luck whenever he has had to meet him.

In the Finnish epic *The Kalevala*, Vainamoinen, the oldest of the ancient wizards, is injured as he performs impossible tasks demanded by Louhi's (Mistress of the North Country or Pohja) daughter. How he cures himself (through a folk remedy) is included in the story of the creation of the magic Sampo (a magic mill that provides food, money, and other good things). The story also illustrates the magic power of words, songs, and story knowledge.

## The Cure for Axe Wounds in the Knee (Finland)

**V**ainamoinen, the oldest of the ancient wizards, was born of the virgin maiden of the air, a spirit of nature who had come down to the open space. The winds blew her pregnant. It took seven hundred years for this pregnancy to be born as the seas from which she fashioned the Earth and all that is on it. She became known as the Mother of the Sea. Again the winds blew her pregnant and for thirty years Vainamoinen was in her womb. His wisdom helped him find his way out, and he was born into the sea and waves. There he rolled among the billows for eight years. And so, the eternal sage and stout-hearted singer began his adventures.

One of these adventures is the creation of the Sampo, which followed one of his most harrowing run-ins with a vengeful enemy, Joukahainen, who had shot Vainamoinen's blue elk. Vainamoinen was aided by an eagle, neither big nor small. This eagle was the size in which one wing grazed the water and the other swept the heavens. Its tail was in the sea and it whetted its beak on the cliffs.

The eagle found Vainamoinen weak and tired, for even ancient wizards lost their lusty youths. The eagle told Vainamoinen to climb on him because at a better time, Vainamoinen was clearing the trees of Kaleva so the fields could be burned, plowed, seeded, and grow crops. In doing this he left one lonely birch tree as a resting place for the birds. The eagle had remembered this kindness and so, on the wing tip of the eagle Vainamoinen traveled along the path of the cold spring wind to the North Farm. Louhi, Mistress of the North Country, took him to her home and fed the weakened hero. She presented him with a feast of salmon and pork. She gave him a warm bath and rubbed life back into his muscles.

Vainamoinen was deeply depressed from his recent and past trials and tribulations. He wanted only to be back in his own lands near his own sauna, listening to the songs of his own birds. He knew the Pohja, or the North Farm, was a place where other heroes told of people who ate each other and even drowned their own heroes.

"If you can forge a Sampo, a magic mill that grinds out all good things, beat out a lid of many colors from the tips of the shaft of a swan's feather, from the milk of a farrow cow, from a single barleycorn, from the fleece of a summer ewe, then I will give you my own daughter to marry and return you to your home," said Louhi.

Vainamoinen, weary and tired told her, "I don't have the skill to do that but my old friend and brother Ilmarinen the craftsman can do such a thing. He forged the heavens, beat out the firmament with such skill that there is no trace of a hammer and no spot where his tongs gripped the heavens."

Louhi pledged, "I will give my daughter to whosoever forges me the Sampo. If you bring such a craftsman here, I will let you go to your home. You must keep this promise." Saying this, she harnessed a stallion to a huge sleigh and warned Vainamoinen, "Do not raise your head as you travel home or disaster and evil will overtake you."

As the sled traveled over the cold, frozen northland, Vainamoinen saw a dazzling maiden sitting on the edge of a rainbow weaving cloth of gold and silver and spinning threads of gold and silver with a golden spindle. Not thinking of Louhi's warning, Vainamoinen stopped and spoke to the maiden. "You most beautiful of women, come home with me and be my wife. I am the eternal singer, sage, wizard, and wiseman. You will live graciously with me.

"Old singer of songs, I would only be a slave in your home as your wife. I would be like a dog in chains in another's house. No, I will not marry you," she merrily told him.

Steadfast Vainamoinen insisted, "I entreat you, while you remain at your home you are only a child. It is only when you marry that you will become a woman."

Being Louhi's daughter, she replied (with a cold gleam in her eyes), "If you can do some tasks, I might consider it. How much of a wizard are you? Tie a knot in this egg with an invisible knot and show me what kind of a wise man you are."

Vainamoinen knew that this was an easy thing to do. He sang songs that made vipers and snakes inside the egg tie themselves in a knot. When this was done, the dazzling maiden gave the eternal sage more tasks. However, one of the tasks was almost his undoing. She told him to, "fashion a boat from bits of my distaff."

He sang songs of bravado and arrogance as he shaped the boat. He sang for three days and as the boat was almost finished, his axe slipped and gouged into his knee. Blood poured from the wound in buckets and barrels. It stained the snow of the North Country. Vainamoinen started to speak the magic words of healing but forgot some of the important charms. In bloody anguish he got back into the sled and whipped the horse to speed so he could find someone who could heal wounds made by iron.

At the third house where he stopped, he found an old man who knew the magic to heal him. The old graybeard growled the charms to staunch the blood. "I am not familiar with the beginning, the origin of iron, where it came from. Without this information I cannot recite the charm."

Vainamoinen sang the origins of iron and its creation for the old man. With this information the old man recited the charms to heal a wound made by iron. When Vainamoinen was healed he said, "I warn you old man about the dangers of bravado and arrogance. I was guilty of using them as I sang songs to build a special boat. Never make the mistake I did of singing charms with bravado and arrogance."

He said farewell to the healer and got back into the sled. As he traveled home Vainamoinen knew he would have to trick Ilmarinen into forging the Sampo. As he drew near to the fields of Osmo, Vainamoinen sang up a bush-crowned birch tree. It was crowned with golden leaves that rose through the clouds to the heavens with its foliage spreading in all directions. He sang a moon to gleam in the gold-crowned tree and put the stars of the Great Bear in its branches. Satisfied that this would tempt Ilmarinen, he went straight to the smithy.

"Ho Vainamoinen. You have been gone a long time," Ilmarinen greeted him. "Where have you been and what mighty things have you done?"

Vainamoinen replied, "I have been staying in the gloomy North Farm skiing about on Lappish skis in the land of the north magicians. There are many amazing things to see there. If you can forge a Sampo with a lid of many colors you can win the comely maiden of the Pohja, daughter of Louhi, as your wife. Many pursue her but she will have none of them. With the Sampo, she would be yours."

Ilmarinen became suspicious. "Vainamoinen, old stout-hearted singer, I fear you have promised that I would create a Sampo as ransom for your freedom. Can this be?"

"Dear brother Ilmarinen, the things I tell you are true. The North Farm is full of marvels and I brought one of them back with me. Come see it." Saying this Vainamoinen tempted Ilmarinen to look at the tree crowned with golden leaves, with the moon in the crown of the leaves, and the Great Bear sparkling on its branches.

"It truly is a marvel," agreed Ilmarinen.

"Look to the heights at the moon. Even you could climb up there and gather the moon in your arms as a prize," said Vainamoinen.

At this idea, Ilmarinen quickly threw off his blacksmith apron and started to climb the tree. "While I am up here I will get the Great Bear too." He climbed higher and higher into the gleaming tree and then Vainamoinen sang the winds to a fury to carry Ilmarinen to the North Farm. The winds carried the tree and Ilmarinen over the moon, under the sun, and on the shoulders of the Great Bear. They dropped him in one of Louhi's fields. Her dogs just stood there amazed. Louhi came outside to see what the winds were about and saw Ilmarinen.

"Come into my house," she said. "You must be the greatest of craftsmen I have heard about." As she came into the house with him she went upstairs and told her daughter to dress in her best gown made of gold, silver, and copper.

When the maiden of the North appeared in her incredible dress, Ilmarinen could not take his eyes off of her. She was lovelier than Vainamoinen had told him. He must have her for his wife, so he agreed to make the Sampo.

Ilmarinen had to build a forge and begin from the beginning. After he added the tip of the shaft of a swan's feather, the milk of a farrow cow, the tiny ear of barley, and the fleece of a summer ewe to the furnace, he saw things forming. But Louhi said of the gold that appeared, "These nuggets are just children's playthings." Of the silver objects she announced, "These are just a horse's jingling bells. Make me the Sampo!"

And so for seven days Ilmarinen broke and returned to the furnace things that appeared until he finally saw the Sampo being born. He skillfully lifted it out and forged a grain mill on one side, a salt mill on a second, and a money mill on the third side. He formed a lid of many colors that spun around and held a bin of things to eat, a bin for things to sell, and a bin for household supplies.

Louhi was delighted. The North Country would never be poor or hungry again. She took the Sampo to a special place for safekeeping. It was placed inside a hill of rock, inside the copper mountain, behind nine doors with locks. It grew three roots nine fathoms deep. One root went into solid rock, a second into the seashore and the third into the earth near Louhi's house.

"Now that the Sampo is done, I will take my beautiful bride and return to my own land," smiled Ilmarinen.

"Oh wonderful creator of the Sampo," started the girl, "I do not have the time to leave here. The land and the birds need me. Besides, I am not ready to marry."

Ilmarinen knew that there was no way he would be able to persuade her to change her mind. Downcast, he only wanted to go home. Louhi conjured a craft with a copper paddle in which Ilmarinen could travel home. "This ship will be a gentler way to travel on the gales of the north wind than a tree. Use it to make your way home."

Much time and many adventures and wives later, Vainamoinen and Ilmarinen were talking about how bad things were in their homeland now. Crops died. Cold had taken over the land, and the people suffered. "While we are in bad times, the people living at the North Farm are in the midst of plenty because of the Sampo," complained Ilmarinen. "They have things to eat, see, and store in their homes. There is plowing, sowing, and all sorts of increase and everlasting good fortune in Pohja. All from the Sampo I made."

Vainamoinen decided that they needed to share the riches of the Sampo. "Let us go back to Pohja and get part of the Sampo for our needs."

"That would be impossible," warned Ilmarinen. "The Sampo is in a hill of rock inside the copper mountain, behind nine doors with huge locks and with enormous roots.

Vainamoinen finally convinced Ilmarinen that it was the only thing they could do to help their people. They set out by boat for the North Farm. When they got there they told Louhi that they needed to share the riches of the Sampo and the lid of many colors.

"The Sampo is mine alone," screamed Louhi. "It is mine!"

The eternal sage Vainamoinen replied, "If you won't share with use, we will have to take it all." With that, he took out his harp made from a pike's jawbone and started to play and sing such marvelous music that the people of the North Farm fell asleep. While they were sleeping, he sang the nine solid doors open into the mountain of copper. Vainamoinen and Ilmarinen got Louhi's steer to plow and pull up the roots of the Sampo. They took the Sampo to their boat for the trip to the end of the foggy island at the tip of the misty headland to a space there unvisited by humans.

However, a young romantic, headstrong fellow who had traveled with them on this adventure started to sing a boastful song of victory. This reckless youth's raspy, roaring, quavering voice frightened a crane, which flew off. The crane flew over Louhi's house squawking loudly, waking Louhi from her sleep.

Louhi discovered that the Sampo was missing. She beseeched the Spirit of the Mist to help her stop Vainamoinen and Ilmarinen. She evoked fog, gales, and a malevolent sea spirit to help her. The trials of the heroes were fought by Vainamoinen with magic songs of his own. However, the pikebone harp was lost overboard in the storm, but that is another story.

Louhi created a warship with thousands of archers and men with spears. When Vainamoinen sang the warship's ruin, Louhi gathered the splinters of wood from the boat and made herself into an eagle. She flew to the ship of the heroes, but Vainamoinen defeated her again. With only the part of one talon left, Louhi seized the Sampo and threw it into the sea, where it and the lid broke into pieces. With the Sampo sinking to the bottom of the sea, the waters would never again lack for treasures.

In misery, Louhi set out for Pohja. Her prestige was now gone and she was defeated. That was how poverty came to be throughout the North Country.

After Louhi was vanquished, Vainamoinen went ashore and gathered pieces of the Sampo and its lid. He took them to the tip of the misty headland at the end of the foggy island. Singing magic charms, he was able to make them grow. He also sang songs for good fortune for all times.

Many, many, many adventures later, Vainamoinen left his people, traveling in a copper boat to a place between heaven and Earth where he is to this day. He bequeathed his harp made of birch wood and great songs as a heritage for all people. When he left, he blazed a trail, broke off the tops of trees, and showed the way for the new young singers. Vainamoinen has gone. No one knows where he is or when he will return. His music has not been heard of late, but parts of his songs are remembered and sung even now. If you are worthy, you may one day hear them yourselves.

Medical professionals tell us that some people alleviate pain and may actually be cured because of their mental outlook. No one knows where the following modern apocalyptic tale about attitude originated. But the story has traveled like an urban legend. Here is a version of it.

## Dance Like Nobody Is Watching (American Urban Myth)

Dave is the kind of fellow you don't trust. You keep trying to find out why he is always in such a good mood. He never has anything negative to say, all the words that come out of him are positive. For instance, if someone asks him, "How are you doing, Dave?" he will always reply, "If I were any better, I would be twins!" We all have aches and pains and people that irritate us whom we can whimper about, but Dave never did.

Another common Davism, when asked, "How are you feeling," is "Fine as frogs' hair." We all know how fine frogs' hair is!

Professionally, he was a restaurant manager. It was typical that if he moved on to manage another restaurant, the waiters would follow right along with him. It was even known that patrons followed along too. Somehow, when he managed a restaurant the food was outstanding, and the ambiance was warm and—just like Dave—positive.

The reason people followed Dave was because of his attitude. He could motivate anyone to do anything. If an employee was having a bad day, Dave always had a way of turning his or her attitude into one of a positive nature. "Let's look on the positive side of this," he would say as he changed the complainer's attitude. "What's good in your life?"

Seeing him in action over the years, I asked him one day, "I don't get it! You can't be such a positive person all of the time. How do you do it?"

Dave replied, "It's easy. Every morning I wake up and say to myself, "Dave you have two choices today. You can choose to be in a good mood or you can choose to be in a bad mood. I choose to be in a good mood. Every time something bad happens, I can choose to be a victim or I can choose to learn from it. I choose to learn from it."

He continued, "Whenever anyone comes to me complaining, I can choose to accept their complaints or I can point out the positive side of life. I always choose the positive side."

I protested, "Yeah right! It's not all that easy."

"Yes it is," Dave answered. "Life is all about choices. When you cut away all the stuff, every situation is a choice. You choose how you will react to everything. You choose how you will let people affect your mood. You choose whether you will be in a good mood or a bad mood. The bottom line is it's your choice how you live life."

That made me stop and think about how we do make choices each day. Shortly after this conversation, I moved away and we lost touch, but I often thought about Dave when I made a choice about life instead of just reacting to things.

Several years later, I heard that Dave did something people in the restaurant business are *never* supposed to do. One morning when he was in the restaurant alone, he left the back door open. Then, as luck would have it, three armed robbers came in and held Dave up at gunpoint.

While following their directions to open the safe, Dave's hand was shaking so badly from nervousness, his fingers slipped off the combination. The robbers panicked and shot him.

Luckily, Dave was found relatively quickly and rushed to the local hospital emergency room. After more than eighteen hours of surgery and weeks of intensive care, Dave was released from the hospital with fragments of the bullets still in his body.

I saw Dave about six months after the shooting. When I asked him how he was doing, he said, "If I were any better, I'd be twins. Wanna see my scars?"

I chose not to see his wounds but asked him, "What went through your mind as the robbery was taking place?"

"The first thing that went through my mind was that I should have locked the back door." Dave replied. "Then as I was stretched out on the floor in my own blood, I remembered that I had two choices. I could choose to live, or I could choose to die. I chose to live."

"Weren't you scared," I asked. "Did you lose consciousness?"

Dave's answer was, "The paramedics were great. They kept assuring me that I was going to be fine. When they wheeled me into the emergency room, though, I saw the expressions on the faces of the doctors and nurses. Then I really got scared! I read 'He's a dead man' in their eyes. I knew that I needed to take action."

"What on earth kind of action could you take?" I asked.

Dave answered, "Well there was a big, burly Brunhilde-like nurse shouting questions at me."

"What is your name? Are you allergic to anything?" she shouted.

"My name is Dave." Dave went on, "As I said this I could see the doctors and nurses hesitated in their work as they waited for my reply to her question about allergies. I sucked in a deep breath and yelled at the nurse, 'Bullets! I'm allergic to bullets!'"

Dave's eyes crinkled in a grin as he continued. "They were all laughing. I told them I was choosing to live and that they should operate and work on me as if I were alive, not dead."

Dave lived, thanks to the skill of his doctors but also because of his amazing attitude. I learned from him that every day we have the choice to live to the fullest. Attitude after all, is everything. You can choose to work like you don't need the money, love like you've never been hurt, and, above all—dance like nobody's watching.

In stories women don't just survive but also can develop strength and heal themselves. This next story is about women's initiation into becoming whole. In it, the maiden becomes a warrior-heroine. What is the symbolic significance of the loss of hands? And what is the lesson to be learned in order to become whole?

## The Maiden Without Hands (Grimm Brothers, Germany)

A miller, who had gradually become very poor, had nothing left but his mill and a large apple tree behind it. One day when he went into the forest to gather wood, an old man, whom he had never seen before, came toward him, and said, "Why do you take the trouble to cut down wood? I will give you great riches if you will promise to let me have what stands behind your mill."

"That can be no other than my apple tree," thought the miller. "I possess nothing else." So he said to the old man, "Yes, I will let you have it."

Then the stranger smiled maliciously, and said, "In three years I will come again to claim what belongs to me," and after saying this he departed.

As soon as the miller returned home, his wife came toward him and said, "Miller, from whence have all these riches come so suddenly to our house? All at once every drawer and chest has become full of gold. No one brought it here, and I know not where it came from."

"Oh," replied her husband, "I know all about it. A strange man whom I met in the wood promised me great treasures if I would make over to him what stood behind the mill. I knew I had nothing there but the large apple tree, so I gave him my promise."

"Oh, husband!" said the wife in alarm, "that must have been the wizard. He did not mean the apple tree, but our daughter, who was behind the mill sweeping out the court."

The miller's daughter was a modest and beautiful maiden, who lived in innocence and obedience to her parents for three years, until the day came on which the wicked wizard was to claim her. She knew he was coming, and after washing till she was pure and clean as snow, she drew a circle of white chalk and stood within it.

The wizard made his appearance very early, but he did not dare to venture over the white circle, therefore he could not get near her. In great anger he said to the miller, "Take away every drop of water, that she may not wash, otherwise I shall have no power over her!"

The frightened miller did as he desired, but on the next morning, when the wizard came again, her hands were as pure and clean as ever, for she had wept over them. On this account the wizard was still unable to approach her. He flew into a rage, and said, "Chop her hands off, otherwise I cannot touch her."

Then the miller was terrified, and exclaimed, "How can I cut off the hands of my own child?"

Then the wicked wizard threatened him, and said, "If you will not do as I desire you, then I can claim you instead of your daughter, and carry you off."

The father listened in agony and in his fright promised to obey. He went to his daughter and said to her, "Oh, my child, unless I cut off your two hands the wizard will take me away with him, and in my anguish I have promised. Help me in my trouble and forgive me for the wicked deed I have promised to do."

"Dear father," she replied, "do with me what you will. I am your child."

Thereupon she placed her two hands on the table before him, and he cut them off. The wizard came next day for the third time, but the poor girl had wept so bitterly over the stumps of her arms that they were as clean and white as ever. Then he was obliged to give way for he had lost all right to the maiden.

As soon as the wizard had departed the miller said, "My child, I have obtained so much good through your conduct that for your whole lifetime I shall hold you most precious and dear."

"But I cannot stay here father," she replied. "I am not safe. Let me go away with people who will give me the sympathy I need so much."

"I fear such people are very seldom to be found in the world," said her father. However, he let her go. So she tied up her maimed arms and went on her way at sunrise.

For a whole day she traveled without food, and as night came on found herself near one of the royal gardens. By the light of the moon she could see many trees laden with beautiful fruit, but she could not reach them, for the place was surrounded by a moat full of water. She had been without a morsel to eat the whole day, and her hunger was so great that she could not help crying out, "Oh, if I were only able to get some of that delicious fruit! I shall die unless I can obtain something to eat very soon."

The girl knelt down and prayed for help. While she prayed a guardian fairy appeared and made a channel in the water so that she was able to pass through on dry ground.

When she entered the garden, the fairy was with her, although she did not know it. She walked to a tree full of beautiful pears, not knowing that they had been counted.

Being unable to pluck any without hands, she went quite close to the tree and ate one with her mouth as it hung. One and no more, just to stay her hunger. The gardener who saw her with the fairy standing near her thought it was a spirit and was too frightened to move or speak.

After having satisfied her hunger, the maiden went and laid herself down among the shrubs and slept in peace. On the following morning the king to whom the garden belonged, came out to look at his fruit trees. When he reached the pear tree and counted the pears, he found one missing. At first he thought it had fallen, but it was not under the tree. He went to the gardener and asked what had become of it.

The gardener said, "There was a ghost in the garden last night who had no hands and ate a pear off the tree with its mouth."

"How could the ghost get across the water?" asked the king. "What has become of it after eating the pear?"

To this the gardener replied, "Some one came first in snow-white robes from heaven. They made a channel and stopped the flow of the water so that the ghost walked through on dry ground. It must have been an angel," continued the gardener. "Therefore, I was afraid to ask questions or to call out. As soon as the specter had eaten one pear, it went away."

The king said, "Conceal from every one what you have told me. I will watch myself tonight."

As soon as it was dark, the king came into the garden and brought a priest with him to address the ghost. They both seated themselves under a tree with the gardener standing near them. They waited in silence. About midnight, the maiden crept out from the bushes and went to the pear tree. The three watchers saw her eat a pear from the tree without picking it while what they thought was an angel, stood nearby in white garments.

Then the priest went toward her and asked, "Are you from heaven or Earth? Are you a spirit or a human being?"

Then the maiden answered, "Ah, me! I am no ghost. Only a poor creature forsaken by every one but God."

The king said, "You may be forsaken by all the world but if you will let me be your friend, I will never forsake you."

So the maiden was taken to the king's castle. She was so beautiful and modest that the king learned to love her with all his heart. He had silver hands made for her and very soon after that, they were married with great pomp.

About a year after, the king had to go to battle. He placed his young wife under the care of his mother, who promised to be very kind to her and to write to him.

Not long after this the queen had a little son born and the king's mother wrote a letter to him immediately. In order that he might have the earliest news, she sent it by a messenger.

The messenger however, after traveling a long way, became tired and sat down to rest by a brook. He soon fell fast asleep. Then the wizard came. He was still trying to injure the good queen. He took away the letter from the sleeping messenger and replaced it with another in which it was stated that the little child was a changeling.

Knowing nothing of the change, the messenger carried this letter to the king. When he read it he was terribly distressed and troubled. However, he wrote in reply to say that the queen was to have every attention and care till he returned.

The wicked wizard again watched for the messenger and while he slept exchanged the king's kind letter for another. He wrote to the king's mother with an order to kill both the queen and her child.

The old mother was quite terrified when she read this letter, for she could not believe the king meant her to do anything so dreadful. She wrote to the king again but there was no answer for the wicked wizard always interrupted the messengers and sent false letters. The last was worst of all for it stated that instead of killing the mother and her child, they were to cut out the tongue of the changeling and put out the mother's eyes.

But the king's mother was too good to follow these dreadful orders so she said to the queen, while her eyes streamed with tears, "I cannot kill you both as the king tells me to do. I must not let you remain here any longer. Go now, out into the world with your child. Do not come here again." Then she bound the boy on his mother's back and the poor woman left, weeping as she went.

After walking some time she reached a dense forest and knew not which road to take. She knelt down and prayed for help. As she rose from her knees she saw a light shining from the window of a little cottage, on which was hung a small sign-board with these words, "Every one who dwells here is safe."

Out of the cottage stepped a maiden dressed in snowy garments who said, "Welcome, queen wife," and let her in. Then she unfastened the baby from her mother's back and hushed him in her arms till he slept so peacefully that she laid him on a bed in another room. She came back to his mother.

The poor woman looked at her earnestly and said, "How did you know I was a queen?" The white maiden replied, "I am a good fairy sent to take care of you and your child."

So the queen remained in that cottage many years and was very happy. She was so good that her hands were allowed to grow again. The little boy became her great comfort.

In the meantime, not long after she had been sent away from the castle, the king returned and immediately asked to see his wife and child.

His old mother began to weep and said, "You wicked man, how can you ask me for your wife and child when you wrote me such dreadful letters. How could you tell me to kill two such innocent beings?"

The king, in great distress, asked her what she meant. She showed him the letters she had received which had been changed by the dreadful wizard. Then the king began to weep so bitterly for his wife and child that the old woman pitied him and said, "Do not be so unhappy. They still live. I could not kill them. But your wife and child have gone into the wide world, never to come back for fear of your anger."

"I will go to the ends of the Earth to find them and I will neither eat nor drink till I find my dear wife, even if I should die of hunger," vowed the king.

He started on his expedition and traveled over rocks and valleys, over mountains and highways, for seven long years. He did not find her. He thought that she must have starved to death and that he would never see her again.

He neither ate nor drank during the whole time of earthly food. Heaven sent him help. At last he arrived at a large forest and found the little cottage with a signboard that read, "Everyone who dwells here is safe."

While he stood reading the words, the fairy in her white dress came out, took him by the hand, and led him into the cottage saying, "My lord the king is welcome here. Why are you here?"

"I have been for seven years traveling about the world hoping to find my wife and child. I have not yet succeeded. Can you help me?" he asked.

"Sit down," said the fairy. "Take something to eat and drink first."

The king was so tired that he gladly obeyed, for he truly wanted to rest. He laid himself down and slept. The fairy in white covered his face. Then she went into an inner chamber where the queen sat with her little son whom she had named, "Pain-bringer."

"Go out together into the other chamber. Your husband is here," said the fairy.

The queen went out, but still sorrowfully for she remembered the cruel letters his mother had received. She did not know that he still loved her. Just as she entered the room, the covering fell off his face, and she whispered to her son to replace it.

The boy went forward and laid the cloth gently over the face of the strange man. The king had heard the voice in his slumber and moved his head so the covering fell off again.

"My child," said the queen. "Cover the face of your father."

He looked at her in surprise and said, "How can I cover my father's face dear mother? I have no father in this world. You have taught me to pray to God and I thought my father was God. This strange man is not my father. I do not know him."

When the king heard this, he started up and asked who they were. The queen said, "I am your wife, and this is our son."

The king looked at her with surprise. "Your face and your voice are the same," he said. "My wife had silver hands and yours are natural."

"My hands have mercifully been allowed to grow again," she replied. He still doubted until the fairy entered the room carrying the silver hands that she showed to the king.

Then he saw at once that this was indeed his dear lost wife and his own little son. He embraced them, full of joy, exclaiming, "Now a heavy stone has fallen from my heart!"

The fairy prepared dinner for them that they all ate together. After a kind farewell, the king started with his wife and child to return home to the castle. His mother and all the household received them with great joy.

A second marriage feast was prepared, and the happiness of their later days made amends for all they had suffered through the wicked demon who had caused them so much pain and trouble.

NOTE: An in-depth analysis of the levels of meaning in this tale can be found in *Women Who Run with the Wolves* by Clarissa Pinkola Estes (Ballantine Books, 1992).

In this story the hero meets death and
discovers that death is not a punishment.

## A Journey to the Underworld
## (Bantu)

In a village in the lower Kuanza River region, there
lived two brothers, Ngunza and Maka. Ngunza was the oldest
brother and was very close to his younger brother. He was so
close that while on a journey Ngunza had a dream about
Maka. "Maka, your dear younger brother is dead," the voice
told him in the dream.

Ngunza returned to his village and went straight to
his mother. "I was told Maka is dead. What caused his
death?" he asked her.

"Kalunga-ngombe, the master of the Land of the
Dead, killed him," his mother answered.

A defiant Ngunza announced, "I will go to the Land
of the Dead and fight Kalunga-ngombe." To prepare for this
encounter, Ngunza went to the village blacksmith and asked
him to make an iron trap. The blacksmith was a skilled
worker of iron, and the finished trap was strong—just what
Ngunza needed.

Ngunza took the trap and traveled to Kalunga, the Land
of the Dead. He discovered the path that Kalunga-ngombe
used and placed the trap in such a way that Kalunga-ngombe
would surely become its victim. Ngunza hid in some nearby
bush with his gun. He waited patiently and sure enough, after
a short while he heard a voice cry out in pain.

"I am dying! I am dying!" was the next cry Ngunza
heard. He came out from the bushes and aimed his gun at
the person caught in the iron trap. "Do not shoot me! Free
me from this trap!" demanded the person.

"Who are you? Who is asking to be set free?" asked
Ngunza.

The answer was, "I am Kalunga-ngombe, the master
of Kalunga, the Lord of Death."

"So, I have caught you, Kalunga-ngombe. You have
killed my dear younger brother, Maka!" replied Ngunza.

"I do not seek people to kill and bring them back to the Land of the Dead. The people are brought to me so that they may live on, here in this land. I did not go searching for your brother. He was brought here," answered Kalunga-ngombe.

"Nevertheless, since you are keeping Maka here in the Land of the Dead, I am going to kill you," Ngunza told him.

"If you release me from the iron trap and remain here for four days, on the fifth day you can take your brother Maka and leave with him," promised the wounded Kalunga-ngombe.

"I will agree to that," Ngunza said, and he opened the trap to set Kalunga-ngombe free.

The two traveled to Kalunga, and the leader of the Place of Death took Ngunza to his home. They sat together and person after person came by Kalunga-ngombe. Kalunga-ngombe asked the first person, "What killed you?"

"In the land of the living, on Earth, I was a rich man. My riches corrupted me and that was the cause of my dying." the man replied. Then he moved on.

The next person was a woman. Again Kalunga-ngombe asked, "What killed you?"

"I was killed by my vanity," she answered. "I wanted a man to choose me as his wife. I did everything to attract a man and I did not behave properly. For this reason, I died and came to Kalunga." She moved on.

Kalunga-ngombe looked at Ngunza and said, "You see how it is. I do not go out looking for people to kill. The tribes and villages of the people send them here to me."

"Yes, I do see how it is," Ngunza said quietly.

"Go over there. You will find your brother Maka in one of the houses. Take him home with you," Kalunga-ngombe told Ngunza.

Ngunza went to the house Kalunga-ngombe pointed out. There was Maka. The brothers exchanged greetings. "I have come to take you back to the land of the living Maka. Let us leave," said Ngunza.

To his surprise, Maka answered, "I do not wish to return there. Life here is good. I have everything I want and need. In the land of the living I have nothing. If I return with you, life will be worse for me than it is here. I am quite satisfied to stay here in Kalunga. I will stay here."

Ngunza prepared to return to his village and Kalunga-ngombe gave him presents to take with him to the land of the living. Not only was Kalunga-ngombe the Lord of the Dead but he was also a spirit of fertility. In this role, he gave Ngunza seeds. Among them were seeds of maize, pumpkin, cashew, okra, orange, and the seeds of many other plants and trees.

As Ngunza departed, Kalunga-ngombe told him, "Eight days from now I will come to visit you at your home."

And so Ngunza returned to his village. Just before the eight days were up, Ngunza remembered that Kalunga-ngombe was coming to visit him. Before the eighth day, Ngunza left his house and traveled toward the east. He reached the place of the spirit-being Ludi dia Suku, who had supernatural powers. Ngunza stopped there.

On the eighth day, Kalunga-ngombe discovered that Ngunza had left his village and gone to the east. He followed him. He came to the house of Ludi dia Suku. "Is Ngunza here?" he asked. Meanwhile Ludi dia Suku was quietly eating some maize.

Ludi dia Suku quietly answered, "No, Ngunza was here some time ago. We were planting our maize then. As you can see we are already eating our maize." Of course, Ludi dia Suku, being a spirit-being, could make the maize grow fast, so he spoke the truth.

Kalunga-ngombe left and came to the house of another spirit-being, who was also called Ludi dia Suku. Ngunza was inside and Kalunga-ngombe yelled at him, "I am going to kill you, Ngunza!"

"I did not commit any crime against you." answered Ngunza. "Why do you want to kill me? You were always saying that you never go seeking people to kill them and that those who came to Kalunga were sent to you by the villages and the tribes. That is what you said, but now you have come looking for me to kill me just the same."

With that, Kalunga-ngombe took his throwing-axe in his hand. "I will kill you with this axe," he roared.

But Ngunza was under the protection of the spirit-being Ludi dia Suku. Quickly, before Kalunga-ngombe could throw his axe, Ngunza transformed himself into a spirit. He was now invisible and beyond the reach of Kalunga-ngombe. And so, Kalunga-ngombe returned to the Land of the Dead without Ngunza.

Stories are still told of Ngunza. The people call him Hero-Spirit because he defied Kalunga-ngombe after he was transformed into a spirit. That is why, every year, in one village or another, people set out food offerings to Hero-Spirit to commemorate his brave actions.

One of many stories of three brothers, in which the youngest brother is looked down upon, shows us how foolishness can be healed through experience. The youngest brother proves himself and becomes a hero.

# Salt
## (Russia)

Long ago in Russia when the Tsar ruled the land and the people, there was a great merchant who had three sons. The merchant sent his ships far over the seas, traded here and traded there, in countries whose names are now lost to memory. We only know the name of the youngest brother because his older brothers always referred to him as Ivan the Silly. (Older brothers are like that to their younger brothers, it seems.) They called him that because he was always playing and singing—never working. If there was something silly to do, off he would go and do it.

When the brothers grew up, the father sent the two older ones off, each in a fine ship laden with gold and jewels and rings and bracelets, laces and silks, and spoons with patterns of blue and red, as well as anything else you could think of that costs too much for most people to buy.

The merchant did not give a ship to Ivan the Silly. And so it was that Ivan the Silly watched his brothers go sailing off over the sea on a summer morning to make their fortunes and come back rich men. For the first time in his life he wanted to work and do something useful. He went to his father and kissed his hand, then kissed the hand of his little old mother, and he begged his father to give him a ship. "I want to try my fortune like my brothers," he begged.

"You have never done a wise thing in your whole life, and there is no one who could count all the silly things you've done if he spent a hundred days in counting," replied his father.

"That is true," answered Ivan the Silly. "But now I am going to be different. I will be wise and sail the sea and come back with something in my pockets to show you that I am not just a silly anymore. Give me a little ship, father—just a little ship for myself."

Ivan's little old mother said to her husband, "Give him a little ship. He may not be just a silly after all."

"Very well," said his father. "I will give you a little ship. However, I will not waste good money by giving him a rich cargo."

"Thank you father," said a very happy Ivan. "Give me any cargo you like."

So his father gave Ivan a little ship—an old, well-used ship—and a cargo of rags and scraps and things that were not fit for anything but to be thrown away. He also gave him a crew of ancient old sailormen who were past the ability to do hard work. Ivan went on board at sunset and sailed away like the silly that he was.

The feeble, ancient, old sailormen pulled up the ragged, dirty sails, and away they went over the sea to learn what fortune, good or bad, was in store for a crew of old men with a silly for a master.

They had sailed for four days when suddenly a great wind came over the sea. The feeble sailors did the best they could with the ship, but their best was not enough. The old ragged sails tore from the masts, and the wind did what it pleased, throwing the little ship on an unknown island in the middle of the sea. Then, just as quickly as the wind had risen, it dropped and left the little ship on the beach. Ivan the Silly and his ancient old men were amazed that they were still alive.

"Well, my children," said Ivan, showing he knew how to talk to sailors, "stay here and mend the sails and make new ones out of the rags we carry as cargo, while I go inland and see if there is anything there that could be of use to us."

The ancient old sailormen followed his orders and sat on deck with their scrawny old legs crossed, making sails out of rags, of torn scraps of old brocades, of a soiled embroidered shawl, of all of the rubbish that they had with them for a cargo.

You have never seen such sails! The tide came up and floated the ship. The ancient sailors threw out anchors at bow and stern and sat there in the sunlight, making sails and patching them and talking of the good old days when they were young. All this time Ivan the Silly went walking off into the island.

He found, in the middle of the island, a high mountain. A very high mountain it was. It was so white that when he came near it, Ivan the Silly began thinking of sheepskin coats although it was midsummer and the sun was hot in the sky. The trees were green all around, but there was nothing growing on the mountain itself at all. It was just a great, white mountain piled up into the sky in the middle of a green island.

Ivan walked a little way up the white slopes of the mountain, and then, because he felt thirsty, he thought he would let a little snow melt in his mouth. He took some in his fingers and stuffed it in his mouth. Quickly enough, it came out again, for the mountain was not made of snow but of good salt.

Ivan the Silly did not stop to think twice. The salt was so clean and shone so brightly in the sunlight. He turned around and ran back to the shore and called out to his ancient sailors, "Empty everything on board and throw it into the sea."

They did as they were told. Over it all went rags and tags and rotten timbers, until the little ship was as empty as a soup bowl after supper. Then those ancient old men were set to work carrying salt from the mountain and taking it on board the little ship. They stowed it away below deck until there was not room left for another grain. Ivan the Silly would have liked to take the whole mountain but there was not room in the little ship.

The ancient sailors were glad of that because their backs ached and their old legs were weak. They said they would have died if they had had to carry any more.

"Hoist the sails," ordered Ivan the Silly. With the sails patched together out of the rags and scraps, they sailed away once more over the blue sea. The wind was a fair one for sailing, and the old sailors rested their backs and told old tales. They took turns at the rudder.

They sailed for many days until they came to a town with towers and churches and painted roofs. The town sat on the side of the hill that was near a quiet harbor. They sailed into the harbor and moored the ship. Somehow, the ship looked better when they hauled down their patchwork sails.

Ivan the Silly went ashore and took with him a little bag of clean white salt to show what kind of goods he had for sale. When he came upon someone walking on the road he asked, "Which way is it to the palace of the Tsar of this town?" After he got the directions he finally made it to the palace and went in and bowed to the ground before the Tsar.

"Who are you?" asked the Tsar.

"I, oh great lord, am a Russian merchant. I have here in a bag some of my merchandise. I beg your leave to trade with your subjects in your town."

"Let me see what you have in your bag," ordered the Tsar.

Ivan the Silly took a handful from the bag and showed it to the Tsar.

"What is that?" asked the Tsar.

"Good clean salt," answered Ivan the Silly.

It happened that in that country they had never heard of salt, and the Tsar looked at it, looked at Ivan, and then he laughed. "Why this," he said, "is nothing but white dust, and we can pick that up for nothing. The people of my town have no need to trade with you. You must be silly!"

Ivan's face turned very red, for he hated what his father and brothers called him. Now the Tsar too! He was ashamed to say anything so he bowed to the ground and went away out of the palace.

When he was outside, he thought to himself, "I wonder what sort of salt they use in these parts if they do not know good clean salt when they see it. I will go to the palace kitchen."

He went around to the back door of the palace and put his head into the kitchen. "I am very tired," he said. "May I sit down here and rest a little while?"

"Come in," answered one of the cooks. "But you must sit there and not put even your little finger in our way. We are the Tsar's cooks and we are in the middle of making his dinner." The cook put a stool in a corner out of the way, and Ivan slipped in around the door and sat down in the corner. He looked about him. There were seven cooks at least, boiling and baking and stewing and toasting and roasting and frying. The scullions were as thick as cockroaches. There were dozens of them, running to and fro, tumbling over each other and helping the cooks.

Ivan the Silly sat on his stool with his legs tucked under him and with the bag of salt on his knees. He watched the cooks and the scullions, but he did not see them put anything in the food that he thought might take the place of salt. No. The meat was without salt, the kasha was without salt, and there was no salt in the potatoes. Ivan turned nearly sick at the thought of the tastelessness of all that food.

Then came the moment when all of the cooks and scullions ran out of the kitchen to fetch the silver platters on which to place the food. Ivan slipped down from his stool and running from stove to stove, from saucepan to frying pan, he scattered a pinch of salt in every one of the dishes. Then he ran back to the stool in the corner and sat there. He watched the food being put on the silver platters and carried off in gold embroidered napkins to be the dinner of the Tsar.

The Tsar sat at his great wooden table and took his first spoonful of soup. "The soup is very good today," he said and he finished the soup to the last drop.

"I've never known the soup to be so good," said his wife the Tsaritza as she finished all of her soup.

The beautiful young princess said, "This is the best soup I have ever tasted." She finished her soup with a final slurp. She could be forgiven for doing this because she was the prettiest princess who ever had dinner in this world.

It was the same with the kasha and the same with the meat. The Tsar and the Tsaritza and the princess wondered why they had never had such a good dinner in all of their lives before. "Call the cooks," ordered the Tsar.

All the cooks came in, bowed to the ground, and stood in a row before the Tsar. "What did you put in the food today that you have never put in before?" asked the Tsar.

"We did not put anything unusual in the food, your greatness," said each of the cooks as they bowed to the ground again.

"Then why does the food taste better?" demanded the Tsar.

"We do not know your greatness," answered each of the cooks.

"Call the scullions," ordered the Tsar. The scullions came and they too bowed to the ground, standing in a row before the Tsar. "What was done in the kitchen today that has not been done there before?" asked the Tsar.

"Nothing, your greatness," they all said, except one. That one scullion bowed again and kept on bowing, and then he said, "Please your greatness, please great lord, there is usually no one in the kitchen but ourselves. Today there was a young Russian merchant. He sat on a stool in the corner and told us he was tired."

"Call the merchant," ordered the Tsar.

Ivan the Silly was brought in and he bowed before the Tsar and stood there with his little bag of salt in his hand.

"Did you do anything to the food?" asked the Tsar.

"I did your greatness," answered Ivan.

"What did you do?"

"I put a pinch of salt in every dish."

"That white dust?" asked the Tsar.

"Nothing but that." was the answer.

"Have you any more of it?"

"I have my little ship in the harbor laden with nothing else but salt," said Ivan.

"It is the most wonderful dust in the world," exclaimed the Tsar. "I will buy every grain of it that you have. What do you want for it?"

Ivan the Silly scratched his head and thought. He thought that if the Tsar liked it as much as all that, it must be worth a fair price. So he said, "We will put the salt into bags and for every bag of salt, you must give me three bags of the same weight—one of gold, one of silver, and one of precious stones. Cheaper than that your greatness, I could not possibly sell."

"Agreed," the Tsar said quickly. "And a cheap price too, for a dust so full of magic that it makes dull food tasty and tasty food so good that there is no equal."

The ancient old sailors bent their backs under sacks of salt and bent them again under sacks of gold and silver and precious stones all day and far into the night. When all of the salt had been put in the Tsar's treasury—yes, with twenty soldiers guarding it with great swords shining in the moonlight—and when the little ship was loaded with riches so that even the deck was piled high with precious stones, the ancient old men lay down among the jewels and slept till morning. Ivan the Silly went to bid goodbye to the Tsar.

"Where will you sail now?" asked the Tsar.

"I am off to Russia in my little ship," answered Ivan.

The beautiful princess asked, "A Russian ship?"

"Yes," was Ivan's answer.

"I have never seen a Russian ship," the princess stated. Then she begged her father to let her go to the harbor with her nurses and maids, to see the little Russian ship before Ivan sailed off.

Ivan and the princess went to the harbor and the ancient old sailors welcomed them on board. She ran all over the ship, looking at everything. Ivan told her the names of things such as the deck, mast, and rudder.

"May I see the sails?" she asked. The ancient old men hoisted the ragged sails, and the wind filled the sails and tugged at the boat.

"Why doesn't the ship move when the sails are up?" asked the princess.

Ivan explained, "The anchor holds her."

"Please let me see the anchor," begged the princess.

"Haul up the anchor, my children, and show it to the princess," Ivan said to the ancient sailors.

As the men hauled up the anchor and showed it to the princess, she said, "That is a very good little anchor." Of course, as soon as the anchor was up, the ship began to move. One of the ancient old men bent over the tiller, and, with a fair wind behind her, the little ship slipped out of the harbor and sped away to the blue sea.

When the princess looked around, thinking it was time to go home, the little ship was far from land, and away in the distance she could only see the gold towers of her father's palace. They glittered like pinpoints in the sunlight. Her nurses and maids wrung their hands and made an outcry. She used a dainty handkerchief to wipe the tears from her eyes, and she cried and cried and cried.

Ivan the Silly took her hands in his and comforted her. He told her of the wonders of the sea and land that he would show her. She looked up at him while he talked. His eyes were kind and hers were sweet. They were both quite content and as things progressed, and they agreed to marry as soon as the little ship brought them to the home of Ivan's father. That was an extremely merry voyage. All day long Ivan and the princess sat on the deck and told sweet things to each other. At twilight they sang songs and drank tea and told stories. As for the nurses and maids, the princess told them all to be glad. They danced and clapped their hands and ran about the ship and teased the ancient old sailormen.

When they had been sailing many days, the princess was looking out over the sea. She cried out to Ivan, "See, over there, far away, are two big ships with white sails, not like our sails of brocade and bits of silk."

Ivan shaded his eyes with his hands and said, "Those are the ships of my older brothers. We will all sail home together."

He had the ancient old sailormen give a hail in their cracked old voices. The brothers heard them and came on board to greet Ivan and his beautiful bride. When they found out that she was a Tsar's daughter and that the very decks were heaped with precious stones, they greeted Ivan—but the two brothers had already developed a plan.

"How can this be?" they said to each other. "Ivan the Silly brings back such a cargo, while we in our fine ships have only a bag or two of gold."

"And what is Ivan the Silly doing with such a beautiful bride?" asked the other. They ground their teeth and waited until Ivan was alone in the twilight. They picked him up by his head and his heels and threw him overboard into the dark blue sea.

Not one of the old men had seen this happen, and the princess was not on the deck. In the morning the brothers said that Ivan the Silly must have walked overboard in his sleep. Then, they drew lots. The eldest brother won the princess and the second brother won the little ship loaded down with gold and silver and precious stones.

With that, the brothers sailed home very content. The princess sat and wept all day long, looking down into the blue water. The elder brother was not able to comfort her, and the second brother did not even try. The ancient old sailormen were only able to mutter in their beards. Even though Ivan was a ninny and made them carry a lot of salt and other things, they loved him because he knew how to talk to ancient old sailormen.

Ivan, however, was not dead. As soon as he had splashed into the water, he crammed his fur hat a little tighter on his head and began swimming in the sea. He swam until the sun rose. And then not far away, he saw a floating timber and he swam to it and climbed aboard. There he sat, on the log, in the middle of the sea, twiddling his thumbs, thinking, because he had nothing else to do.

There was a strong current in the sea, though, and that carried him along. At last, after floating for many days without even a bite for his teeth or a drop of water for his stomach, his feet touched dry land. He landed at night, left the log, walked onto the shore, and lay down. There he rested until morning. When the sun rose, he looked around him and saw he was on a bare island. There was nothing on the island but a huge house—as big as a mountain. As he stood looking at the house, the great door creaked with a noise like that of a hurricane among the pine forests. It opened. A giant came walking out and stood there looking down at Ivan.

"What are you doing here, little one?" asked the giant.

Ivan told him the whole story. The giant listened to the very end, pulling at his monstrous whiskers the whole time. "Listen, little one. I know more of the story than you, for I can tell you that tomorrow morning your eldest brother is going to marry your princess," rumbled the giant. "But there is no need for you to take on about it. If you want to be there, I will carry you and set you down before the house in time for the wedding."

With that, he picked Ivan the Silly up and set him on his great shoulders. He set off striding through the sea. He went so fast that the wind he created blew off Ivan's hat.

"Stop a minute," Ivan shouted. "My hat has blown off."

"We can't turn back for that," roared the giant. "We have already left your hat far behind us." He rushed on through the sea. Before the sun had climbed to the top of the blue sky he had splashed on shore, lifted Ivan from his shoulders, and placed him gently on the ground.

"Now, little man," the giant said, "off you run and you will be in time for the feast. There is only one thing. Don't you dare to boast about riding on my shoulders. If you open your mouth about that, you'll pay for it, even if I have to travel back here again."

Ivan the Silly thanked the giant and promised that he would not boast. He ran off to his father's house. Long before he got there he heard the musicians in the courtyard playing as if they wanted to wear their instruments out before darkness came.

The wedding feast had begun and Ivan ran in. The princess was sitting at the high board beside his eldest brother. His mother, father, other brother, and all the guests were there. Everyone was celebrating except the princess. There she sat, as white as the salt he had sold to her father.

When she saw him, she jumped up, and blood once more flushed into her cheeks. "There, there is my true love. Not this wretch of a man who sits beside me at the table!"

"What is this?" exclaimed Ivan's father after he heard the whole story. He turned the two older brothers out and gave their ships to Ivan. Ivan and the princess were married, and the wedding feast began again. Ivan even sent for the ancient old sailormen to come take part. They wept with joy when they saw Ivan and the princess, like two sweet pigeons. They lifted their goblets with old shaking hands and cheered with their old cracked voices.

That is the story about salt and how it made Ivan the Silly a rich man. Best of all, it gave him the loveliest wife in the world.

*Sometimes we don't know what we are seeing because we don't understand what we see. The same is true about healing— the prescription is understanding.*

## Guru's Advice
## (Tibet)

In a small mountain village, there lived a man who was admired and loved by all for his good works and kindly deeds. He was very kind and generous. And yet, his life wasn't all that he wanted it to be. He was passionate about becoming an enlightened being, both compassionate and wise. Then, one day he heard that a legendary guru was coming to his village.

The man drew up all of his courage to ask for a meeting with the great guru. He joined his hands, touching first the crown of his head, then his throat, and finally his heart with his joined hands. He then slid fully outstretched onto the floor. In this way he surrendered his body, speech, and mind to the guru.

The guru asked him what he wished. "Oh, most wise of all, I desire to become an enlightened being. I want to be compassionate and wise and help all living beings. I want to devote my life to learning and helping others. Help me gain this wisdom."

After several other questions, the guru was content that this man was sincere and worthy, so he said, "Go to the mountains and spend each day praying and meditating. I will give you a special prayer to chant. If you do this constantly and with great dedication, you will become an enlightened being. Then you will be able to help all others through your wisdom, compassion, and sincere behavior."

The joyful man thanked the guru and again prostrated himself before him. He climbed up to the top of the highest mountain that surrounded the village. He searched until he found a cave with a suitable stone slab that would be his bed, cushion, and table. He began to meditate and pray. For many years he did this, but he did not gain enlightenment. Twenty years passed in this manner.

Someone who had climbed the mountain to seek his advice informed him that the great guru was coming to the village again. When the kind man heard this, he went down from his mountain cave to again seek advice from the guru.

Many days passed. People lined up to see the famous guru and seek his blessings. At last it was the kind man's turn to see the holy man. He prostrated himself three times at the guru's feet. "Here is a *kata*. With this felicity scarf of white I pledge my dependence on your wisdom."

"Have I not counseled you years ago?" asked the guru.

"Indeed. It was twenty years ago. You told me to meditate and pray and through this I would become enlightened. For twenty years I have done as you told me and I have not reached enlightenment."

"Oh," whispered the great guru. "That will be of no use at all. I must have told you the wrong things to do. You will never reach enlightenment following those directions."

This pronouncement crushed the kind man. He fell to the feet of the guru and cried.

"I am quite sorry," the guru told him. "There is absolutely nothing I can do for you in your search for enlightenment."

The kind man slowly got up to a standing position and suddenly felt quite old. He shuffled back up to his cave convinced that twenty years of his life had been wasted. As he climbed he thought, "What am I to do? For all these years I believed that I would reach enlightenment, and now I have no hope of reaching that goal." He reached his cave and sat down on his familiar stone slab, crossed his legs, closed his eyes and began to pray and meditate as before. "I may as well continue. What else is there left for me to do?"

The kind man began to meditate and chant the prayers that had become so familiar to him. Although he no longer had any hope of reaching enlightenment, he prayed and chanted. Immediately, he became enlightened. Amazingly he saw the world in its reality and everything was clear. It was necessary for him to give up in order to attain his goal.

He now realized that grasping at enlightenment prevented him from attaining it.

With this profound knowledge, he left his cave and gazed at his village below. For an instant he thought he heard the gentle laughter of the guru as he looked up at the sky and saw a huge rainbow that stretched across the snowy peaks. "I see, you must give up in order to succeed," he said. And the kind man went back to the world to do all of the things that he had dreamed of doing for so long.

That trickster Anansi was full of greed.
It wasn't until he had lost all he sought
that good was attained. Anansi left a
legacy for all to share.

## Anansi's Greed for Common Sense
## (Jamaica)

Anansi the trickster decided one hot day that he
knew how he could get plenty of money and all of the power
anyone could want. With those things, everyone would bring
their worries to him and beg for his help. He would give
them advice and then charge them a high price for it. All he
needed to do was collect all the common sense there was in
the world and keep it for himself.

And so, even though it was quite hot, Anansi started
to collect all of the common sense in the world and store it
in one huge calabash. He searched all of the gourd trees to
find the largest calabash of them all. When he found it, he
put all of the common sense he discovered into it. He
searched everywhere for common sense. There was a little
of it in some places and lots of it in others. He stuffed all that
he could find into his giant calabash. When Anansi could
find no more common sense left in the world, he put the top
on his calabash.

"Where can I put this precious calabash of common
sense so no one else can find it?" Anansi thought. Then Anansi
came up with a plan. He tied a strong rope around the neck
of the calabash and then with the ends of the rope. He tied
them so he could hang the calabash around his neck. He
searched for the tallest tree he could find, all the while the
calabash bumping along on his stomach.

When he found a satisfactory tree, he started to
climb it. It was hard climbing, for the calabash kept bouncing
off the tree and onto his stomach, and off his stomach and
onto the tree. It was hard, slow climbing, but he was determined to hide his calabash on the very top of the tree.

He was breathing hard as he bumped, climbed, and bumped. Below him, he suddenly heard a little boy who was standing on the ground looking up at him. "You are such a silly!" the boy laughed. "Look at you bumping and banging your way up the tree. Why don't you do it the easy way and put the calabash behind you?"

What was this he heard? Anansi grew furious hearing this common sense coming from the mouth of the little boy. After all, didn't he collect all of the common sense in the world? It would seem that he hadn't—and the little boy was proof of that.

Furiously, Anansi slipped the calabash over his head and smashed it into pieces. As he did that, little bits of common sense fell out, were caught up in gentle breezes, and scattered all over the world again. That is how everyone got a little bit of common sense, but no one got it all. We can all thank Anansi for that!

Sometimes we think taking the easy way
out is the best way, but what do we lose
in doing that? The Dog and the Wolf
give us examples of what is lost and
gained. Does freedom help us heal
ourselves?

## The Dog and the Wolf
## (Aesop, Greece)

Aesop, a slave in the sixth century B.C., collected
and told many fables. It was said that he won his freedom by
his storytelling talents. "The Dog and the Wolf" is adapted
from Aesop's fable of the same name.

A wolf, half-dead with hunger, comes upon a house
dog.

"Hey, brother wolf, what's happening?" the dog
asked politely.

The wolf replied in a very sad voice, "Nothing lately.
In fact, I haven't had anything to eat for days."

"I can see that!" replied the house dog. "Look at you.
You can hardly manage to stand up. You must be weak from
hunger."

In a weak voice, the wolf answered, "I know, but
what else can I do? I can never know when or where I'll get
my next meal."

"Now that is a problem," mused the house dog.
"Maybe I have a deal for you. Come with me to my master
and share my work. The work is hard but the food is regular
and good."

And so they went, the jovial, well-fed house dog
gaily leading the frail, weak wolf. As they were making their
way toward the town, the wolf noticed something peculiar
about the house dog.

"Hey, dog," he questioned him. "How did the hair on your neck get worn away?"

"Oh, this?" asked the house dog as he pointed to one side of his neck. "That's nothing. That's where my master puts the collar on me at night when he chains me up. Yes, it rubs a bit, but I do get fed each day. You don't get something for nothing."

When he heard this, the wolf suddenly stopped, turned around, and started slowly walking back to where they came from.

"Hey," yelled the house dog impatiently. "Where are you going? You can't leave now. We are going to work together."

"No way! Good-bye, house dog," shouted the wolf over his shoulder. "To me it's better to starve free than to be a fat slave."

With that, the wolf went on his way to enjoy his free—if sometimes hungry—life.

# HEALING RELATIONSHIPS

**R**elationships play a significant role in stories, and healing relationships with spouses, parents, and children are common themes in folk literature all around the world. We also find numerous tales about childless couples, orphans, grandparents, and siblings. These tales not only reflect the customs, circumstances, and values of the times, they also share truths that transcend the times. As abbreviated forms of distinguishing right from wrong, how to live the good life, which behaviors will be rewarded and which will be punished, these stories contain many layers of moral teaching. They also teach us the importance of family, its problems, and the pain of breaking family ties.

The value of families is clearly conveyed in the many tales of childless couples who long for a child and invariably become parents in some unique way. There are familiar tales, such as "Tom Thumb" and "Pinocchio," as well as the more obscure and unusual "The Greedy Youngster," which I included in the previous chapter of this collection. It offers an interesting variation on the theme of children. Other tales (e.g., "The Doll") relay the plight of orphans and demonstrate how this unfortunate circumstance can be surmounted.

Stories about stepparents and stepsiblings seemed archaic not long ago. In the far past, stepparents were fairly common because of disease, death, and other unfortunate circumstances. Today, with marriages, divorces, and remarriages, many youngsters are again living with stepparents. The cautionary message of these stories is clear—take the role of parenting seriously and be as fair as possible to all the children.

97

Stories also have a great deal to teach us about the relationship of spouses. There are many examples of faithfulness and trust, often demonstrated through everyday behaviors. Lessons for all relationships can be gleaned from such tales as "The Tiger's Whisker," which shares a wonderful healing message of patience and self-trust. "The Lute Player" teaches us of the constancy of love.

Sibling rivalry is another theme found in traditional tales. Think of all the stories there are about three sons, with the youngest being mistreated and ridiculed. These are usually accounts of a fool's transformation into a hero. Other tales, such as "The Seven Swans," teach us about family loyalty.

Finally, folktales underscore the importance of intergenerational relationships. They teach that respect for elders—by children and grandchildren as well as by the community—is both right and virtuous. The wisdom of the elders renders strength to the family and to society.

Virtually all stories in some way concern relationships. The lessons they teach us—about honesty, being true to oneself, being generous and kind—are good medicine for today's families, just as they were when the stories were first told.

A mother's health and her relationship with her son are threatened when he marries. A doctor suggests an interesting cure for both problems.

## The Cure
## (Syria)

An old widow had only one son. When he grew to be a man she found him a bride, but she was jealous of her daughter-in-law and began to complain of imaginary sicknesses. Every day she would nag her son and say, "Bring me the doctor, my boy. Let the doctor come." The son did nothing for a while, but eventually he gave in and went to fetch the doctor. While he was out, the widow washed herself and lined her eyes with *kohl.* She put on her best gown and wound a sash of silk about her waist. She donned a velvet vest and her daughter-in-law's wedding headdress and placed an embroidered kerchief over it. Then she sat and waited. When the doctor arrived and asked for his patient, the son showed him in and said, "There she is. It is my mother. Since the moment I was married she has been grumbling like a hen, and not one day has brought her joy or pleasure." "This lady needs a husband," said the doctor. "But she is my mother!" "Yes," said the doctor, "and she needs a groom." "She is over ninety years old! Surely she can't be thinking of marriage again!" "You are wrong, my son," said the doctor. "As often as her skirts are lifted by the wind, the thought of a bridegroom enters her mind." "Sir," said the son, "if she had wanted a husband, she could have married long ago. Why don't you examine her and see what is the matter with her." "I have already told you what is wrong." At this, the old woman sprang up from her corner and said to her son, "My boy, may you find favor in the sight of God, do you fancy yourself a greater expert than the wise doctor?"

From *Arab Folktales* by Inea Bushnaq, copyright © 1986 by Inea Bushnaq. Used by permission of Pantheon Books, a division of Random House, Inc. This story also appears in *Gray Heroes: Elder Tales from Around the World,* edited by Jane Yolen (Penguin Books, 1999).

In this tale relationships can be healed not only in this lifetime but in the next lifetime. Communication holds the key.

## A Bird Couple's Vow
## (Hmong)

**M**any, many New Year's festivals ago, there were a couple of birds who vowed to love each other for life and never to leave each other. They needed to build a nest and ended up laying their eggs in the beard of a spirit man. One evening the male bird flew off to find food. He landed on a lotus flower and sucked the nectar from it for quite a while. But suddenly the sky became dark, and the flower closed up, *whoomp,* with the bird inside. He couldn't get back to the nest that evening and had to spend the night inside the flower. When the male bird didn't return, the female bird thought that her husband had left her.

In the morning, when the sun came up and shone on the flower, so the flower opened and the bird was able to fly back home. But when he arrived, his wife said to him, "Why were you out so long? Were you out talking with other girls?"

"No," said the male bird. "I didn't talk to anyone. I went to suck nectar from a water lily and, while I was sucking, it closed up and I couldn't get out."

The female bird didn't believe him. Being very persuasive, the male bird said, "I swear this is true. If it isn't true, may something bad happen to the spirit man." When the spirit man heard that, he was quite angry, so he cut off the nest from his beard and threw it away in a valley of long, tall grass, the kind that was used to make thatch for roofing.

Shortly thereafter, the bird couple's eggs hatched. Then one day the people came to the valley to burn the grass where the birds were living. As the fire burned closer and closer, the female bird said to the male, "Let me stay on top of the chicks and you stay on the bottom. Let both of us die with our chicks."

The male said, "No. Let me stay on top and you stay on the bottom." Finally the female let the male stay on the top. The fire burned up to their nest and then finally burned it, but just before the nest caught fire, the male flew away, letting the female die with the chicks. The female died, but she saw that her husband had left her to die in the nest with their little chicks.

The female bird was reincarnated as a king's youngest daughter. She remembered her life as a bird, and she couldn't forget the things that her bird husband had done. In fact, it made her so mad that she couldn't speak.

After the male bird had flown away from his wife and chicks, he also died. He was reincarnated as a man.

One day the king proclaimed, "If anyone can make my daughter talk, I will let her marry that person."

Shortly after that, a young man, who was the reincarnation of the bird husband, heard about the king's promise. He went to the *shoa* (which means "wise prophet" in Hmong) and said, "*Shoa,* I want to marry the king's daughter. Please help me and tell me what I can say to this lady that would make her talk to me."

*Shoa* remembered the birds and said, "Don't you remember when fire burned the valley of the long, tall grass? You flew away and let her die with your chicks. You only need go to her and tell her what you did. But instead of saying that you flew away and left her and the chicks to die, you should say that the female flew away and the male died with the chicks. Then she will answer you, of course."

So the young man traveled to the king's palace. He said to the king's daughter, "Let me tell you a story. A long time ago, there were a couple of birds. They made a nest on the spirit man's beard. But the spirit man cut off their nest and throw it into the valley of the long, tall grass. When people burned the valley of grass, the male bird said that he should stay on top of the chicks and that both he and his wife would die with the chicks in the fire. The female disagreed, so the male let the female stay on top of the chicks, and he stayed under them. But when the fire burned their nest, the female flew away and left the male to die with the chicks."

The girl spluttered and cried, "You are wrong! The male bird was on top!" The man answered, "No, the female was on top."

They kept arguing back and forth about which bird was on the top. The king heard them and said, "This young man has succeeded in getting my daughter to talk. I will keep my promise and let him marry her."

So they were married, and that is how the couple once again became husband and wife.

In this story, the wife proves her love through a clever rescue. She doesn't depend on others who might not have the best intentions to save her husband. She does it herself.

## The Lute Player
## (Russia)

Once upon a time there lived a king and a queen. They were happy, comfortable, and very fond of each other and had nothing to worry them, but at last the king grew restless. He longed to go out into the world, to try his strength in battle against some enemy, and to win all kinds of honor and glory.

So he called his army together and gave orders to journey to a distant country where a heathen king ruled. This heathen king mistreated or tormented everyone he could lay his hands on. The king then gave his parting orders and wise advice to his ministers, took a tender leave of his wife, and set off with his army across the sea.

I cannot say whether the voyage was short or long; but he finally reached the country of the heathen king and he marched on with his troops, defeating all who came in his way. But his victories did not last long, for in time he came to a mountain pass, where a large army was waiting for him. The army put his soldiers to flight, and took the king himself prisoner.

He was carried off to the prison where the heathen king kept his captives, and now our poor friend had a very bad time indeed. All night long the prisoners where chained up, and in the morning they were yoked together like oxen and forced to plough the land till it grew dark.

This state of things went on for three years before the king found any means of sending news of himself to his dear queen. But at last he contrived to send this letter: "Sell all our castles and palaces, and put all our treasures in pawn and come and deliver me out of this horrible prison."

102

The queen received the letter, read it, and wept bitterly as she said to herself, "How can I deliver my dearest husband? If I go myself and the heathen king sees me he will just take me to be one of his wives. If I were to send one of the ministers!—but I hardly know if I can depend on them."

She thought and thought, and at last an idea came into her head. She cut off all her beautiful long brown hair and dressed herself in boy's clothes. Then she took her lute and without saying anything to anyone, she went forth into the wide world.

She traveled through many lands and saw many cities, and went through many hardships before she got to the town where the heathen king lived. When she got there she walked all round the palace and at the back she saw the prison. Then she went into the great court in front of the palace, and taking her lute in her hand, she began to play so beautifully that one felt as though one could never hear enough.

After she had played for some time she began to sing, and her voice was sweeter than the lark's.

> I come from my own country far
> Into this foreign land,
> Of all I own I take alone
> My sweet lute in my hand.
>
> Oh! who will thank me for my song,
> Reward my simple lay?
> Like lovers' sighs it still shall rise
> To greet thee day by day.
>
> I sing of blooming flowers
> Made sweet by sun and rain;
> Of all the bliss of love's first kiss,
> And parting's cruel pain.
>
> Of the sad captive's longing
> Within his prison wall,
> Of hearts that sigh when none are nigh
> To answer their call.

My songs beg for your pity,
And gifts from out your store,
And as I play my gentle lay
I linger near your door.

And if you hear my singing
Within your palace, sire,
Oh! give, I pray, this happy day,
To me my heart's desire.

No sooner had the heathen king heard this touching song sung by such a lovely voice, than he had the singer brought before him.

"Welcome, O lute player," he said. "Where do you come from?"

"My country, sire, is far away across many seas. For years I have been wandering about the world and gaining my living by my music."

"Stay here then a few days, and when you wish to leave I will give you what you ask for in your song—your heart's desire."

So the lute player stayed on in the palace and sang and played almost all day long to the king, who could never tire of listening and almost forgot to eat or drink or to torment people. He cared for nothing but the music, and nodded his head as he declared, "There's something about playing and singing. It makes me feel as if some gentle hand had lifted every care and sorrow from me."

After three days the lute player came to take leave of the king.

"Well," said the king, "what do you desire as your reward?"

"Sire, give me one of your prisoners. You have so many in your prison, and I should be glad of a companion on my journeys. When I hear his happy voice as I travel along I shall think of you and thank you."

"Come along then," said the king, "choose whom you will." And he took the lute player through the prison himself.

The queen walked about among the prisoners, and at length she picked out her husband and took him with her on her journey. They were long on their way, but he never found out who she was, and she led him nearer and nearer to his own country.

When they reached the frontier, the prisoner said, "Let me go now, kind lady. I am no common prisoner, but the king of this country. Let me go free and ask what you will as your reward."

"Do not speak of reward," answered the lute player. "Go in peace."

"Then come with me, dear boy, and be my guest."

"When the proper time comes I shall be at your palace," was the reply, and so they parted.

The queen took a short way home, got there before the king, and changed her dress.

An hour later all the people in the palace were running to and fro and crying out, "Our king has come back! Our king has returned to us."

The king greeted everyone very kindly, but he could not so much as look at the queen.

Then he called all his council and ministers together and said to them, "See what sort of a wife I have. Here she is falling on my neck, but when I was pining in prison and sent her words of it, she did nothing to help me."

And his council answered with one voice, "Sire, when news was brought from you, the queen disappeared and no one knew where she went. She only returned today."

Then the king was very angry and cried, "Judge my faithless wife! Never would you have seen your king again if a young lute player had not delivered him. I shall remember him with love and gratitude as long as I live."

While the king was sitting with his council, the queen found time to disguise herself. She took her lute, and slipping into the court in front of the palace she sang, clear and sweet

> I sing the captive's longing
> Within his prison wall,
> Of hearts that sigh when none are nigh
> To answer to their call.
>
> My song begs for your pity,
> And gifts from out your store,
> And as I play my gentle lay
> I linger near your door.

And if you hear my singing
Within your palace, sire,
Oh! give, I pray, this happy day,
To me my heart's desire.

As soon as the king heard this song, he ran out to meet the lute player, took him by the hand and led him into the palace.

"Here," he cried, "is the boy who released me from my prison. And now, my true friend, I will indeed give you your heart's desire."

"I am sure you will not be less generous that the heathen king was, sire. I ask of you what I asked and obtained from him. But this time I don't mean to give up what I get. I want you—yourself!"

And as she spoke she threw off her long cloak and everyone saw it was the queen.

Who can tell how happy the king was? In the joy of his heart he gave a great feast to the whole world, and the whole world came and rejoiced with him for a whole week.

I was there too, and ate and drank many good things. I shan't forget that feast as long as I live.

⚮ From *Troubadour's Storybag* by Norma J. Livo (Golden, CO: Fulcrum Publishing, 1996).

We all admire those who are loyal and those who persevere. In this story a young couple is rewarded for faithfully adhering to these virtues. Themes of reconciliation and the constancy of love take to the heavens.

## The Seventh Night of the Seventh Month (China)

If you look to the heavens on the seventh night of the seventh month, you will see some very special stars. One of the stars is called Herding Boy Star and the other is called Weaving Girl Star.

Many turns of the Earth ago, a silver river separated the heavens and the Earth. In the celestial heavens lived a girl called Weaving Girl. She was the most beloved grand-child of the Queen Mother. The Weaving Girl was not only beautiful, but also very gentle. Her hands were slender and she could weave the most beautiful cloth of any weaver.

Weaving Girl had six sisters who also could weave. Each day they would weave different patterns of cloth and sometimes they would weave a cloud for the heavens.

At this same time, on earth there lived a young orphan boy. His parents had died when he was very young. His name was Herding Boy and he lived with his older brother and his wife. They were very poor.

One day the elder brother decided to divide the property they had. Naturally, he kept everything for himself and gave Herding Boy only a very old ox. Herding Boy did not complain, and he brought his ox to a lovely plain to eat grass and then took him to a watering hole. He took very good care of his ox. The ox somehow seemed to understand the boy's problems.

The ox worked diligently for his new master. He tilled and plowed the earth. Soon after, the area where the ox had plowed became extremely fertile ground so that anything Herding Boy planted grew. With the money that Herding Boy saved from the crops, he bought a house and built a large corral for his ox.

Even though Herding Boy was happy, he was lonely because he had no one to talk with. One day he remarked to the ox, "I wish I had a companion."

To Herding Boy's surprise, the ox answered, "That's not such a difficult task." The ox continued, "There are seven fairies now swimming in the river. Their clothes are on the banks of the river. If you quickly go to the river unseen and gather up the clothes of one of the fairies, she will have to remain and be your wife. Quickly now, get on my back and I will take you to the river."

It was just as the ox had said. There in the river were seven beautiful fairies playing. It was the Weaving Girl and her six sisters having a bath in the river. There were seven garments, all of different colors on the river bank—red, green, blue, yellow—and Herding Boy decided to take the garment that was all white.

As he ran away, the fairies saw him and were frightened. They ran onto the shore and put their clothes on, but Weaving Girl could not find her clothes. She started sobbing and begged the young man to return her clothes. Herding Boy answered, "Only if you will be my wife will I return your clothes."

There was nothing Weaving Girl could do but nod "yes." After receiving her clothes and putting them on, she returned with Herding Boy to his home and became his wife.

Ten years passed. The couple now had two beautiful children, a girl, age five, and a boy, age six. The ox was very old when Herding Boy got it and by now it was even older and was about to die. The ox said to Herding Boy, "When I die, skin my hide and put the hide on whenever you have any troubles." With that, the ox died. The couple mourned the ox and were filled with grief. Herding Boy skinned the hide of the ox just as he had been told to do.

In heaven, ten years was like only ten days. Since Weaving Girl had disappeared, no more clouds were woven. The Queen Mother was very upset and ordered, "Weaving Girl must be brought back to the heavens."

At that very moment, on Earth, Weaving Girl was busy weaving some very beautiful cloth. Her children were at her side when suddenly the sky became very dark. Lightning flashed across the sky, and the thunder was horrendous. The children started to cry when a magpie flew down from the heavens.

"You have sinned and must return to the heavens," said the magpie. "The Queen Mother says you must come back."

Weaving Girls' face turned white and she blurted, "I will not return. I will not return."

"If you do not return, your whole family here on Earth will be punished," cautioned the magpie.

As the thunder continued to boom, heavenly soldiers came down to Earth and started to take Weaving Girl to heaven. Her children sobbed, "Don't take our mother away."

At the same time, Herding Boy chased the heavenly soldiers shouting, "Return my wife!" He put his children in a basket and carried them with him. He ran hard and fast and chased the heavenly soldiers to the silver river.

The Queen Mother, seeing that Herding Boy was close to her soldiers, quickly removed the silver river and threw it into the sky. With this act, Herding Boy could no longer give chase to the soldiers.

Suddenly Herding Boy remembered the hide of the ox. He threw the hide onto his back and was able to run into the heavens. He was almost near the silver river, now in the sky, when the Queen Mother threw a golden hairpin into the river.

At once the river became very wide. So wide in fact that Herding Boy could not get across it. The expression on his face was filled with despair. Weaving Girl tried to express her love for him. They both showed their anguish about being apart.

Seeing all of this, the Queen Mother was deeply moved. It was then that she agreed that once a year on the seventh day of the seventh month, the two could cross the silver river and meet again. She asked the magpies to stretch their wings to make a bridge on that day so the couple could meet.

Now, when you look into the sky on the seventh day of the seventh month, you will see a very bright star and two little stars. These are Herding Boy and his two children. The other star, separated by the Milky Way, is the Weaving Girl star. At a certain time of the night, the Milky Way, which is the silver river, will appear. Then in an instant, you will see the star of Herding Boy and the star of Weaving Girl meet, only to be separated again by daylight.

Today, children often make seven flowers, seven chairs, and seven dresses in miniature for the seven fairies. It is considered a time when young girls pray for the right husband-to-be. Everyone looks into the sky to try to find the stars of Herding Boy and Weaving Girl. Do you think you can find them?

❧ This story is a variation on the legend of the Blue Willow dinnerware pattern.

This story appeared in the *Dublin and London Magazine* in 1825. Strange things happen near the Loughleagh, or the Lake of Healing, in Ireland. A son braves many dangers for his mother.

## The Lake of Healing or Loughleagh (Ireland)

"Do you see that bit of a lake," said my companion, turning his eyes towards the acclivity that overhung Loughleagh. "*Troth* [truth], and as you think of it, and as ugly as it looks with its weeds and its flags, it is the most famous one in all Ireland. Young and *ould* [old], rich and poor, far and near, have come to that lake to get cured of all kinds of scurvy and sores. The Lord keeps our limbs whole and sound, for it's a sorrowful thing not to have the use o' them. 'Twas but last week we had a great grand Frenchman here; and, though he came upon crutches, faith he went home sound as a bell; and well he paid Billy Reily for curing him."

"And, pray, how did Billy Reily cure him?"

"Oh, well enough. He took his long pole, dipped it down to the bottom of the lake, and brought up on the top of it as much plaster as would do for a thousand sores!"

"What kind of plaster?"

"What kind of plaster? Why, black plaster to be sure; for isn't the bottom of the lake filled with a kind of black mud which cures all the world?"

"Then it ought to be a famous lake indeed."

"Famous, and so it is," replied my companion, "but it isn't for its cures neither that it is famous; for, sure, doesn't all the world know there is a fine beautiful city at the bottom of it, where the good people live just like good people. Troth, it is the truth I tell you; for *Shemus-a-sneidth* [Shemus of the fairy ground] saw it all when he followed his dun cow that was stolen."

"Who stole her?"

"I'll tell you all about it: Shemus was a poor *gossoon* [simpleton], who lived on the brow of the hill, in a cabin with his ould mother. They lived by hook and by crook, one way and another, in the best way they could. They had a bit of ground that gave 'em the *preaty* [grain], and a little dun cow that have 'em the drop o' milk; and, considering how times go, they weren't badly off, for Shemus was a handy gossoon to boot; and, while minden the cow, cut heath and made brooms, which his mother *sould* [sold] on a market-day, and brought home the bit o' tobaccy, the grain of salt, and other *nic-nackenes* [knickknacks], which a poor body can't well do widout. Once upon a time, however, Shemus went farther than usual up the mountain, looken for a long heath, for town's people don't like to stoop, and so like long handles to their brooms. The little dun cow was a'most as cunning as a sinner, and followed Shemus like a lap-dog everywhere he'd go, so that she required little or no *herden*. On this day she found nice *picken* [picking] on a round spot as green as a leek; and, as poor Shemus was weary, as a body would be on a fine summer's day, he lay down on the grass to rest himself, just as we're resten ourselves on the *cairn* [pile of rocks] here. *Begad* [Golly], he hadn't long lain there, sure enough, when what should he see but whole loads of *ganconers* [a kind of fairy appearing in lonesome valleys] dancing about the place. Some o' them were *hurlen* [hurling], some kicking a football, and others leaping a kick-step-and-a-lep. They were so *soople* [supple] and so active that Shemus was highly delighted with the sport, and a little tanned-skinned chap in a red cap pleased him better than any o' them, *bekase* [because] he used to tumble the other fellows like mushrooms. At one time he had kep the ball up for as good as half-an-hour, when Shemus cried out, 'Well done, my hurler!' The word wasn't well out of his mouth when whap went the ball on his eye, and flash went the fire. Poor Shemus thought he was blind, and roared out, '*Mille murdher!*' [a thousand murders] but the only thing he heard was a loud laugh. '*Whay* [Why] is this?' says he to himself, 'what is this for?' and *afther* [after] rubbing his eyes they came to a little, and he could see the sun and the sky, and, by-and-by, he could see everything but his cow and the mischievous *ganconers*. They were gone to their rath or *mote* [hillside]; but where was the little dun cow? He looked, and he looked, and he might have looked from that day to this, bekase she wasn't to be found, and good reason why—the ganconers took her away with 'em.

"Shemus-a-sneidh, however, didn't think so, but ran home to his mother.

"'Where is the cow, Shemus?' *axed* [asked] the ould woman.

"'*Och* [Oh], *musha* [term of endearment], bad luck to her,' said Shemus, 'I *donna* [don't] know where she is!'

"'Is that an answer, you big blaggard, for the likes o' you to give your poor ould mother?' said she.

"'*Och, musha,*' said Shemus, 'don't kick up *saich* [such] a *hollhous* [ruckus] about nothing. The ould cow is safe enough, I'll be bail, some place or other, though I could find her if I put my eyes upon *kippeens* [a stick or twig], and speaking of eyes, faith, I had very good luck o' my side, or I had *naver* [never] a one to look after her.'

"'Why, what happened your eye, *agrah* [term of endearment]?' axed the ould woman.

"'Oh! didn't the ganconers—the Lord save us from all hurt and harm!—drive their hurlen ball into them both! and sure I was stone blind for an hour.'

"'And may be,' said the mother, 'the good people took our cow?'

"'No, nor the devil a one of them,' said Shemus, 'for by the powers, that same cow is a knowen as a lawyer, and wouldn't be such a fool as to go with the ganconers while she could get such grass as I found for her to-day.'

"In this way, continued my informant, they talked about the cow all that night and the next mornen both o' them set off to look for her. After searching every place, high and low, what should Shemus see sticking out of a bog-hole but something very like the horns of his little beast!

"'Oh, mother, mother,' said he, 'I've found her!'

"'*Wherem alanna* [Where about]?' axed the ould woman.

"'In the bog-hole, mother,' answered Shemus.

"At this the poor ould *creathure* [creature] set up such a *pullallue* [noisy ruckus] that she brought the seven parishes about her; and the neighbours soon pulled the cow out of the bog-hole. You'd swear it was the same, and yet it wasn't, as you shall hear by-and-by.

"Shemus and his mother brought the dead beast home with them; and, after skinnen her, hung the meat up in the chimney. The loss of the drop o' milk was a sorrowful thing, and though they had a good deal of meat, that couldn't last always; besides, the whole parish *faughed* [looked down] upon them for eating the flesh of a beast that died without *bleeden* [bleeding]. But the pretty thing was, they couldn't eat the meat after all, for when it was boiled it was as tough as carrion, and as black as a turf. You might as well think of sinking your teeth in an oak plank as into a piece of it, and then you'd want to sit a great piece from the wall for fear of knocking your head against it when pulling it through your teeth. At last and at long run they were forced to throw it to the dogs, but the dogs wouldn't smell to it, and so it was thrown into the ditch, where it rotted. This misfortune cost poor Shemus many a salt tear, for he was now obliged to work twice as hard as before, and be out cutten heath on the mountain late and early. One day he was passing by this cairn with a load of brooms on his back, when what should he see but the little dun cow and two red-headed fellows herding her.

"'That's my mother's cow,' said Shemus.

"'No, it is not,' said one of the chaps.

"'But I say it is,' said Shemus, throwing the brooms on the ground, and seizing the cow by the horns. At that the red fellows drive her as fast as they could to this steep place, and with one leap she bounced over, with Shemus stuck fast to her horns. They made only one splash in the *lough* [lake], when the waters closed over 'em, and they sunk to the bottom. Just as Shemus thought that all was over with him, he found himself before a most elegant palace built with jewels, and all manner of fine stones. Though his eyes were dazzled with the splendour of the place, faith he had *gomsh* (sense) enough not to let go his *holt* [hold], but in spite of all they could do, he held his little cow by the horns. He was axed into the palace, but wouldn't go.

"The hubbub at last grew so great that the door flew open, and out walked a hundred ladies and gentlemen, as fine as any in the land.

"'What does this boy want?' axed one o' them, who seemed to be the master.

"'I want my mother's cow,' said Shemus.

"'That's not your mother's cow,' said the gentleman.

"'*Bethershin!*' [that is impossible] cried Shemus; 'don't I know her as well as I know my right hand?'

"'Where did you lose her?' axed the gentleman. And so Shemus up and tould him all about it: how he was on the mountain—how he saw the good people hurlen—how the ball was knocked in his eye, and his cow was lost.

"'I believe you are right,' said the gentleman, pulling out his purse, 'and here is the price of twenty cows for you.'

"'No, no,' said Shemus, 'you'll not *ould birds wid chaff* [hold birds with chaff]. I'll have my cow and nothen else.'

"'You're a funny fellow,' said the gentleman; 'Stop here and live in a palace.'

"'I'd rather live with my mother.'

"'Foolish boy!' said the gentleman, 'stop here and live in a palace.'

"'I'd rather live in my mother's cabin.'

"'Here you can walk through gardens loaded with fruit and flowers.'

"'I'd rather,' said Shemus, 'be cutting heath on the mountain.'

"'Here you can eat and drink of the best.'

"'Since I've got my cow, I can have milk once more with the *praties* [potatoes].'

"'Oh!' cried the ladies, gathering round him, 'sure you wouldn't take away the cow that gives us milk for our tea?'

"'Oh!' said Shemus, 'my mother wants milk as bad as anyone, and she must have it; so there is no use in your *palaver* [idle talk]—I must have my cow.'

"At this they all gathered about him and offered him bushels of gold, but he wouldn't have anything but his cow. Seeing him as obstinate as a mule, they began to thump and beat him; but still he held fast by the horns, till at length a great blast of wind blew him out of the place, and in a moment he found himself and the cow standing on the side of the lake, the water of which looked as if it hadn't been disturbed since Adam was a boy—and that's a long time since.

"Well, Shemus drove home his cow, and right glad his mother was to see her; but the moment she said 'God bless the beast,' she sunk down like the *breesha* [breaking] of a *turf rick* [grass pile]. That was the end of Shemus-a-sneidh's dun cow.

"'And sure,' continued my companion, standing up, 'it is now time for me to look after my brown cow, and God send the ganconers haven't taken her!'"

Of this I assured him there could be no fear; and so we parted and left Loughleagh or the Lake of Healing.

I told this story at a workshop. Afterward, a woman came up to me in tears. She told me her family was just going through such an emotional time. She thanked me for the story and confided, "It will definitely change my life." Her family was experiencing similar troubles, and the story gave her a new respect for the elders in her family.

## Grandfather's Corner
## (Germany)

Once upon a time, a long time ago, there was a very old man who lived with his son and daughter-in-law. His eyes were dim and watery, his knees tottered under him when he walked, and he was very deaf. As he sat at the table his hand shook so that he would often spill the food over the tablecloth or on his clothes, and sometimes he could not even keep it in his mouth when it got there.

His son and daughter-in-law were so annoyed to see his conduct at the table that at last they placed a chair for him in a corner behind the screen, and gave him his meals in an earthenware basin quite away from the rest of the family. He would often look sorrowfully at the table with tears in his eyes, but he did not complain.

One day, while he was thinking sadly of the past, the earthenware basin, which he could scarcely hold in his trembling hands, fell to the ground and was broken. The young wife scolded him for being so careless, but he did not reply, only sighed deeply. Then for a penny she bought a wooden bowl and gave him his meals in it.

Some days after that, his son and daughter-in-law saw their little boy, who was about four years old, sitting on the ground and trying to fasten together some pieces of wood.

116

"What are you making, my boy?" asked his father.

"I am making a little bowl for papa and mamma to eat their food in when I grow up," he replied.

The husband and wife looked at each other without speaking for some minutes. At last they began to shed tears, and went and brought their old father back to the table and from that day he always took his meals with them and was never again treated unkindly.

Mother and daughter relationships can be difficult sometimes, but this story points out the gifts of mother to daughter. We all experience loss and need to heal from it.

## The Doll
## (Ukraine)

Beyond the Dnipro and beyond the Dniester, there lived a happy family—a mother, a father, and their daughter, Paraska. Together they prospered without a care in the world. Then one day the mother became sick. Pale and weak, she wasted away. They called the doctors and they called the wise women of the village, but no one could do anything for her. Soon everyone realized that the mother would die, and they all grieved sorely. But none grieved more than Paraska and her father.

As the mother lay on her deathbed, she called her daughter to her side, "Paraska," she said, "you are still a young girl. When I am gone, you will have no mother to protect you, but I will give you a mother's blessing. Remember, a mother's blessing can save you from the bottom of the sea, while a mother's curse brings nothing but trouble. Paraska, my blessing will always be with you."

Paraska stood silently, holding her mother's hand, tears streaming from her eyes. Then her mother handed her a doll. The doll looked just like Paraska's mother, with dark hair and round green eyes. As Paraska stood admiring the doll, her mother continued.

"Take care of this doll, Paraska. Feed her and care for her and always keep her with you. If you ever need anything, take your dolly from your pocket and tell her what you need. She will help you. Good-bye now, my love. Take the doll and go. Send your father to me, for I must talk to him, too."

Paraska put the doll in her pocket, as her mother had told her, and went to fetch her father. When the father came and stood at his wife's side, she took her wedding ring from her finger and handed it to him.

"My beloved husband, we have been together only a short time. I am sorry I must leave you now, but it is the will of heaven. I know how hard it will be after I'm gone, but do not pine for me too long. The sorrow of the living weighs heavily on the dead and disturbs their eternal rest. Mourn for me for one year only. When the year is over, seek another wife. Take my wedding ring for the new wife you will find. The woman whom my ring fits will be the perfect bride for you. And she will bring you happiness as I have for this short time."

The mother closed her eyes. Her breathing became harsh and slow and finally it stopped. Her husband stood still, turning the ring over and over in his hands as tears poured from his eyes. Paraska rushed back into the room and threw her arms around her father, and together they wept. Then they laid out the body and buried it as was the custom in those parts. The two kept vigil at the mother's grave. Forty days passed and they celebrated her memory, her *molebin'* (a supplication, church service, or litany of grati-tude celebrating the final rest of the dead) as it is called. Nine months passed and the mother's grave bloomed with flowers. Ever so slowly the sorrow began to lift from the hearts of Paraska and her father.

On the anniversary of her mother's death, Paraska's father remembered his wife's dying wishes. He took the wed-ding ring from the drawer and looked at it. Then he showed the ring to Paraska and told her of his wife's wishes.

"You know, Paraska, you look more and more like your mother each day. Try on the wedding ring and see how it looks on your hand." Paraska hesitated at her father's request, but did not want to disobey. She took the ring and slipped it on her finger. Lo and behold, the ring fit perfectly! Paraska's father was overjoyed.

"Paraska," he said, "look how well it fits! Your mother must have known. So, you see, I need look no further. You were meant to be my bride."

At first Paraska thought her father was joking and she laughed, but he kept insisting and Paraska's laughter changed into alarm. "Father, you can't mean this. You cannot marry me! I am your own flesh and blood. A father does not marry his own daughter. Who ever heard of such a thing?"

But Paraska's father had made up his mind. He was going to marry Paraska and that was that. He told his daughter that she would be very happy as his wife and that he would be happy too. Didn't she want to be happy? Then he started the wedding preparations. He brewed beer and ordered food, and Paraska, seeing that her father meant to go through with it, worried desperately. What could she do? She could not marry her own father, but how could she get out of it? The more she thought about it, the worse she felt, and with her mother gone, Paraska had no one to talk to. Finally, she began to cry.

As Paraska wept, she felt something stirring in her pocket—almost as if it were tapping to get her attention. Then she remembered, "The doll!" Her mother's deathbed wishes had gotten her into this predicament. Maybe they could get her out too.

"Dolly, dolly, in my pocket," she whispered, "I need your help. Father wants to marry me and I don't know what to do—my own father, my own flesh and blood. It is wrong."

"I'm hungry," said the doll. "Take me out and feed me. Then we'll talk."

When Paraska went to dinner that night, she ate quickly and hid some of her food in her apron. Her father kept looking at her and smiling.

"Tomorrow's our wedding day, my love," he said. "After our wedding, we will not be just father and daughter, but also husband and wife." Paraska's heart shuddered.

"Please excuse me, father," the girl said. "I have so many things to do before tomorrow. May I go to my room?"

"Of course," her father agreed, again smiling.

Once she was in her room, Paraska took the doll from her pocket and the food from her apron. She fed the doll. Then the doll opened its round green eyes even wider and looked straight at Paraska as it spoke. "Tomorrow your father will come to take you to the church for the wedding. When he knocks on your door, tell him you're not quite ready. Tell him you need a few more minutes, then spit into each of the corners. Your spit will cover for us while we escape."

Paraska put the doll back in her pocket and went to bed. She woke early the next morning and had just gotten out of bed when she heard a knock on her door. It was her father.

"Come, my darling," he said. "Today is our wedding day. Come and I will take you to church."

"Just a minute, father," Paraska answered, "I'm not quite ready. Give me a few more minutes." Then she quickly spat into all four corners of the room as the doll had told her to do. She felt the doll stir in her pocket and took it out.

"Give me a piece of bread and put me in the middle of the room," said the doll. Paraska again did as she was told. The doll stamped three times and the floor opened to a dark, narrow staircase. Down, down, down it went. As Paraska stood with her mouth gaping, the doll spoke again.

"Hurry! Hurry down the staircase," it said. But the staircase looked so dark and foreboding that Paraska held back. Just then her father knocked again.

"Come, my darling. We must go to the church now."

To Paraska's surprise, the spittle answered him in her own voice, "Just a minute, father, I'm not quite ready. Give me a few more minutes." Paraska stood frozen in astonishment.

"Quick!" urged the doll. "We must escape before the spittle dries. Once it dries, it will not be able to speak."

So Paraska grabbed her doll and started down the stairs. She heard her father knock again and again the spittle answered, "Just a minute, father, I'm not quite ready. Give me a few more minutes." Paraska hurried on, her heart pounding and her feet clattering down the steps. When her father knocked the third time, Paraska could hear the impatience in his voice. The spittle tried to answer, but it was drying out and all it could say was, "M-m-m F-f-f."

Then Paraska heard her father burst into her bedroom. Of course, the room was empty. No Paraska there, only bits of dry spittle in the corners and a dark stain on the floor where the staircase had been!

So that was the last Paraska heard of her father. She continued down, down, down, and as she descended her eyes grew accustomed to the dim light and she became less afraid. When she reached the bottom, a horseman went by. He was all white: his saddle was white, his bridle and stirrups were white, and his whip was white. Even his face was a strange luminescent white. As he rode by, the darkness lifted and it became day. Paraska sighed and reached into her pocket to make certain her doll was still there. Yes, she felt better now. She went on.

Paraska had no idea where she was going; she just walked. She walked and she walked. She did not know how long she had walked and she did not know how far she had walked. Maybe it was far and maybe it was not, but after a time she heard hoof beats and saw a plume of red dust in the distance. She saw as it got closer that it was another horseman. This one was completely red—as red as the first horseman had been white. He was dressed in red, his horse was red, and on the horse was a red saddle. Even his face was a ruddy, glowing red. When he galloped by, the sun rose to its highest point. It was high noon.

As the sun bore down upon her, Paraska grew tired. She was hungry and thirsty too, but there was nowhere to rest and nothing to eat. Soon the girl found herself surrounded by a dark, dense forest. On and on she walked, hoping to find something—a stream or a soft meadow perhaps—but every turn she made was like the last.

Still she walked on. Suddenly, and without warning, a third horseman rode by. He was as black as the others had been white and red. His horse was black and everything on his horse was black. He was black too, and so were all his clothes. He rode in silence and as he passed Paraska, the darkness fell and it became night.

Now Paraska began to worry. She had no idea where she was, except that she was in the middle of a forest in a strange land, and now it was nighttime. How had she gotten herself into this predicament? Had her doll misled her? Paraska shuddered. No, there could be nothing worse than having to marry her own father. Tears filled Paraska's eyes, but through them she glimpsed a light in the distance. Ah, she thought, maybe she was not going to perish after all!

Paraska hurried toward the light. The forest was so thick and overgrown that it was hard to stay on the path. As she approached the light, Paraska saw a small hut surrounded by a high fence. When she drew nearer, she saw that on each fence post was a strange beacon. Paraska strained to see. Could it be?

Yes, they were human skulls! Their eyes glowed with an eerie light that illuminated the hut and its yard.

Paraska stopped dead in her tracks. Should she run? She looked about frantically. She wanted to leave, but there was nowhere to go, so she crept slowly toward the yard. The eyes of the skulls turned toward her and stared. Trembling, she opened the gate and entered the yard. With the eyes upon her, she was drenched in a strange light. As she crossed the yard to the hut, the eyes followed her. Finally she took a deep breath and knocked on the door.

A harsh, crackling voice answered, "Who's there? Who dares disturb my rest?"

"My name is Paraska," the girl replied. "I'm lost and I need food and shelter. Can I stay here for the night?"

"Why, yes," the voice said. "There is food on the stove. After you eat and sleep, we'll talk."

Paraska opened the door carefully and entered the cottage. Inside was a huge old woman. This woman was thin as a rail, but so tall that she had to hunch over and bend her knees to fit inside her own hut. She had a few whisps of white hair on her head and a few long hairs on her chin. Her wrinkled lips clung to her gums and her arms and legs seemed to have no flesh at all. Paraska stood silent before the old woman. This must be *Baba Yaha* (a witch or hag figure common in Ukrainian, Russian, and Eastern European tales—also known as *Baba Yaga*) she thought to herself. Then the old woman spoke.

"There—the food is on the stove." She pointed a long, bony finger. "Take what you need, then rest till tomorrow." Paraska obeyed and ate from the pot. Then she curled up on a bench. She was still shaky and thought she would never fall asleep, but her eyes closed and the next thing she knew, she was waking to the sound of horses' hooves upon the ground. It was morning.

Paraska looked about. The old woman was out in the yard puttering. The girl tiptoed to the door and stood watching quietly. Then the old woman turned around.

"Ah, awake at last!" she cried. "Now here is what you will do. You will work for me, my young one, and if you work, you will eat. And I will pay you as well. If you work hard, I will give you a spindle and a loom such as you have never seen."

"Thank you, grandmother," Paraska replied shyly, "I will do as you say."

*Baba Yaha's* eyes blazed. "And if you don't, your head will join the many on my fence, my precious." The hag pointed her chin to the skulls on her fence and cackled. Then she said, "My horses need oats. See that bag over there?" Paraska nodded and the old woman went on, "Take those oats and go to the field on your left. Plow it. Sow the oats. Reap the oats, thresh them, and roll the oats. You must have them ready for me when I return at sunset, for my horses will be hungry and so will I!"

The old woman then jumped into a huge mortar that stood by the gate. She grabbed the pestle and pushed herself off. The mortar lifted from the ground and flew up into the air, only to disappear behind the clouds. *Thump, swish* . . .

*thump, swish. . . .*" Paraska heard *Baba Yaha* row her mortar through the sky. When the old woman had disappeared from sight, the girl broke down and wept.

"I can't grow a field of oats in one day," she thought. "It's impossible, even in this strange land." Paraska sobbed and sobbed until she remembered her doll. She went to the stove and got some food saying, "Dolly, dolly, in my pocket." Then she set the doll on the table and fed it. After the doll had eaten, Paraska told it what the old woman had said. The doll nodded as Paraska spoke.

"It can be done, it can be done," the doll repeated. "With a mother's blessing and good will and diligence, it can be done."

"But how?" Paraska whimpered.

"Don't worry," said the doll. "You clean and sweep *Baba Yaha's* house. Gather some wood, make a fire in the stove, and cook a meal. By the time you finish and the old woman returns, the oats will be ready."

Paraska did as she was told. In the meantime, the doll went outside. It turned to the left and looked at the field then stamped its foot three times. Suddenly the soil began churning. It plowed itself into long, deep furrows. Then the doll walked over to the bag of oats and clapped its hands three times. The bag opened and oats flew into the furrows, covered themselves, and sprouted. The grain grew and grew, and then it turned yellow and lay on its side as though it had been mowed. The doll clapped its hands again. Stalks of grain lifted from the ground and gathered themselves into sheaves. The sheaves marched into the barn. There each sheaf beat itself till it was threshed and then swept the oats under the millstones to be rolled. Three empty bags glided up to the millstones and oats poured into each.

By the time Paraska had finished her chores inside the house, it was growing dark. Three bags of oats stood by the gate where the old woman parked her mortar and pestle. As the girls stood washing her hands she heard hoof beats, then the *thump* and *swish* of the mortar and pestle. Down from the clouds came *Baba Yaha*.

When the old woman saw the three bags of rolled oats, she did not know whether to be happy that the work was done or sad that she could not punish Paraska. After dismounting from her mortar she began to squeeze herself into the hut. First she stuck her head through the door, then her shoulders. Hunching her back, she bent her knees so they almost touched her chest. Then she squirmed inside. The old woman cast her eyes about the hut suspiciously. She could not believe what she saw! The house was spotless and a pot of soup was on the stove, ready to eat. *Baba Yaha* took a big slurp. Yes, it was good. Then she ate her fill, saying, "You eat too, my child. Eat and rest, for you will need your strength tomorrow. If you work, then you eat. That's how things go around here. You will have plenty to do tomorrow."

Paraska ate and stowed some food away for her doll. Then she curled up on the bench and slept soundly. In the morning, the old hag called to the girl through the window. "Wake up, wake up! Today you must work on the middle field. I need wheat and I need bread." Paraska stumbled outside, squinting in the light. The old woman pointed to a bag of wheat and said, "Take that bag of wheat. Sow it in the middle field and have some fresh bread ready for me by the time I get home." *Baba Yaha* drew her long, red tongue over her mouth and smacked her lips. Then she got into her mortar and picked up her pestle. *Thump, swish,* she was gone.

This time Paraska did not cry. She took her doll out, fed it, and told it about the day's tasks. The doll said, "With a mother's blessing and good will and diligence, it can be done. You clean the house. Gather wood for the stove and build a fire. By the time the fire is ready for cooking, the loaves will be ready to bake."

Paraska got to work and the doll went outside. The doll looked at the middle field and stamped its foot three times. The soil plowed itself into furrows. Then the doll went to the bag of wheat and clapped its hands three times. The wheat flew into the furrows, covered itself, and sprouted. It grew, turned yellow, and lay on its side as though it had been mowed. When the doll clapped its hands again, the wheat gathered itself into sheaves and the sheaves marched to the barn. There the sheaves beat themselves till they were threshed and swept the grains between the mill-stones to be ground into flour. Three bags slid into place and flour poured into each one. The doll took one bag. It clapped its hands three times and the flour poured into a bowl with water, yeast, eggs—everything for the most delicious bread.

By the time Paraska had finished her chores, it was growing dark. Two bags of wheat stood by the gate where *Baba Yaha* parked and three loaves of bread were baking in the oven. As Paraska pulled the steaming loaves from the oven, she heard the sound of a galloping horse, then the *thump* and *swish* of *Baba Yaha's* mortar and pestle. She glanced out the door just in time to see the old woman descend to Earth.

*Baba Yaha* looked at the bags of wheat. She sniffed the air and poked her nose into the hut and smelled the freshly baked bread. Then she ate heartily, telling Paraska to eat, eat, and rest too. Again Paraska saved some of her food for the doll and then went to sleep on her bench.

The next morning, Paraska woke to the old woman's voice wheedling in her ear.

"Your task today, my precious," she said, "is to plow the third field—the field on the right. Sow it with flax seed. Mow the flax and soak it. Beat it and pull the fibers. Then cure them, spin them, and weave me a new *rushnyk* (an embroidered towel used as decoration and to adorn icons and holy images, as well as in engagement ceremonies and other rituals).

Paraska rubbed her eyes and stretched. She watched the old woman fly off into the clouds then fed her doll and told it the task. While Paraska worked in the house, the doll went outside. As before, the doll plowed and sowed the field. Then it marched the flax to the river to soak and clapped its little hands. The flax beat itself to fiber, combed itself, and presented itself to the spindle. At the doll's command, the spindle whirred, spinning the flax, and then the loom wove the *rushnyk*.

By the time Paraska had finished her chores, it was growing dark and a beautiful new *rushnyk* lay across the table. Then the girl heard the sound of horses and the *thump* and *swish* of the old woman's mortar and pestle. *Baba Yaha* was home.

The old woman again bent herself like a pretzel to get into the house. She hunched her back and lifted her knees and squeezed inside. There she saw the lovely *rushnyk* on the table. The house was clean and dinner was cooked and ready to eat. *Baba Yaha* turned to the girl and said, "I see you have earned your keep, but I must ask you how you accomplished this, for never before has a human done what I required."

"I will answer your question if you will answer mine," Paraska replied. The old woman nodded.

"When I was coming through the forest, three horsemen crossed my path—a white horseman, a red horseman, and a black horseman. Who were they?"

"Ah, those were my horsemen," said the witch, "morning, noon, and night. But young girls should not ask too many questions. So tell me, how were you able to do my tasks?"

Paraska looked down and looked into the old woman's eyes. "I had my mother's blessing," she said, "and with a mother's blessing and good will and diligence, anything can be done."

"What?" *Baba Yaha's* eyes flared with anger. "A mother's blessing, eh? A mother's blessing?! No, no, no, we cannot have any blessings around here! Now you must go. Take your pay and leave. And ask no more questions."

The old woman handed the girl a spindle and a loom. Paraska checked her pocket to make sure the doll was still there then headed back the way she had come. When she arrived at the edge of the forest, she found the stairs that led to the world above. Paraska stopped. What if her father was there, waiting to marry her? Still, the witch had told her she could not stay in the underworld. She touched the doll in her pocket and when she felt no objection, she headed up the stairs.

As Paraska emerged from the underworld, she was dazzled by the light. She found herself in a large field. Her old house was gone without a trace and her father was nowhere to be seen. Paraska did not know that she had been gone for a long, long time. What had seemed like days to the girl had actually been years. In that time, her father had married and moved away and their little mud and thatch hut, whipped by the winds and washed by the rains, had crumbled and become one with the earth. Paraska saw nothing but the field.

So she began walking again. She did not know how long she walked or how far. Perhaps it was far, or perhaps it was not, but after a time she saw a city in the distance. Paraska approached the city and entered it. She wandered into the poor section of the town, where she found an old widow woman. The woman had no children and was all alone. When Paraska asked her for shelter, the old woman agreed.

So Paraska lived with the old widow. Their lives were peaceful and routine and time passed; no one noticed how long Paraska stayed. The young girl did all the chores and whenever she had a free moment she would take out her spindle and loom and spin or weave. The spindle produced the finest thread ever seen. It was thin and even and almost shone in the dark. The loom produced the most exquisite cloth—fine and strong and of the most beautiful white color.

Before long, Paraska had several measures of cloth. She called the old widow and said, "Take this cloth to the market, grandmother. Sell it and see what you can get. It is fine cloth. Perhaps it will make some money for us."

So the old widow went to the market and sat down near the stalls where vendors were selling cloth and fabric. Everyone who came by looked at the cloth and marveled. They touched it and rubbed it against their cheeks and sighed. "This is much too fine for us," they said. "We cannot afford such cloth. Only a king can have cloth like this. Take the cloth as a present to the king."

The old widow did not know what to do. True, the cloth was fine enough for royalty, but she had been hoping to get some money for it. Anyway, she was just a poor old woman. She did not know if she would even be allowed into the palace. But again and again people told her the same thing, until finally she set off to see the king. As she passed through the gates, she trembled. Almost instantly, two guards seized her.

"This is no place for the likes of you!" they shouted, and they were about to push her out when she managed to pull some of Paraska's cloth from the wrapper.

"Th-this is a gift for the king," she stammered, her hand trembling as she held the cloth before their eyes. The guards stared and then led her into the king's chambers.

The old woman bowed low and without saying a word, laid the cloth at his feet.

"Where did you get this?" asked the king. "You didn't steal it, did you? Surely you did not make this yourself with your old, twisted hands!" At first the old woman was so frightened that she could not speak. Then she blurted out that the cloth was indeed hers, but this only confused the king and that in turn made the woman even more afraid. Finally she managed to tell him about Paraska, a poor orphan, a young woman who lived with her and did spinning and weaving in her spare time.

"Ah!" The king's face softened and his eyebrows raised. He touched the cloth to his cheek and caressed it. Then a hint of a smile crept across his lips. After ordering his carriage, he seated the trembling old widow in it beside him and told the coachmen to follow her directions to her home. As they approached the widow's house, they saw Paraska standing in the doorway. When the king saw the young woman, his smile broadened and he became almost cheerful. He stepped out of the carriage and bowed before Paraska.

Then he kissed her hands and asked the old widow for Paraska's hand in marriage.

"If it is Paraska's wish to marry you, then so be it," answered the widow. "If my adopted daughter gives her consent, I will not stand in the way."

So Paraska and the king were married. They lived happily together and had no trouble and no sorrow, just beautiful children to bless their marriage. The doll stayed in Paraska's pocket till the end of her life, when Paraska gave her mother's blessing away to her own daughter. And so it is that the mother's blessing is passed from generation to generation.

∾ Natalie O. Kononenko, *The Magic Egg and Other Tales from Ukraine,* retold by Barbara J. Suwyn (Englewood, CO: Libraries Unlimited, 1997).

NOTE: For a different version of this tale and a detailed interpretation of it, refer to *Women Who Run with the Wolves* by Clarissa Pinkola Estes (Ballantine Books, 1992).

This story of wisdom demonstrates how gentleness and patience can overcome seemingly impossible problems. It also tells us to trust in ourselves.

## The Tiger's Whisker (Korea)

Long ago, in ancient Korea, there was a time of warfare, battles, warriors, and those left behind waiting for it all to end. One particularly fierce warrior returned home after fighting battle after battle for many years.

His wife greeted him with kisses, embraces, and tears of happiness. The man who returned home wasn't the same as the man who had left years ago. He was now going through each day in a gloomy, detached way. There was no joy or liveliness left in his emaciated body. He didn't respond to his wife's relief and joy. In fact all he did was sit at the table with his eyes cast down at his feet.

She told him what had happened since he had been gone, but he just sat there, unresponsive. Before him, she placed all of his favorite foods to please him, but he just played with the food and pushed it back away from him.

In their bed at night, he turned his back to her and ignored her touch and attempts to comfort him. He curled himself up into a ball and just lay there. His wife didn't know how to reach him anymore. "What has happened, dear husband? What can I do to help you? Please don't turn from me," she pleaded.

Pleas had no effect on him. Finally, in total frustration, the wife went to the old wise man, who healed people's sicknesses with potions and magical charms and provided solutions to their problems. "What am I to do, oh wise one?" she begged. "My husband has returned from years of battle and is not the same man I married. There is no love left in him."

130

The wise man listened to her story, stroked his beard and thought for a while. "I may have the answer to your problem. You must win back your husband's love, but to do this I will need some very special ingredients for the potion that will help you. I need the whisker of a fierce tiger. When you bring me such a whisker, I will mix the remedy."

The distraught wife stared at him in alarm. "What did you say? A tiger's whisker? A fierce tiger's whisker? I cannot get such a thing."

The old man placed one gnarled hand in his other and studied them. Then he said, "You must bring me what I need or I cannot help you win the love of your husband."

The warrior's wife didn't even thank the wise man for his guidance. She left his place and muttered to herself "This is impossible. How am I to get the whisker of a fierce tiger and survive?" She went to the market and bought a chunk of fresh meat. Instead of returning home, she went into the jungle. She knew where the cave of the tiger was. From the sounds coming out of the cave, the tiger was in there, sleeping. He slept in the mouth of the cave with the sun just reaching him. She softly walked closer to the cave.

"Look how sharp his claws are," she thought. She sat down nearby and watched the heaving of the tiger's chest as he breathed in his sleep. After a while, she carefully set the chunk of meat on the rock where she had been sitting. She softly left, and returned home.

The next day, she did the same thing. Daily she got meat, went to the cave and left the meat a few inches closer to the sleeping tiger. It took several weeks of this and then the tiger, who was awake, didn't move as she approached him. He almost seemed to say, "Place the meat right in front of me."

More time passed, and the wife continued her daily trip to the tiger's cave. One daring time, she sat right next to the tiger. He watched her closely. More time passed and on one of the visits, she stretched her hand out, let the tiger sniff it, and then petted him. Several visits later, the tiger put his head near her lap and made a sound like a giant purr.

Many trips later, she carefully took her pair of tiny scissors from her pocket, leaned over to the tiger and ever so carefully cut one of his whiskers.

She felt so triumphant as she returned home with the tiger's whisker. She had done the impossible. Early the next morning she trotted to the wise man's place and triumphantly gave him the whisker. "I did not forget your instructions.

Here is the tiger's whisker that you need to make the magical potion that will win my husband's love back for me."

The wise old man, accepted the whisker, studied it, and said, "Hmmm, ah, and oooh." He turned it over in his fingers. Quietly he asked her, "How did you manage to get this tiger whisker?"

The wife answered, "At first, I thought it was an impossible task. Then I decided to try anyway. I knew where the tiger's cave was, and I took a chunk of meat each day to him and patiently got closer to him each trip. I was very patient about it. We seemed to accept each other carefully and then seemed to come to trust each other. It almost seemed like he let me cut his whisker like a precious gift."

What the wise old man did next shocked the wife. He threw the whisker into his cooking fire. "That is a wonderful story you have just told me," he said.

"How could you throw the whisker in the fire? After all I have been through to get it? Why did you do such a thing?" the wife wailed. "Now how can you make the love potion for me?"

"Ah, dear patient one, you do not need magic and spells. Anyone who can tame a fierce animal like a tiger already knows how to win her husband's love. Just look at your husband and remember how you got the tiger to trust you," he advised.

And so, the wife returned home to her very unhappy husband. She no longer whimpered, whined, or scolded. She won his love again with her patience and gentleness. At long last her unhappy warrior husband really returned to her.

In this tale the hero devotes himself to study to win the hand of the girl he loves. When he backslides, the girl in the mirror knows. Love wins out only after our hero learns to earn it.

## The Mirror
## (China)

There was a village in China where country people owned just their plot of ground, their thatched cottage, and a few clothes. The people loved each other and did not dream of riches, which they knew they could never have.

In one of these village homes, however, lived a young girl whose mother insisted that she should learn to read and write along with keeping house, embroidering, and playing on the lute.

"Remember, to hold a high place, one must be a scholar. Learning is the most important thing there is," the mother said. And so, this most unusual family made sure that both their son and daughter studied.

Grandmother told the young girl that she must study hard because she was not as lucky as Lu in the story, who had a lovely maid in the mirror to help him.

The boy and girl knew there was a story they were about to hear from grandmother. They were right.

"Lu was a young man who lived in days long ago. His family was determined that he should be educated, and they worked hard and saved their money to pay for good teachers for him," old grandmother began.

"Lu would rather spend time in games with his friends or walking with his bird under the trees that grew by the banks of the river. He was not a hardworking student even though his family pleaded with him to settle down and pay attention to the teachers," she continued.

"One day, instead of studying, Lu was out with his bird in its cage and he met a young maiden. She glowed and was so beautiful that she was more beautiful than any painting of young women he had ever seen. They greeted each other, 'My name is Tu Chin,' she said. Lu was so struck by her that he knew he must marry her. If he could not, he knew he would never marry. Tu Chin was the answer to all of his dreams of happiness.

"They met on the riverbank and talked and talked for hours. Then, one day Tu Chin told Lu that their meetings must end. 'Dear Lu, you do not study. You are wasting your time so I will not come again until you have passed the Emperor's examinations. I have brought you a present to remind you of me.'

"She took out a box and gave it to Lu. Inside it was a flat, round piece of metal. One side was ornamented with carved animals and flowers, while the other was smooth and shining like crystal. When she put the round mirror into his hand, she told him that he would see her face in the mirror but only after he had studied diligently. Then, she was gone.

"Sadly Lu returned home and went to the room where he studied. He looked at the mirror and there he saw the figure of Tu Chin, with her back turned as if she were moving away from him. He immediately sat down at his study table and took out his books. From that moment, Lu was a changed person. He no longer wasted his time, instead he amazed his teachers with how hard he worked. Whenever he looked in the mirror, he saw Tu Chin's beautiful face.

"Lu did this for quite some time and then he fell into his old ways. He stopped studying, and then one day when he looked in the mirror, he saw Tu Chin, her back to him, just as it had been after she first gave him the mirror. He became ashamed of himself and hurried back to his books. In a few years he was ready to take the Emperor's examinations. Over a period of three days, he took the tests and he triumphantly passed them.

"His family celebrated his success. Meanwhile, a representative of the richest man in the whole city came to arrange plans for a marriage between Lu and the wealthy man's daughter. Everyone else was filled with joy except for Lu. He refused to consider such an event. He went into his study and looked at the mirror and saw his beloved Tu Chin's face in smiles. Then it seemed that she stepped down out of the mirror and told him to agree to the marriage with the rich man's daughter. Then she vanished.

"Lu could not understand why his beloved had told him to marry another. When it came time for the bridal procession to come, Lu's sorrow instantly turned to great joy, for the bride turned out to be Tu Chin herself.

"Lu gained not only a beautiful wife, but a high position and riches—all because he had worked and studied. You two children have heard the story of the mirror and now you must learn to study and work at learning so you too may someday earn great happiness. That is my story."

A faithful, determined sister rescues her seven brothers from enchantment and proves to be a relationship healer supreme.

## The Seven Swans
## (Europe)

**I**n a land by the shore of a restless sea, a king mourned the loss of his wife. She had been more dear to him than the light of day, and in remembrance of her he poured out his love upon his children: They were the sun and stars of his life, and all that could be wished for was theirs. The seven boys grew in time to be youths both strong and gentle, and as for the youngest child, his daughter, she bloomed as merry and as fair as the wild roses running along the castle walls. Her brothers were devoted to her and she to them, and there was no shadow upon their lives. But in the king's heart there was still a sadness that their laughter could not heal.

In time, then, he sought a new wife. The bride he brought into their home was clever and beautiful, but she was a jealous woman, and could not bear to share her husband with the children of his first love. Most of all she hated the young girl, who as she grew was becoming the very image of the woman she wished to replace.

"First, though, to be rid of the sons," she thought, "so that they'll not hinder me." She had learned the trick of charms and spell casting from her mother, and used her witch-wit now to make seven shirts for the brothers, each one lined with swans' down she begged from the king's huntsmen. Then one day, while the king himself was at the hunt, she found the seven youths amusing themselves in the courtyard, and she flung the shirts over their heads. In an instant they were transformed, and seven wild swans rose crying into the air and flew from sight.

The daughter saw all this from her window and she was afraid, sure that her stepmother meant to do her harm as well. She feared, too, that her father would not listen to her words, for she had seen the looks and smiles and soft whispers that passed between the man and his wife, and was for the first time uncertain of his love. So in that very hour she slipped away from the castle and walked far away along the shore. She knew that in time her father would come seeking her, to return her to the home that now held no safety. Yet the kingdom was hemmed in by mountains, forest, and sea: how could she escape? Late in the afternoon, she came across the long, white feathers of swans strewn on the sand, and she wept for her brothers and herself as she twined the feathers into her tangled hair.

Then as the sun spilled itself out of sight, she heard the cries of birds, and the air around her was filled with wings as the seven wild swans came to rest. In the instant that the light faded from the sky, their swan-shapes fell away, and they stood once more before her, her brothers. With tears of joy, they embraced her. Yet as she told them what had befallen her, their faces became grim.

"But can you not come home with me now?" she begged them.

"No," they replied, "for that is a part of the spell: While the sun is in the sky we are wild swans and have the spirits of swans, and even when the sun is set a part of that wildness remains. We may not enter indoors nor sleep beneath a roof, nor may we ever call a corner of sea or land our home. We cannot go back."

"There is worse," the elder brother added, "for the wind and the seasons are calling us away. In the morning we must fly away across the sea, and you will have no protection at all!"

"I wish I had wings as well!" she cried. "I wish I could go with you over the sea."

"Perhaps there is some hope of that," one of the brothers said. "We could weave a net of sea grasses this night, and the seven of us might be able to carry you that way." In the end, that was what they did. As the sun rose above the mountains, the brothers resumed the forms of swans. Quickly, their sister cast braided ropes of grass about them which bound them to the net, and as one creature they spread their seven pairs of wings and, bearing her with them, rose to meet the sky. It was a long flight for her, and a frightening one as well, as she watched the sea surging far below through the spaces in the net. But the youngest of her brothers flew as close to her as possible, the shadow of his wings sheltering her from the midday sun, and she was somehow comforted by that.

So swiftly did they fly that in mid-afternoon she sighted land, and by evening they were winging above a strange countryside. As the day closed itself up the swans came to rest in a wood, and once again became her brothers. They rejoiced in having made the crossing, but at last the oldest brother said, "You are safe now, and we are happy for you. But we cannot stay. There is no rest for us here; we must fly to the south, where the wild swans winter. And you should not come with us: it is a life for swans, not maidens; you should seek a home and happiness." Her brothers were all of one mind in this, and at last, with reluctance, she agreed. They spent that night together in the wood, and as dawn approached, awoke to say their farewells.

As she embraced her youngest brother, she entreated him "Will you be swans forever, then? Is there no way I can break the spell?"

"Oh, no," he replied, "Sister, it is too hard. To break the spell you must pluck nettles from the cemetery of a church and spin them into flax. They you must make shirts for us from the flax, and when they are done, cast them over us. And for all that time you must neither speak nor laugh, for if a sound escapes you, all the work will be lost. It is too hard, little sister. But do not be sad. Only think of us, some-times, when you hear the swans flying overhead!" And with that, the first light of the sun came through the trees and, wild once more her brothers took wing and were gone.

For a while she remained where they had parted, sunk in her grief. But at last she roused herself, and began to make her slow way through the wood. After a while she came upon a little forest chapel, long abandoned, its yard given over to weeds and the shelter of its eaves to swallows. Here she paused and, gazing at the overgrown graves beyond the church, recalled the words of her brother. She sighed once, and then, without another sound, went forward into the churchyard and began to gather the stinging nettles.

As her brother had warned, it was a hard task. Soon her fair, soft hands were blistered from plucking the nettles. The chapel was a cold and comfortless resting place; she was often hungry, and the cries of wild animals frightened her at night with their strangeness. But in her silence she neither wept nor complained, and in time became accustomed to that life. She worked away at her labors, pulling the nettles in their season and at other times spinning, weaving, and sewing with her makeshift tools.

One spring, the king of that country chose to hunt in the maiden's wood. His huntsmen came across her in the chapel glade; she did not hear them until too late, as she stood watching the wild flocks passing north, seeking the longed-for shapes of swans. Startled, she fled, but the hounds soon brought her to bay in a tree. The huntsmen called off the dogs, and stood amazed. "Who are you?" they cried. "Come down to us!" She only shook her head and, as they persisted, took off her fine gold necklace and dropped it, praying they would take it and go. Still they shouted up to her, so she threw down to them one by one the last remnants of her finery—ring, girdle, and garter—until she had nothing left but her rags. The huntsmen were not diverted, however, and soon climbed the tree and urged her down. They brought her before the king, who was astonished by her beauty. He asked her in all the languages that he knew who she was and where she came from, but she said no word. He wrapped her in his cloak then, and took her to his castle, where he had maids dress her in fine clothes and arrange her hair. When she was brought before him again, he looked on her lovely sad face and knew that he could not rest until she became his bride.

"I wish you to be my wife," he said to her, "Will you not say yes?" But she would not say yes or no, and only sat by her window, gazing out toward the forest. He tried every plea and promise he could think of, every kindness that might woo her, but to all she made no response.

Finally, he led her to a small room in the tower of the castle. He opened the door, and there was all her work from the chapel: spun flax and half-sewn shirts! Even her rustic loom and spinning wheel were there. He said to her, "I have had all your things brought from the forest. Will you smile now? For I only want you to be happy here." And yes, she smiled at last, and it was like the first light of the sun touching a gray sea. She looked at the king and nodded once, and he knew that his long-asked question was answered. In but a few days, they were wed.

Both the king and his new queen were content, but there were others in the castle who were not. Many in the court thought her strange and backward, for she showed little interest in the affairs of the castle, or in the balls and feasts with which the king tried to please her. They whispered about her silence and her unknown past, and her habit of working all the day long on shirts for no one. Others spoke of how she was still fey and wild, springing up from the table and running out of doors at the cries of migrating birds, whether the meal be done or no. The king's elderly mother was especially displeased, and spoke nothing but evil about her, which the queen could not deny.

After a time, she gave birth to a son, and the old mother saw a chance to be rid of her. Soon after the birth, she stole the child away, and smeared her daughter-in-law with blood as she lay asleep. She ran to the king and cried to him, "Did I not warn you against this wife? Come and look, she has murdered your only son!"

The king of course was furious and denied his mother's words, but the evidence seemed quite plain to the people of the court. The young queen was only able to shake her head and weep silent tears in her defense. Her husband would not let any harm her, but in private he begged her to break her long silence. "If they find but one more reason to suspect you a witch," he pleaded, "I will not be able to keep you from them. O beloved, speak to me! Tell me you are innocent," But the queen could say no word to reassure him.

There was another, greater worry on her mind. The end of her task lay almost in sight, but she had no more nettles for the last of the shirts. Finally, despite her husband's vigilance, she slipped away to the town's churchyard and gathered as many as she could find, but she was observed, and accused of grave robbing and witchery. Though he argued, threatened, and entreated, the king was not able to sway his people and grieving, he was forced to deliver her to justice. She was sentenced to die by fire.

She was imprisoned in her tower room, but she cared nothing for that: she had her nettles, and she worked feverishly, racing the day of her sentence. The day came at last and she was almost finished, with only the last of the sewing to be done. When they came for her, she would not let go of the shirts. Even as the cart rolled through the streets, carrying her to the fire, her needle flew. The townspeople yelled and jeered. "See the witch! She is still working her charms!" "Hi! Let us take her evil work away! Let us burn it as well!"

As the cart lurched to a stop, she raised her eyes at last. Before her lay the stake, wood piled high around it, but she looked away from it, up into the sky. It was the fall of the year, and the sky was filled with wings. As the crowd surged forward, shouting, wild cries shook the very air, and down out of the southward flying flocks swept seven great swans in a thunder of white. The crowd fell back, mute with surprise, as the birds winged into the square to surround the condemned woman. In an instant she flung the shirts over their heads, and see! they were swans no more, but seven young men, tall, and as fair as the queen herself. In that same moment, she turned to where her husband stood astonished, and cried out, "Now I may speak! I am innocent!"

There was a great confusion then, but at last the whole story of her labor to restore her brothers was told. The king's mother was brought forward, and forced to admit that it was she who had taken the queen's child; she revealed that he was hidden with a poor huntsman's family, and the king sent for him at once.

The queen and her brothers embraced and kissed each other, yet even in her happiness she still mourned a little, for she had not been able to finish the last of the shirts, and so her beloved youngest brother had a swan's wing in place of his left arm. But he laughed and kissed her face. "O, do not be sad, little sister! A swan's wing is a small price to pay. For we are together again, after all, and all that could be healed, has been. And if your husband is willing, perhaps we shall find our rest here, at last."

And indeed, it was so.

# HEALING THE COMMUNITY

The African adage "It takes a village to raise a child" aptly reflects the folk recognition of the importance of community. In fact, in times past the individual's very survival against the tremendous forces of nature or the invasions of hostile outsiders often depended on the solidarity and support of the community. So it is not surprising that villages and communities play a large role in many folk stories.

The interconnectedness of community and the effects of our actions on others are evident in such tales as "Story of the Owl," while the importance of working together underlies "Stone Soup." We all know the message of such stories as "The Little Red Hen"—those who contribute will be rewarded, and those who don't will go hungry. Articles and books have been written on the phenomenon of the 100th monkey in which the lessons learned by a single monkey spreads miraculously through an entire species. The scientific validity of the story may be questioned, but the underlying truth is one to which most people can relate. "The Holmolaiset Build a House" offers a more humorous perspective on community, showing us how group efforts can fail.

In stories every member of the community counts—from the smallest babe to the oldest sage. In the legend "Constantine, the Emperor," a mighty ruler acknowledges the value of the powerless child. Such stories as "Abandonment Canyon" and "The Golden Cup" encourage respect for elders. Folk literature also shares the wisdom of the elders, putting our lives into proper perspective. Ray Lucht's poem, "I'd Pick More Daisies," falls into this category.

Diversity is a fact of life, and stories teach us to appreciate our differences—not just age differences, but differences in appearance and ways of living. In "The Ugly Duckling," we discover that differences are not to be despised or even ignored, but prized.

The success of any community depends in part on the generosity and sharing of its members—within the community and with outsiders. How many stories have you heard in which kindness to others—even strangers—is rewarded? In "Silver Heels," we learn how a woman's good deeds bring immortality to her name. On the other side of this coin we find many warnings about the destructiveness of greed, as, for example, in "A Blessing in Fact Might Be a Curse."

Learning to live together, to build a community, is a necessity in today's shrinking world. The lessons of folk tales—of kindness to strangers and the value of diversity—can help heal our communities in a time of wars, ethnic cleansings, and religious strife. The illnesses of our community are evident in tragedies ranging from suicides to mass murders. Even the communities of our young people and schools such as Columbine High School are in dire need of healing. Stories offer children the tools to understand their situation and to cope with problems and fears in healthier ways. I have explored this topic more fully in my book *Who's Afraid? . . . Facing Children's Fears Through Folktales* (Libraries Unlimited, 1994), but it is certainly an issue worth addressing.

Healing the community begins with the children. The forces that threaten communities today come not from the outside, but from the inside. The monsters of collective fear and hatred must be healed if we are to survive. Once again, stories help show us the way.

Greed can lead to the extinction of a community, as demonstrated in the following story. The healing message is a warning of how not to behave.

## A Blessing Might in Fact Be a Curse (Ethiopia and Sudan)

Long before other people came to live in this land, giants roamed the Earth. The stories tell us that the Lord created giants first. Later he made people in the size they are today. These giants were GIANTS. They made water skins out of whole elephant hides. See that tallest of trees, the euphorbia tree? The spears of the giants were that tall. The stones they threw with their slings were not pebbles but large boulders. When they were hungry, they roasted whole cows over their fire, providing only enough for a single meal. They used great wooden tubs when they drank milk.

This tribe of giants killed tribes of smaller people that came into their country looking for water for their cattle and goats. If these visiting tribes were lucky, they weren't killed but driven away. Many courageous warriors from many tribes died trying to hold watering places against the giants.

One day the Lord decided that the giants were the cause for the world being out of balance and full of hurt and anger. Therefore, the Lord sent for the chief of the giants and told him, "It is time for your giant tribe to leave the world."

"Lord, how have we offended you that you tell us we should leave?" asked the chief of the giants.

"Your tribe has been too hard with the small people," the Lord replied. "You have forgotten that water holes were given to all the tribes for their cattle to use. Instead, you drive the people away even though they have done you no harm."

"Master," began the chief of the giants, "All tribes guard their wells. All tribes fight to protect their land. We haven't done anything that is different."

"Because you are so large and the others are so small," the Lord told him, "everything is out of balance. You giants consume everything. You eat a whole cow for your dinner while the other tribes stand on the hilltop watching you swallow down enough food to keep them alive for a month."

"Lord, it is not our fault. It is you who created us as we are," answered the giant's chief.

"You are right, the fault is not yours, but I must send your tribe out of this world," spoke the Lord. "I will be as kind as I can. I will give you a choice. I will let you choose how to depart. You may disappear with my curse or my blessings."

"Who would want to receive your curse?" asked the giant chief. "If we must go, then send us on our way with your blessings."

"Good. Let it be that way," the Lord answered. "I will lay blessings on you. Because sons are a blessing to all families, henceforth all of your children to come will be sons. Because cows are a blessing because of the calves they bear and the milk they give, hereafter all calves that are born will be females."

After hearing this the chief of the giants returned to his tribe. "Here are the blessings the Lord has given us," he told his people. The giants were happy.

And so things came to pass just as the Lord had promised. Women gave birth to only sons and cows gave birth to only female calves. The sons grew up and when it was time for them to marry, there were no young women to become their wives. The female calves matured but there were no bulls for them to mate with. So in time there were no more children born to the giants and no more calves were born to the cattle. People just grew old and died. It was the same for the cattle. They just grew old and died. And so, the tribe of giants withered like a sunflower in the dry desert.

The chief called a meeting of all of the old people who were still alive. "As all men can see, we are dying out from our blessings. Let us not stay here any more waiting for the end," he told them. "Let every person build a tomb for himself and cover it with a roof of stones. Let each one enter his tomb and close up the entrance. In this way we will depart from the world."

So it was as he suggested. Every person built himself a tomb and covered it with a roof of stones. They entered their tombs and closed up the opening and stayed there until they died. In this way, the giants perished and disappeared from the land.

The stone roofs of the tombs collapsed long ago. Even though the giants are gone today, you may see the great stones they used as foundations for their homes. Here and there people find the remains of the enormous tombs that hold the dead giants. The old people still tell the stories about how the giants finally disappeared. People of the tribes remember what happened to the giants. Sometimes they say when life seems too generous to them, "Be careful. Let us not die from blessings like the giants did."

# Mulla Nasreddin
# (Persia)

Every community needs a character like Mulla Nasreddin. He is portrayed as both foolish and wise, naive and shrewd, shady and beyond reproach. He is like the child who says the emperor is naked—innocently speaking the truth that no one else dares to speak.

Mulla Nasreddin is claimed by the Middle Eastern peoples as their own, but he belongs in spirit to all peoples and all times. (The Turks know him as Gogia NaserEddin, and the Arabs call him Haja.) Stories and anecdotes bearing the name Mulla Nasreddin date as far back as the Crusades and are as modern as the present century. If there is a philosophy underlying his humor, it is that in this life it is not worth taking oneself or anything else too seriously, if seriously at all.

This legendary character lives in the imagination of those who have created and recreated him over the centuries. Reflect on these stories and discover that the simple tales contain shrewd ethical meanings useful in the community.

### On Annoying People

Nasreddin taught, "Enjoy yourself, or try to learn—you will annoy someone. If you do not—you will annoy someone."

## Nasreddin's Donkey

Nasreddin went to the marketplace and put up a sign which read

"Someone has stolen my donkey. Whoever stole it, if they return it I'll give it to them."

When asked why he would do this, Nasreddin said, "There are two pleasures in life—to find something you have lost and to give away something you love."

## Nasreddin's Boast

"If someone doesn't say something to entertain me," shouted the tyrannical and effete king, "I'll cut off the heads of everyone at court."

Mulla Nasreddin immediately stepped forward. "Majesty, don't cut off my head. I'll do something."

"And what can you do?"

"I can teach a donkey to read and write."

The king said, "You'd better do it or I'll flay you alive."

"I'll do it," said Nasreddin, "but it will take me ten years."

When the court was over for the day, the grandees crowded around Nasreddin. "Mulla," they said, "can you really teach a donkey to read and write?"

"No," said Nasreddin.

"Then," said the wisest courtier, "you have only brought a decade's tension and anxiety, for you will surely be done to death. Oh what folly to prefer ten years of suffering and contemplation of death to a quick flash of the headman's axe!"

"You have overlooked just one thing," said the Mulla. "The king is 75 years old and I am 80. Long before the time is up, other elements will have entered this story."

### Nasreddin's Fun with
### Fools and Fakes

Nasreddin was asked to give the sermon for the next three Fridays at the local mosque.

Being a lazy man, he hadn't prepared his talk by the time the first Friday rolled around. Looking at the congregation, he asked, "Good people, do you know what I'm going to tell you?"

"No, Nasreddin," said the men seated on the prayer rugs. "No, Nasreddin," whispered the women hidden behind the latticework in the balcony.

"What! If you're so ignorant, I can't be bothered to share my knowledge," huffed Nasreddin. He left.

The next Friday he asked the same question. This time the cunning congregation, remembering the week before, called out, "Yes, Nasreddin!"

"Then I won't waste your time telling you what you already know." Nasreddin smiled and walked out.

By the third Friday the congregation was so confused that some answered, "Yes!" and some answered, "No!" when Nasreddin asked his question.

"Good!" Nasreddin beamed. "Let the people who know, tell the people who don't." He strolled out of the mosque to go home and lie under his shady fig tree.

### One Answer to Forty Questions

Someone asked Nasreddin, "If I ask you forty conflicting questions, can you give me one answer to cover them all?"

Nasreddin agreed, and the man propounded forty complex and contradictory philosophic questions.

"Simple," said Nasreddin. "I can answer them all with seven words."

"What are they?"

"I am ignorant of all forty questions," he said.

This story is a delightful example of what people can do when they work together and each offers their best.

# Stone Soup
# (Ireland)

There was a poor, hungry, and cold traveling man going on the road between green fields and villages. He had been traveling from village to village with his penny whistle and Irish harp, making music, and money, along the way.

One day as he was trudging down the road all he could think of was how good a bowl of hot soup would be. In fact, he knew that a bowl of good soup would fix everything that was wrong with him at that moment.

As he was passing by a farmer's house, he got the great idea that the wife of the farmer there would help him out with his hunger. He decided to try his luck. He went down to the shore of the river and picked up a round river stone about the size of a large apple. He went to the farmer's house, knocked on the door, and was pleased when his knock was answered by the wife.

"Dear woman," he said, "would you give me a pan and a small drop of clean warm water?"

The wife was as kind as he hoped she would be and she did as he asked. He started to wash and clean the stone with great splashing and ceremony until the stone was shining clean.

The wife was curious and told him, "You have certainly done a grand job of washing that stone."

"And why not, kind lady? It is my very special soup stone," he replied. "Not only can I make soup with it, but it will be the best soup," the man said as he fondly rubbed the stone.

"Mercy be to the heavens! How could anyone do that?" she asked.

"There would be no trouble at all to it," he bragged. "All a person would have to do is to watch the one who knows how to make stone soup."

151

"Oh my, oh my!" she exclaimed. "I would be extremely pleased to watch you do it. There is the pot and there is the fire, and there is plenty of water," she told him as she led him into the cozy kitchen.

Things were working out just as he had planned. The man put a half gallon of water in the pot and ceremoniously placed the stone in the water. The two of them stood by the bubbling pot and watched it. Then, the fellow sat down on one of the kitchen chairs, took up his Irish harp and started strumming a song and singing along with it.

A couple of local people heard the music as they were coming down the road and stopped by the kitchen door to see what was happening.

"You know, kind woman," the harpist said as he saw the faces in the door, "a shake of salt and pepper would not do it any harm."

She gave the salt and pepper to him and he made a great show of measuring out just the right amount. Now the faces belonging to the fellows in the doorway, were familiar ones to the good wife. "And what brings you two here after all of your unpleasant actions lately?" she asked.

"Oh, dear Maggie, we came to say we are sorry, to listen to the music, and to see if there is anything we can do to make things better," one answered.

The harpist took the chance to suggest, "We are making some soup. It could stand the bone of a leg of mutton for flavor."

"Maggie," to show you how sorry we are, we will go home and get our wives to come help and we will bring a sturdy meat covered bone back with us."

The frown that was on Maggie's face disappeared, and she answered, "Your apologies are accepted as well as your offer of a meaty bone."

Off the two men went. The harpist turned to the wife and said, "A good handful of white flour would help thicken the soup right now."

She got such a handful and came back to put it right into the pot herself. The fellow sat down with his harp again and played some merry music.

The two fellows returned with their wives and the mutton bone. That was added to the soup and the three women began to talk with each other like there had never been a problem between them. "That's a fine bone," said the harpist. "There is plenty of meat on it and it will make the soup much stronger." And then as if he were musing to himself, "A few potatoes would give it great texture."

One of the wives said, "I can go back to our cottage and get some potatoes."

Not to be outdone, the other wife said, "Maybe a few fine onions would help." I'll get some from our neighbor's garden and bring them back with me."

The potatoes and onions came along with several more people. From what the people were saying, there had been some misunderstandings in the recent past but they were all being forgotten as the women sat down together to peel the potatoes and chop them up and add them to the soup. The onions were sliced and cut and added.

All the harpist had to do at this point was to make more merry music and sing as people added to the pot. It was starting to smell really wonderful by now, but one of the newcomers said, "It needs some carrots and turnips. I'll go borrow some from Mary. Maybe she and her family will want to join us."

Off she went and quickly returned with more people and the carrots and turnips, which were cleaned, chopped, and added to the soup. The soup bubbled and boiled merrily for a little bit longer. The musician played some sentimental songs, and they all joined along in singing as he played.

Pretty soon this gathering of people had forgotten all of their quibbles and were mellow with the music and the smell of soup. The man of the house returned from work and was amazed to see who all was in his home getting along so well together.

The musician stopped playing, jumped up, and got a spoon. He handed it to the husband and said, "You should be the one to taste the soup. What do you think of it?"

"Yes, dear husband, this is special soup made with a special stone to give it flavor."

The husband sipped the soup off the spoon and declared it delicious. "This is truly fine soup but maybe I need to have another taste to make sure," and he dipped the spoon into the soup to get another spoonful.

Quickly, bowls and spoons appeared and everyone there sipped, slurped and slowly enjoyed bowls of the soup. The rascally musician played more music and all the guests were full of good will and happiness.

The housewife said, "I am extremely grateful to you for showing me how to make such good soup."

"What did I tell you?" said the harpist. "I knew that you could make nothing but the finest, richest soup with my special stone."

After the soup was gone, the men set back and lit pipes of tobacco and enjoyed a good smoke together. "It's been a long time since we have done this together," one of the men said to the others.

The traveling musician played a final merry melody on his penny whistle and resumed his travels.

The housewife never stopped bragging about how she could make soup with a stone. All the neighbors complimented her on its discovery. I think it is safe to say that the people enjoyed each other's fine company after that, and it was probably a long time before the man came back to that part of Ireland again.

Acceptance is the message shared by the ugly duckling. Almost everyone can relate to this classic story of growth and transformation and the final acceptance into a special community. Finding the right community is sometimes the key to healing of the individual.

# The Ugly Duckling
## (Hans Christian Andersen, Denmark)

All the fields and meadows were full of summer's beauty and richness of crops. In the middle of it all were some deep lakes. In one of the lakes sat a mother duck on her nest. She had to hatch her eggs, but something was quite unusual. Among all the eggs was one that was quite different from the others. It was so big!

The mother duck sat and sat and sat on her eggs. She was really quite lonely doing that. The father of the ducks never came to visit her or to help her with the sitting on the eggs. An old duck came swimming by the nest and passed the time of day with the mother duck.

"It's such a lovely day, mother duck. When are your babies going to come out and enjoy it all?" the old duck asked.

Mother duck just stood up and flapped her wings for some exercise as well as to dry them off. "I hope it is quite soon," she replied.

"What is that funny egg in your nest?" asked the old duck. "It looks like a turkey egg. I know because I was fooled by a turkey egg once. No matter what I did, it was afraid of the water and would not learn to quack and was a great nuisance."

"Oh," replied the mother duck as she settled back on her nest, "I do not think any turkey would have been able to fool me. I have been sitting on these eggs steady."

Old duck wagged its tail good-bye and swam off.

Finally, a few days later, mother duck felt the little baby ducks breaking through their shells. They all hatched except for the large different egg. "I think I'll give it a few more days to hatch," mother duck said. Meanwhile, her babies were quacking and swimming around the nest. Finally the last egg burst, and a big ugly duck emerged! It did not look like any duck baby she had ever seen. It surely was not a turkey, however, because it swam. With a mother's pride, she quickly decided that it really was not ugly but beautiful in a different way. And so they all went out to see the world.

Other ducks swam over to see her family and pecked at her large baby. "It is peculiar and needs to go," said one of the ducks. Other ducks would fly by and bite it on the neck.

Mother duck was very protective of her baby. "Don't do that," she squawked. "Do you see what a pleasant disposition my baby has?"

Things only got worse as the other ducklings bit, pushed, and taunted her unusual baby. "It is too big and does not belong here with us," one of the ducklings said. Even the little girl who came to the lake with corn and bread to feed the ducks kicked at it whenever it came to her for food. Finally the duckling swam off to hide in the reeds.

Two wild geese glided over to it, and one of them looked at the duckling with respect and said, "Hey, you are so ugly, I like you. Why not fly away with us?" Just as they were taking off there were two loud noises, and both of the geese fell back into the water. There were hunters all around the lake shooting the birds. A big black dog jumped into the lake and started to swim out to the duckling, who closed his eyes and was ready to be eaten. But the dog just swam past him and seized the body of one of the geese that had fallen.

"I am so ugly that even the dog will not eat me," said the duckling. With that, the duckling just lay quiet in the reeds. That evening it left the lake and ran through a booming storm. It ended up in a peasant's hut. The door was just hanging on one hinge, and the whole building was tilted to one side and about to fall over. Even so, inside was a woman with her pets. The next day when the woman saw the duckling, she had it join her household—only because she was thinking of what a delicious meal it would make when it was fattened up. The other animals, as seemed to always happen, expected the duckling to purr, lay eggs, have sensible opinions, and be clever. When it obviously did not do any of these things, the animals in the hut became disagreeable.

Once again, the duckling went to the water, swam, and dived but always was slighted by every creature because of its ugliness. By now it was autumn, and the trees in the forest turned yellow, red, and brown. The winds blew the leaves in straight lines into the forest. There was the sound of the crunch of leaves as animals traveled over them as well as a smell of rotting leaves. Dark clouds appeared, and with them came cold, damp air. Rain fell, and then it turned to snow. The duckling saw amazing things as flocks of birds flew in and swam for awhile before taking off again. One special flock was sparkling white, with long graceful necks, and they flew away with glorious great wings. Oh, how the duckling loved seeing those happy, beautiful birds.

The winter was a harsh one. The duckling had to keep swimming to prevent the lake's surface from freezing solid. In spite of it, though, each night the hole left in the ice kept getting smaller and smaller. The duckling used its legs and did everything possible to prevent the hole from freezing over, but at last he was too tired and froze into the ice.

In the morning a farmer walked by and saw the duckling. He took a stick and broke the ice away from the duckling and carried the duckling home to his wife. But things did not go much better there. The duckling became frightened by the children who wanted to play with it, and it flew, flapped, and fell in a frenzy, knocking things over and creating havoc. He escaped out the door and spent the rest of the winter in misery and sorrow. But, as always, spring came, and it was beautiful. The sun warmed the duckling, and he was able to flap his wings and beat the air. In fact, he flew and ended up in a thicket that looked inviting. To his amazement, three glorious white swans swam over to him. When he saw them, he prepared to fly away to save himself. Surely these splendid creatures would not want the likes of his ugliness around them. He changed his mind, though, and decided that maybe the best thing would be to let these royal birds kill him and settle everything forever. As he swam to them he bent his head down and saw something in the clear water that made him stop and stare. It was his reflection. He was a swan! Suddenly his life was quite different. All the swans accepted him, and the children who went to the water cried, "Look, there is a new one. He is the most beautiful of them all."

As he heard them making up songs about his beauty, he rejoiced from the depths of his heart. "I am a swan. I am a beautiful swan," he thought. "The ugly duckling is gone!"

One of the more popular legends in Colorado history concerns a beautiful dance-hall girl of Fairplay and nearby Buckskin Joe, both mining towns. This tale is a clear example of an unexpected heroine helping others.

## Silver Heels
## (Colorado, United States)

In 1896, when word of the gold discoveries in the mountains got out, the mining camps in Colorado grew rapidly. As stories of endless wealth spread, these mines and towns became famous, and the miners had bright prospects. This news brought a stampede of new miners and their families as soon as the snow began to melt. Some of the stories claimed miners discovered gold veins of solid ore said to be fifteen to twenty feet wide and so pure it didn't need to be sorted. As the towns grew, people built cabins, frame houses, hotels, stores, an assay office, a blacksmith shop, and a saloon.

Among the people drawn to this exciting area was a beautiful dance-hall girl named Silver Heels Jenny. She got this nickname because of the gleaming heels on her shoes. It seemed that she could dance faster and more gracefully than any other girl in the mining district. Men seemed hypnotized when they watched her dance. At first they were fascinated by her flashing heels and then, when they looked at her face and figure, they became smitten with her looks and charm. Jenny was one of the most popular girls in the area.

Shortly after Silver Heels Jenny arrived in Fairplay, she met a handsome young miner. They fell in love and became engaged. Other miners were green with jealousy. They competed with each other to dance with her, hoping to distract her. But Silver Heels Jenny was loyal to her beloved and was just as kind as she was loyal. She was a favorite with the other dance-hall girls because of her special good nature and helpfulness.

Then Fairplay and Buckskin Joe became the targets
of a smallpox epidemic. The disease claimed victim after
victim. Business places closed. The dance halls were deserted.
One of the first people to die was Silver Heels' lover. After
his death, she began to nurse miners who where helpless
and alone in their cabins. She also nursed whole families
who had been struck down with the disease. From house to
house she went, offering help and asking nothing in return.
Along with nursing the people, she cooked, cared for their
homes, and washed their clothing.

Gradually the smallpox epidemic abated. Grateful
miners and their families decided to show their gratitude and
appreciation for all that Silver Heels had done for them. As
life returned to normal, they decided to honor the dance-hall
girl who had ministered to the many sick with complete no
thought for her own well-being. A delegation was appointed
to give her the money. They collected a large sum to present
to her, but they couldn't find her anywhere.

As the people got better, they became busy again.
Their search for Silver Heels slowed down. No one knew
where she was. There were signs that she had taken her few
possessions and gone away leaving no forwarding address.
When she did not return, the miners returned the money
they had collected for her to the donors.

Then rumors started to spread of a woman with
dark, heavy veils who was sometimes seen in the area. Some
claimed it was Silver Heels, hiding from recognition. Others
said that she had become a victim of the smallpox and that
the disease had disfigured her once-beautiful face. But the
mystery woman was never found. Still wanting to show their
appreciation to this kind woman, the miners gave her name
to the highest and most beautiful mountain in the district.
And so today, Mount Silver Heels, crowned with pure white
snow, framed against a blue Colorado sky, is home to beautiful
fields of iris and alive with birds and animals that call it home.
It stands as a tribute to one woman's generous contribution
to her community.

In this tale we can explore the nature of healing and healers. Honesty and greed are its major themes. Certainly these components are crucial in healing the community.

## The Wonder Doctor
## (Estonia)

In olden times there lived a poor peasant who craved, desired, and was determined to become rich. He had, however, no idea how to bring this about. One day he heard a preacher say in his sermon, "whatever you give to the poor will be returned to you tenfold." Straightway the peasant decided to give away everything he had to the poor.

He sold all his meager possessions and distributed the money he got among the poor. Then he waited impatiently for the time when he would get it back tenfold. He waited and waited—but nothing came! He had nothing to eat, and hunger plagued him more and more. Filled with anger against himself and everybody else, he went into the woods and lay down under a tree.

Suddenly a stranger appeared before him and asked, "Why do you lie here idle?"

"What can I do in my moments of dire need? I am hungry. For three whole days I have had no food. A fool that I was, I gave everything to the poor in the hope of getting it back tenfold. Now I am starving. That is all the reward I got for my kindness."

"Sleep never gives a new coat nor a long shirt," said the stranger. "If you had worked, you would not be starving. Just now I have no bread with me but take this sack. It will provide you with everything you wish to have," said the stranger. With that, he vanished.

The greedy peasant hung the sack around his neck and wished to see if what the stranger said was true. "I wish my sack were full of gold!"

Scarcely had he uttered his wish, when the sack grew heavy and almost dragged him to the ground. He peeped into it and oh, joy! Gold! Pure gold to the very brim of the bag! The peasant wished to skip about in his happiness but the heavy sack hindered him and he sat down. He pondered over what he would do now that he had become rich.

"I will buy myself a mansion and live there like a lord. I will eat pork three times a day and will sleep between two fur coats. Oh, what a happy life it will be! Now I believe the preacher when he said that gifts to the poor would be returned tenfold! For me, I have been rewarded thousands of times."

The peasant would have dreamed like this for weeks had he not been so hungry.

He tugged and strained with the bag of gold but he could not lift the sack up even a little bit. Not a single soul was around who could help him. "Should I hide the sack in the woods? No! Never! Someone might find it!" He thought and thought but not one idea came into his mind.

And so he spent the night and the following day there in the woods, in the same spot, with the bag of gold hanging heavily about him. He preferred to die by the side of his gold than to be separated from it.

On the third day, the stranger returned.

"Help, father, help! I am dying!" begged the peasant.

"What is your trouble now? Did I not give you the magic sack which would make all your wishes come true?"

"True enough, you gave it to me but the sack of gold is so heavy that now I cannot move it at all. Here I am—helpless and starving."

"Why were you so greedy and asked only for gold? Well, I will help you once more. Here is a piece of bread, take it and eat!"

The peasant ate the bread gratefully. In the meantime the stranger took the sack of gold upon his back as easily as if it were filled with feathers and said, "I see you are unable to do anything for yourself. You should enter my service and at least you will never be starving again."

The stranger set out and the peasant followed him munching his bread. Soon they arrived at a river. Quick as lightening the stranger poured the sack full of gold into the water. He handed the empty sack back to his new servant.

"What have you done! You must be mad to pour the gold into the river!" yelled the peasant and he jumped into the water after the gold. But it was too late. All the gold had disappeared.

So it was that with great sighs and groans the servant followed his master upon his wanderings. One evening they came to a city and decided to stay overnight. Here they learned that the son of a rich merchant was dangerously ill and that no doctor could help him. A barrel of gold was promised to anyone who could cure him. Thousands of doctors had tried and failed and the merchant drove them from his house with a whip.

The next morning the master and servant set out for the merchant's house and offered to cure the youth.

"Begone!" cried out the merchant in annoyance, "thousands have cheated me! You are no different!"

But the stranger insisted and the merchant at last gave his consent. The master started with the cure. A trough was brought in. The master took out a sharp knife and a bottle of medicine from his bag. He cut open the patient's side and said, "It is necessary to cut out the disease."

Trembling with fear, the servant washed the wound, while his master sewed it up himself. Then the master told his servant to dress the body. "What use is it to dress the body? The poor lad is dead as a doornail and anyone who is dead is dead!" mumbled the servant.

The doctor took a bottle from his pocket and poured a drop of medicine into the youth's mouth. A shiver and a tremor went through the dead body of the youth, and his pale cheeks grew pink. At the second drop, the lad moved and opened his eyes. At the third drop, the youth was on his feet and said, "It seems that I have slept too long today."

"Do you still feel pain in your bones?" asked the wonder doctor.

"Not in the least. I feel perfectly well," was the answer.

Three hours later the merchant came in and stood speechless with amazement. His son met him at the door, looking as well as a fish swimming in water.

The happy father offered lavish gifts as a reward for healing his son. The servant whispered eagerly into the ear of his master, "Take it! Take it! It is gold he offers!" but the wonder doctor refused to accept any reward.

"We do not want anything!" he said. "We have all we need. But if you give us something to eat, we would be grateful."

After they had dined, the wonder doctor and his servant went on their way again. They had covered a good many miles and the servant began to whine about being hungry. They saw a flock of sheep grazing in the woods by the roadside. There were no buildings or houses in sight.

"I will go and kill a lamb, roast it, and take care of our hunger." declared the servant.

"Take one if you wish. But do not eat it before I return. I will go to speak with the owner of the sheep or to a shepherd about it," said the doctor.

The servant killed the lamb, made a bonfire, and roasted the meat, but the master still had not returned.

The servant thought, "Why should I wait for him any longer? I will eat the heart of the lamb and the doctor will never notice."

When he returned, the doctor knew that his servant had not obeyed him.

"Where is the lamb's heart?" he asked.

"A lamb doesn't have a heart," the servant replied.

"You ate it?"

"No! No! How could I eat something that doesn't exist?"

They argued for a long time. The master, insisting that a lamb has a heart, while the servant claimed there was no heart. At last the doctor said, "There is no use arguing with you. He who is wiser yields."

They continued upon their way and the doctor healed many sick people just as he had healed the young son of the rich merchant. They finally came to the capital city of a famous and powerful king. All the people looked sad, and the whole city was gloomy.

"Our king's daughter is very ill! There is no doctor who can heal her. The king has promised to give away half of his kingdom and his daughter in marriage to anyone who can heal her. Up to now, no one has been able to do that."

That night, before they went to bed, the doctor announced to his servant that they would go to the palace to cure the princess the next morning.

The servant could not rest that whole night. He was sure that he had seen enough of the doctor healing people that he now knew how it was done and decided to do it himself. When his master was fast asleep, the servant stole out of the room, took the medicine bag, and hurried to the palace.

He wakened the king and announced, "I am a famous doctor. I have heard about the illness of your daughter the princess and I am here to help her. Tomorrow might be too late if we wait!"

The king looked him over from head to heel and remarked with contempt, "You a doctor? A swine doctor you may be, but that is all."

"In three hours' time, your daughter will be as well as ever or you may hang me," declared the impostor. He was so sure that he could heal the princess.

At length the king gave in, and the servant started immediately with his work. He was led into the bedroom of the princess. The king locked the door so that the "doctor" could not escape in case anything went wrong.

The servant did everything his master used to do on similar occasions. When he was finished he dropped some medicine into the mouth of the princess. One, two, three . . . ten drops, but the princess neither moved nor did her cheeks change their color. In his growing terror, he poured the whole bottle of medicine into her mouth. It was all in vain because what is dead, is dead.

Now he was really frightened. Over and over he sighed, "Oh the unlucky wretch that I am! If only my master were here!" He tried to escape but the room was locked, and he could not get out. He knew for certain that they would hang him. After all, wasn't he the one that proposed this?

In his despair, he crept into the stove and closed the door.

Three hours later the king entered the chamber. When he beheld the sight of his dead daughter, his grief became boundless. He ordered the arrest of the fake doctor. The guards looked all around the room, but the man had vanished.

The stove in which the servant had hidden chanced to be too short, so that his legs were up tight against the door. The trembling of the desperate, frightened man made the stove door rattle. "Clink, clink, clink!" The guards noticed this noise, looked into the stove and dragged the quivering man out.

The furious king shouted, "To the gallows. You wished to go if you failed. Now—go! Just as you said earlier, you will be rewarded!"

The guards led the phony doctor out to be executed.

In the morning when the wonder doctor awoke, he missed both his servant and his medicine bag. Because they had talked about the ailing princess, he concluded that his servant must have gone to heal her. He went straight to the palace. When he got there, he was informed as to what had taken place during the night.

He requested that he be led to the body of his dead servant. He carefully gave him a few drops of his wonderful medicine. Instantly the servant was on his feet and as lively as he had been before.

Those who witnessed the miracle pleaded, "You are a wonderful, great healer! None but you could possibly heal our princess. Have pity on us. Help her and our king!"

They led him into the palace where the king joined with them in their pleas for help.

Three drops of his amazing medicine sufficed. The princess jumped out of her bed, merrily laughing and in her usual happy mood.

The king was overcome with joy and declared that he would keep his promise to reward the healer with half of his kingdom, along with the hand of his daughter in marriage.

"We are not in need of anything. Cherish your daughter and rule over your kingdom for many years to come," said the doctor as he refused any reward.

"No, no! The princess belongs to me!" cried the servant.

An angry look from his master silenced him and he muttered to himself, "What a fool! He takes nothing himself, neither does he allow me to take anything. What a waste! What a shame."

Again, the wonder doctor walked on while his servant, carrying the bag, kept up with him.

"Why did you steal my bag?" questioned the master.

"I did not steal it."

"How did my bag get to the palace?"

"It went by itself."

"A bag never goes by itself."

"But your bag did. I only went after it and by chance began the healing."

As he said this, the servant pondered and pondered, but he could not understand why he had failed to heal the princess. He concluded that he must have taken the wrong bottle by mistake and that was what spoiled everything. In the future he would have to be more careful, he thought. Soon after coming to this conclusion, he decided to leave his master and become a doctor on his own.

One night, when his master had fallen asleep, the peasant again took the medicine bag and hurried away. He ran and ran. After a while, he believed he was safe from every possible pursuit. Then a river gave him his next problem. How would he cross it?

He decided the river did not seem to be deep, so he sprang into it. But the bottom was soft and muddy. Deeper and deeper he sank through the dark water. Soon the water was up to his mouth.

He screamed with all his might, "Help! Help! Anyone who hears and sees me, help!"

Unexpectedly, his master appeared on the shore. He held out a long pole and helped drag the servant out of the muck and water.

"Why did you again steal my bag?"

"My dear master, I did not steal it. I just went for a little walk and fell into the water."

"I do not believe this tale! Give me my bag. I will carry it myself so that you will never again feel tempted to steal it."

They went on again. Suddenly the master stopped, took a shovel out of his bag, gave it to the servant and ordered him, "Dig here, under this bush. You will find something there." The master himself put his bag under his head and went to sleep. The servant dug and dug. True enough! Soon he saw a big iron chest brimful with golden coins.

"All this is mine for all of my troubles," gloated the servant. "Why should I share with my master? I will deny that I found the chest," and he hurriedly covered the chest with soil.

After a while the wonder doctor opened his eyes and looked around. "Did you find anything?" he asked.

"Nothing at all. I dug and toiled very hard, but all I saw was sand and earth."

"No? You did not find anything? Then I myself must dig." said the master.

Hardly had he taken the shovel in his hands when the treasure chest came into sight. Together they dragged it out of the ground. Now the master told his servant to divide the money, and the greedy man began to separate it into two piles.

"Stop, stop!" interrupted the master. "Divide the money not in two, but into eight heaps."

"Why? There are not eight of us!"

"Of course not. But we must share with some others. Do as I tell you to do."

When the money was finally divided, the servant quickly grabbed one part and then slyly asked, "Who will get the other six heaps?"

"The poor will get one part, the eater of the lamb's heart, the second, he who wanted to steal my things gets the third, the thief of my bag gets the fourth, the church gets another part, and to him who found the treasure chest, the sixth."

When he heard this the servant exclaimed victoriously, "All of this belongs to me! I ate the lamb's heart. I wanted to steal your things. I stole your bag. I found the treasure chest!"

The master shook his head gravely and said, "How can I believe you? Hundreds of times you have assured me of the opposite. In the hope of getting the money you purposely declare yourself guilty of crimes you have never committed."

"But I have done everything I told you." repeated the servant again and again.

"If that is so, then we cannot stay partners any longer. Take your share and go. With liars and cheaters I do not work," said the wonder doctor sadly. Then he vanished with all of the gold. For the servant, he left behind exactly as much money as he had given away to the poor.

All over the country the servant sought the wonder doctor and asked everyone if they had seen him. When he was told that his master had gone to heaven, the servant went there. When he got to the gate of heaven, it was closed. He knocked tentatively. He was met by none other than the wonder doctor.

"Let me in, let me in," begged the servant.

"No! No! Liars and cheaters are not admitted. I gave you the wonder sack. What else do you need?"

The servant took his sack off of his neck and hung it on a peg just by heaven's gate. Again he pleaded to be let in.

"You have everything in your sack. Why do you wish to enter heaven?"

"Maybe if I were in the sack to see what treasures it contains," said the servant. No sooner had he said this when—plop!—into the sack he went. He found nothing in it at all. He struggled frantically to get out of the sack, but he could not. In the sack he was, and there he remained—watching all the happiness of life in heaven from his deep, dark sack.

And if St. Peter has not taken the sack from the peg, the greedy peasant hangs there still.

This legend explores the importance of mercy, along with the value of the young to the community. It is the wise emperor who recognizes these crucial issues and acts on them.

## Constantine, the Emperor of Rome (Ancient Rome)

**N**oble Constantine, Emperor of Rome, was in his prime—young, handsome, strong, and happy. Then a great and sudden affliction came upon him—leprosy!

The horrible disease first showed itself on his face. There was no way he could hide the disease. In fact if he had not been the emperor, he would have been driven out to live in the forest and wilds as other lepers were forced to do.

The leprosy spread from his face until it entirely covered his body. It became so bad that he could no longer ride out in public or show himself to his people.

When all possible cures had been tried and had failed, Constantine withdrew completely, abandoned his imperial duties and shut himself up in his palace. There he lived a secluded life. The people of Rome talked of his illness and prayed to their gods to heal him.

When there seemed to be no hope and no way out of his disease, Constantine summoned to Rome all the doctors, learned men, and physicians from every realm. He begged them to consider his illness and try to find any cure for his malady.

A proclamation went throughout the world and great rewards were offered to any man who should heal the emperor. Tempted by the rewards and the great fame to be won, there came leeches and physicians from Persia and Arabia, and from every land that was under Rome. Philosophers came from Greece and Egypt, and magicians and sorcerers from the unexplored desert of the east.

Constantine hopefully tried all the remedies suggested or recommended, but his leprosy did not improve. In fact, it grew worse. Again, the learned men assembled and consulted with each other. They were determined not to abandon him in his great distress. However, they were all at a loss as to what to do next.

The healers sat in silence until at last one very old and very wise man, a great physician from Arabia, said, "Now that all else has failed, I will tell you of a remedy that I have heard. I believe that it will certainly cure our beloved emperor, but it is a very terrible solution. I dreaded to name it until every other means had been tried and failed. It is a cruel thing for any man to do." The old healer paused, and the group turned to him in anticipation. He lowered his voice and continued. "Let the Emperor dip himself in a full bath of the blood of infants and children who are seven years old or under. Then he will be healed, and his leprosy will fall from him. His malady is not natural to his body and it demands an unnatural cure."

A gasp went through the group. At first, none of those assembled would agree to this terrible proposal. But after they considered and discussed at length that nothing else would heal the emperor, they reluctantly gave in. Two of them brought the news to Constantine in his darkened room. The emperor was horrified when he heard the recommendation and refused to carry out such an evil plan. His friends and leaders kept repeating that he had great work to do in the world and that he must take the necessary steps to heal himself. Constantine finally agreed, with many tears, to try the terrible remedy.

Council drew up letters with the emperor's hand and seal and sent them out to all the world, bidding mothers with children of seven years or under to bring them with haste to Rome. There, they were told, the blood of these innocents might prove the needed remedy to the emperor's disease.

Throughout all the lands there rose a wailing and crying of mothers. Women clasped their children close to them. They reviled Constantine and called him terrible names. But though the mothers lamented bitterly, they had no choice but to bow to the emperor's order. With their babies and young children the women journeyed to the great courtyard of the imperial palace at Rome. They were so heart-broken and woebegone that many fainted on the spot.

The mothers wailed, the children cried, and the tumult grew until Constantine heard it in his lonely wretched darkened room. He looked out of his window at the mournful sight. He viewed the sobbing mothers and children, the sentinels of his palace suffering along, and he thought, "Who am I that my health is to outweigh the lives and happiness of so many of my people? Is my life of more value to the world than those of all the children who shed their blood for my healing? Surely each babe is as precious as Constantine the Emperor!"

At that moment, Constantine chose to die rather than to commit so great a slaughter of innocent children. He summoned his council and announced to them, "He who will be truly master must be ever the servant to pity!"

Without delay, the mothers were told that their children were free and safe. There was rapture and rejoicing. Songs of praise and thanks floated up through the windows of his palace. "Feed and clothe all of these children. Let them return home untouched by any loss and give them rewards for their anguish and sufferings!" Constantine ordered.

The women and their children went home bearing the rich gifts they had received. Each one thanked and blessed the emperor and sang his praises. Everyone in the Roman Empire prayed for the healing of their great lord.

That same night, Constantine saw a vision of two strangers. They told him, "Oh Constantine, because you have obeyed the voice of pity, you deserve pity. Therefore you will find mercy and be saved. You will be healed not only in your body but your very soul will be made whole."

Constantine called for all the clergy to come to the palace. There, he greeted them kindly. The clergymen took the great vessel of silver that had been made for the children's blood and filled it with pure water from the well. Constantine stood in the water until it reached his chin. As he did so, a great light shone upon him. The scales of his leprosy, which were like those of a fish, fell from his body until there was nothing left of his horrible disease. He had been purified in body and soul. Through his compassion, this great emperor was healed—and so was his empire.

The unique people of Holmola see their problem solved by a traveler and then proceed to take his solution to excess. This humorous story shows communities "how not to be."

## The Holmolaiset Build a House (Finland)

**I**n a very remote part of Finland, there was a little village called Holmola. The people of Holmola, the Holmolaiset, never traveled away from their town. They were happy there and had no need for anything else. Very seldom did anyone visit Holmola, so the people there became quite different from the rest of the people in Finland. They became simple-minded and extremely conservative. In fact, you might even call them not only unique, but weird.

Making decisions was extremely difficult for the Holmolaiset as they pondered this way versus that way. They would talk, argue, discuss, and consider things for weeks before they ever got around to any action.

You could say the Holmolaiset were similar to the people in stories told about the Men of Gotham or the Fools of Helm. They were unpredictable and they always some-how managed to make easy jobs difficult. These noodleheads would follow an idea to its extremes.

As our story begins, the Holmolaiset are getting ready for a new project. Everyone is arguing with each other and raising a ruckus. It has been like this for a year. It's all because the people got tired of living in houses shaped like wigwams. After a lot of discussion they decided to build houses that were different. They wanted to make houses that looked like log houses do today.

The Holmolaiset organized people into teams for the different jobs. One team would cut down the trees, another group would trim the branches off, and a third bunch would peel the bark off of the trees. Another man would take out his homemade tape measure and measure the trees for the right length. There were men whose job was to cut the tree into the measured lengths, and yet another gang would carry the logs to the place where the house was to be built.

Two fellows notched the ends of the logs so they would fit together tightly. It took four more men to lift the logs into place to make the walls. Women came along and chinked the places where the logs rested on each other with moss. When all the walls were up, the roofing group got to work.

Once they had decided how they would get the work done, the Holmolaiset got busy on it. They worked slowly but carefully, until the log house was finished, and then the workers went inside the finished house and closed the door. But something was terribly wrong.

"What happened?" they asked. They hadn't counted on it being pitch-black inside. After all, wasn't this log house built in the sunshine? "We chinked all of the walls so the sunshine would stay inside and not leak out," said the women.

The people all gathered together to solve this problem. What had happened to the sunshine? Where had it gone? They started to blame each other for making a mistake that helped the sun escape.

They brought in their local wise man to fix things and get the sunlight back. The wizard drummed on his drum while he chanted and sung spells to bring back the sun. He was a good wizard—the best they had. But his songs, chants, spells, and drumming didn't change a thing. It was still dark, dark, dark inside the house.

After several months of arguing, discussing, considering, and deciding, the Holmolaiset decided that they had to carry sunlight into the house. This would be a very simple thing to do. All they had to do was to make great woolen sacks, fill them up with sunlight, twist the top of the sacks, and carry the sacks inside the house. Then they would open the sacks and let the sunlight fill the house.

Everyone worked hard to fill the house with sacks of sunlight, but when they opened the bags, nothing happened. It was still dark, dark, dark inside the house.

About this time a stranger named Matti happened to come to their town. Everyone was arguing and shouting. Matti asked them, "Is there something that I could help you with?"

The Holmolaiset told him what had happened and moaned about how everything had gone wrong, even after all of their careful planning.

"That's no problem, people of Holmola," declared Matti. "Where I come from we have been living in log houses with sunlight for a long time. I'll help you get the sunlight into the house if you pay me one thousand marks."

After a lot of loud bickering, the people of the village agreed.

"Fine," said Matti. "Watch what I do," he told them. He walked into the house, kept the door open so he could see, took his axe from his belt, and chopped out a square hole in the wall. When he was done, the sun streamed into the house and gave enough light that everyone could see all the empty sacks they had used, lying on the earthen floor. Everyone was delighted. They paid Matti and thanked him for his idea and his help.

Matti continued on his trip. But no sooner was he out of the village limits and heading into the forest than the people got to talking again. Since Matti's idea had worked so well they decided to improve upon it. Before they had properly discussed, argued, considered, and thought of all the possibilities, they set about improving the house. They started to hack out more windows in the house. They cheered as they saw more sunshine stream in the house. Those noodleheads cut so many windows that before you could say "crash" the whole roof came tumbling down.

And that is why you will never find a log cabin in Holmola even to this day. The Holmolaiset keep telling the story of they time they let more sunshine in the log house and everyone learned from the story. No log houses in Holmola!

This poem was written by an eighty-five-year-old man named Mr. Ray Lucht and has been published in magazines and newspapers, on the Internet, and in other venues where aging is a topic. It is a lesson from the elder.

## I'd Pick More Daisies
## (United States)

If I had my life to live over,
I'd try to make more mistakes next time.
I would relax. I would limber up.
I would be sillier than I have been on this trip.
I know of very few things I would take seriously.
I would be crazier. I would be less hygenic.
I would take more chances. I would take more trips.
I would climb more mountains, swim more rivers, and watch
    more sunsets.
I would burn more gasoline.
I would eat more ice cream and less beans.
I would have more actual troubles and fewer imaginary ones.
You see, I am one of those people who lives prophylactically
    and sensibly hour after hour, day by day.
Oh I have had my moments.
And if I had it to do over again, I'd have more of them.
In fact, I'd try to have nothing else. Just moments one after
    another instead of living so many years ahead of each day.
I have been one of those people who never go anywhere
    without a thermometer.
If I had it to do over again, I would go places and do things.
And travel lighter than I have.
If I had my life to live over, I would start barefooted earlier
    in the spring.
And stay that way later in the fall.
I would play hooky more.
I would ride merry-go-rounds.
I'd pick more daisies.

175

**POT SHOTS®**  Ashleigh Brilliant

IF YOU STAY HEALTHY,

the longer
you live,
the more
alive
you can become.

This story shows what elders have to offer to both the community and their families.

## Abandonment Canyon
## (Japan)

**T**here was a time when the warlord of the country decreed that whenever anyone became sixty years old, they were to be taken into a mountain canyon and abandoned. He reasoned that when people became sixty years old they were unable to work or do anything constructive.

Shortly after, a farmer became sixty years old, and so it was the time for his family to take him to Abandonment Canyon. His son sadly accompanied with him on the trip. On the way up the mountain, the old man had trouble walking in the boulder field. His son was filled with compassion and set his father on his back.

As they climbed through the forest, the old man broke off limbs of trees. "Why are you doing that, father?" asked his son. "You know you will not return home and use the trail to guide you."

The answer, "Oh no, son, it would be too bad if you didn't find your way back home. I am simply marking the trail for you."

The son was a good man with a good heart, and he felt it break inside of him with his father's words. The son also knew how gentle his father was, so he decided to take him back home. He dug a place for the old man under the porch and laid mats on the earth for comfort. Hidden there, no one would know the old father still lived with his son.

Now the warlord of the area took pleasure in giving the people difficult tasks to accomplish. One of those times came and he called the men folk to come to his stronghold. When all were gathered, he gave the order, "Tomorrow you must each bring me a rope woven from ashes."

"How can we do such a thing?" the men asked each other. They were all deeply troubled.

The young man went back home and crawled into his father's hiding place. "Bad news! The lord has commanded everyone bring him a rope woven from ashes tomorrow. I am sure there will be some terrible punishment for failure to do this task."

The old father consoled his son. "Do not worry. That can be done easily. Follow my directions. You must weave a rope very tightly, then carefully burn it until it turns to ashes. You will take that to the lord."

The son was relieved to get this solution to the task. He did just as his father had told him to do. He made the rope of ashes and took it to the lord the next day. As it turned out, he was the only man who had accomplished this task. No one else had been able to do it. The lord praised him highly "You are a very clever man." But moments later he roared, "Everyone must bring a conch shell with a silken thread passed through it."

The son returned home and again, joined his father under the porch. "This time the task is truly impossible," he said as he told his father what the latest demand was.

"Ah, son, do not despair. Get a conch shell and point the tip toward the sun. Take your silken thread and stick a piece of rice on it. Find a hungry ant and give him the rice and make it crawl into the mouth of the shell. You will see how quickly the ant will pull the thread through the conch shell."

Again, the son did as his father told him. He was amazed at how fast the ant pulled the silken thread through the shell. The next day, he took the shell to the lord, who was again very impressed.

The lord demanded, "How were you able to do what I thought would be impossible?"

The son fell to his knees before the lord and bowed low. "The things that you asked us to do were difficult. Taking my father to Abandonment Canyon, though, was more difficult. I have hidden him under our porch. The things that you ordered us to do were not difficult for my father. He told me what to do and that is why I have been successful in solving the tasks."

The lord pondered his answer. "I am very impressed with your honesty and caring. I see now that old people have wisdom for us and should be honored instead of abandoned." Following that, the lord decreed that abandonment in sixty-year canyon be abolished.

Following is another story observing the wisdom of the elders and the need of the community for their accumulated knowledge.

## The Golden Cup
## (Buryat)

A group of nomads were told by their mighty Khan that they must move to new lands. "The camping sites there will be better. The pastures will be richer," he old them.

The trip to these new lands, though, would be long and hard. In preparation for the trip, the Khan ordered all the old people to be killed. "If you do not carry out my command to kill all the old people, you will be severely punished. The old ones will hold us back and be a burden to us. They must die."

The people lived in terror of the Khan. They knew if they disobeyed him what would happen to them. What a dilemma!

Among the Khan's subjects was a brave young man, Tsyren, who silently vowed, "I will not kill my old father!" He turned to his father and said, "Hide in my large leather sack. I will carry you in secret." Tsyren never considered what might happen to them later.

The Khan with his people and herds left the old camping site for the new lands in the north. Tsyren's old father traveled with them in a large leather sack slung across his horse's back.

When they camped for the night, Tsyren untied the sack and let his father out to stretch his aching joints. "Here father, eat this food to keep up your strength."

One night, the group camped near water. One of the Khan's loyal subjects saw a large golden cup of unusual shape at the bottom of the water. He faithfully took the news of it to the Khan. People were reluctant to dive into the sea for it. "Draw lots to see who will dive and get the golden cup," ordered the Khan.

179

The man who drew the lot dived into the sea, but he never returned, disappearing in the water. The men drew lots again. This time the man with the lot jumped into the sea from the top of a sheer cliff. He, too, disappeared.

Many of the Khan's people lost their lives attempting to recover the cup. The Khan was determined that he would get it. One after another, men dived into the sea and were swept away. At last it was Tsyren's turn. Before his attempt, he went to his hidden father and said, "Farewell Father. We are going to die now—both of us."

The old man asked him, "Why is that? What is the problem now?"

Tsyren told his father about his upcoming dive to get the cup. "No one who has tried to get it ever returned. They have all died. I, too, will perish following the Khan's orders. I fear that his servants will find you here and kill you."

His father listened carefully, then told him, "There is no cup at the bottom of the sea. Look at the mountain. Can you see the golden cup standing at the top? What everyone sees in the water is only the reflection of the cup."

He continued, "Climb the mountain. It will be steep and hard to do. If you find that you can't climb it, wait for some female deer and frighten them. In their mad dash to avoid you, they will knock the cup down. Make sure you don't let it fall into a deep ravine."

Just as his father had predicted, the climb was hard. Tsyren had to grab shrubs, trees, and sharp rocks as he climbed. He saw he would never be able to reach the mountaintop. He stopped and followed his father's directions to wait for some deer.

When they appeared, the deer gazed down at Tsyren. He jumped up and gave a loud shout. Just as his father had predicted, the startled does knocked the golden cup, and it came rolling down.

With the cup tucked safely under his arm, Tsyren made his way down the mountain. He went straight to the Khan and set the cup down before him.

"How were you able to do what all the others failed to do? They all died, and here you are with a grin on your face," the Khan asked him with a puzzled look.

"The cup was not at the bottom of the sea but instead on the top of the great mountain. What we saw in the water was really the reflection of the cup," answered Tsyren.

The Khan's eyes narrowed as he looked at Tsyren. "Did you think of this yourself?"

Tsyren nodded, "Yes."

The Khan dismissed Tsyren and asked him nothing more. The next day the Khan ordered his people to move on. After a long hot trip to a great desert where the earth was dry and cracked and no vegetation grew, they stopped. There was no water to be seen. There was no oasis. All the men along with their cattle suffered from thirst.

"Spread out in all directions to search for water," the Khan ordered. But the search was futile. There was no water anywhere.

"What will we do now," the men asked in despair. Tsyren left the group and went to his father.

"What are we to do father?" Tsyren asked. "All of the people and cattle will die of thirst."

"I have a possible answer," Tsyren's father told him. "Let a three-year-old cow roam about. Leave it loose and study it closely. When it stops and sniffs at the ground, dig in that spot."

Tsyren followed his father's direction. When the cow stopped to sniff at the ground, Tsyren gathered the other men, "We must dig here." When they did, they found cool, clear water that gushed from an underground spring. It flowed out over the parched ground. Everyone cheered Tsyren, drank their fill, and filled their water carriers.

Khan observed what had happened and called Tsyren to come to him. "You have done the impossible again. How were you able to find water in this desert?" he asked.

"Ah, my lord, certain signs told me what we must do," answered Tsyren. Everyone drank more water, rested, and then moved on. They didn't stop to make camp again for many days. That night, a surprise heavy rainfall hit and put the campfire out. The people were now wet, chilled to the bone, and unable to get another fire started.

Someone saw what seemed to be the light of a campfire on the top of a faraway mountain. Khan ordered his men to bring the fire down from the mountain. Or course, everyone rushed to do as he ordered. At the top of the mountain they found the fire, which flamed beneath the thick branches of a large spruce tree. There was a hunter warming himself at the fire. Each of the Khan's men took away a burning log but as they traveled to their camp, the heavy rains put out the fire.

The Khan ordered everyone who returned without fire to be put to death. It was Tsyren's turn to go up the mountain. Before he left, he went to his hidden father. "Now what can I do father? How can I bring a burning log down to our camp?"

The old man thought for a short while then directed his son, "Do not take the logs. They will only smolder, and the rain will put out any fire. Take a large pot with you and fill it with burning coals. In this way you will be able to bring fire back to our camp."

Again, Tsyren followed his father's direction and succeeded in bringing a pot full of live coals from the mountain. He started a fire, and everyone warmed themselves by it and cooked food over it.

"Who brought the fire?" demanded the Khan. When he found out that it was Tsyren, he had the young man brought to him. "How did you know how to bring the fire back? Why did you not speak up immediately?"

"I did not know how to do it myself," Tsyren told the Khan.

"Then how were you able to do it?" roared the Khan.

The Khan kept demanding Tsyren tell him how he accomplished the things no one else could do. He was so insistent that Tsyren finally confessed "I only followed my father's wise advice."

The Khan's mouth dropped. He demanded to know where the father was. "I carried him all the way here in a large leather sack," was Tsyren's answer.

For a moment the Khan was quiet. Then he ordered the old man to be brought before him. He sat stroking his chin and looking at Tsyren's father. "I have decided to take back my order. Old people are not a burden for the young. Age has wisdom. You need hide no longer but you may travel with us openly. Welcome."

This cumulative tale illustrates the connectedness of community and the folly of blame.

## The Story of the Owl (Hmong)

**L**ong ago, the owl could see during the day as well as other animals could. One day, the owl was sitting by himself on the branch of a huge tree without much to do. He saw a monkey eating corn in the field. The owl decided to make fun of the monkey, so he suddenly made a very loud noise. "Hoot!" the owl cried.

The monkey was frightened and immediately ran away as fast as he could. As he ran, he accidentally stepped on the stem of the pumpkin vine, which caused the pumpkin to drop and roll very fast down the field until it hit a nat plant (sesame). The nat plant had very tiny seeds, and they all fell to the ground. In fact, some of the tiny seeds fell into a rooster's eyes, and the rooster was blinded.

The rooster ran aimlessly, pecking the ground, and unintentionally picked up a few ants from a group of worker ants. The other ants started rushing around and then dug into their anthill to hide themselves.

This caused the anthill to collapse, and it crushed and killed a mother hen's two chicks. The mother hen was very angry because, of course, she loved her babies very much.

The mother hen was so upset that she decided to investigate what had killed her babies. She first started to question the anthill. "Why did you kill my babies?"

The anthill told her, "I was standing in my place and did not do anything wrong. But the ants started digging into me and I collapsed and fell down and squashed your chicks. I never meant to do it."

Then she went to the ants. "Why were you digging in the anthill? It fell down and killed my babies," she said.

"It was not our fault. We were busy working and the rooster pecked a few of our workers, so we dug into the anthill to hide ourselves. We did not want the rooster to catch us," snapped the ants.

So the hen went to the rooster and demanded, "Why did you peck the worker ants? They started to dig into the anthill to hide from you, and it collapsed on my two chicks and killed them!"

"I did not intend to peck the ants," the rooster answered. "I was on my way to look for food and some seeds suddenly fell into my eyes and blinded me. I could not see anything. I pecked around with my beak trying to figure out where I was and I accidentally pecked the ants."

The mother hen waddled straight to the nat plant to find out why its seeds had fallen down and into the eyes of the rooster. The nat plant told her, "I was holding all my seeds in place, but the pumpkin rolled down the hill and hit me. It hit me so hard I could not hold onto my seeds, so I lost them."

Now the mother hen half-flew and half-hopped to the pumpkin plant. "Why did you roll down the hill and hit the nat plant? It lost all of its seeds and some fell into the eyes of the rooster, so he pecked some worker ants who started digging at the anthill to hide from him. The anthill fell down and killed my two chicks!"

The bruised pumpkin plant answered, "I was hanging on my vine when the clumsy monkey stepped on my stem so I fell down. I rolled down the hill and hit the nat plant. I did not want to do it."

Clucking and squawking, the mother hen ran to the monkey to find out why he had stepped on the pumpkin vine. The monkey chattered, "It was the owl! He made a sudden loud noise and scared me. I was afraid that someone was going to shoot me, so I ran as fast as I could and mistakenly stepped on the stem of the pumpkin vine. I am sorry."

Furiously, the hen marched straight to the owl and demanded, "Why did you make the loud noise that scared the monkey and made him step on the pumpkin vine? The pumpkin fell off and rolled down the hill and hit the nat plant and made all of its tiny seeds fall. Some seeds fell into the rooster's eyes and blinded him, so he pecked some worker ants and the other ants dug into the anthill to hide from him. When they did that, the anthill collapsed and killed my two chicks. Why did you make that noise?"

The owl just stared at the mother hen with his eyes wide open. Finally, she angrily grabbed the owl's neck and twisted his head back and forth. "You are a wretch. From now on you will see only at night because you are not like the other animals."

And that is why the owl can see only at night and why he is able to turn his head all the way around.

# HEALING THE EARTH

**M**any stories contain themes about our wonderful home—the Earth. There are creation stories in every culture, stories of great floods and stories about the natural phenomena that we see regularly, such as thunderstorms and rainbows, and the sun and moon. These stories teach us about the Earth and our connections to it and its creatures. Our experiences with the Earth help us become whole. Enos Mills, father of Rocky Mountain National Park, said "Probably the best way to delay death, the best medicine to lengthen life, is to take to the woods. This life-sustaining prescription is most effective as a preventative and should be regularly used. Like a sermon, it should be taken once in a while whether needed or not." This pioneer environmentalist was right! The Earth is full of greatness and mystery and we are privileged to be part of it all.*

In stories and in the natural world around us, bodies of water (e.g., rivers, lakes) are of special significance as places to revive the spirit. In traditional tales we find many references to "healing waters" and magic wells. Remember the healing water in "The Wonder Doctor"? Consider also "The Lake of Healing or Loughleagh," which we explored earlier. There are also tales in which magical kingdoms exist at the bottoms of rivers and lakes. In "Little Water Medicine," water actually helps restore a man's life.

---

*For further exploration of environmental themes in stories, refer to *Celebrating the Earth* (Libraries Unlimited, 2000).

The Slavic composer, Bedrich Smetana (1824–1884), explored the symbolism of water in his symphonic poem, "The Moldau." Here the river is depicted through sound as a living being. This view directly relates to and draws upon symbolism found in folk literature. Symbolism for Earth's other elements—soil, air, fire—also abound in stories.

You may wonder why animals play the role of characters in stories. It is not because animals are so darn cute; there is much more to it than that. Perhaps animals assume so much importance in folktales because their differences from people make the dramatic events of a folktale or fable a little easier to handle. Animals help us follow the story line while keeping our distance from it; they prevent a frightening story from creating outright terror in the listener. People often use symbolism to talk about important things; the neutrality of animals serves us well. Animals aren't as specific as lazy Uncle John or hysterical cousin Terry. Animals can masquerade as people dressed in fur, feather, or fin, but as characters they make the story's medicine a little easier to swallow. And with stories that rehearse the future, animals as actors ensure smooth rehearsals.

Animal stories fall into several groups: talking beasts (who are not always true to their species); animals true to their species but with the power of speech; and animals objectively reported. In folktales, animals might represent various aspects of human personality. For example, the cow is often a fairy-tale metaphor for the mother. Bees, usually female, represent hard work and sweetness and are therefore also a symbol of maturity. The cat, also usually female, often symbolizes a valuable, lovable, and mature mother figure.

Wily tricksters are often depicted in the form of a coyote, a raven or crow, or a rabbit. These animals might be seen as symbols of human traits—the sly fox, the predatory wolf, the powerful bear. Sometimes it helps to see a small, timid animal such as a rabbit, outsmart a large, strong animal. After all, aren't we all sometimes helpless in the real world? Wouldn't it be easy for us to relate unconsciously to Br'er Rabbit as he outwits the other animals? Doesn't that give us a sense of power—an "I can do it, too" spirit?

Animal characters can serve as metaphors for a coarser side of human nature—with snails, frogs, pigs, and birds of prey, such as vultures, usually cast in the unseemly roles. Other birds (robins and sparrows) are used as symbols of the superego.

Historically people have credited animals with powers far beyond their own, and ranked them among the earliest of the gods. Some gods assumed the forms of animals when they appeared among men; how else could a mortal explain the snakes shedding of its old skin? Wasn't that the stuff of transformation and immortality?

Another way animals are used in stories is to represent natural phenomena. Ancient Egyptians saw the sun as a beetle. The beetle lays its eggs in the sand and wraps them in a cocoon of manure, which it rolls across the ground just as the sun rolls across the heavens. The legendary phoenix also symbolizes the sun. It rises from the tallest trees in the east from the ashes of its former self.

Then again, animals can represent omens and transformed humans. Real and imaginary beasts existed in ancient minds. Could these creatures really have existed and become extinct? Or did ancient people simply embellish ordinary animals with special features and magic powers? Forms of animals shift and change in stories, and language adds confusion in translation. Legendary animals sometimes combine the features of several creatures; often they add human features to their own. Many wear the fabulous masks of invention. These amazing beasts (e.g., unicorns, griffins) usually purportedly possessed supernatural powers and even today maintain an important place in folklore. Writers call them mythical monsters, exotic zoology, fabulous beasts, and beasts of never.

There are many stories of humans being changed into animals or trapped in an animal form—usually the result of a spell or curse. For example, think of the transformation of the prince into a frog. These tales show us our proximity to members of the animal kingdom and also caution us that under some circumstances we can become animals.

In stories there are also many examples of animals as helpers. The fish thrown back into the sea, the trapped bear that is released, the eagle with a broken wing who is nursed back to health—these animals always reappear to help or save the heroes.

Ancient people understood their connection to the natural world, and their stories reveal this understanding. For example, the Native American tradition holds that all things have a spirit or life force and that all these forces are interconnected. The traditional view is that each animal, each stone, each place has a unique spirit that influences all life around it. To use medicine is to use the forces of nature to influence and guide your path in life. You can witness this power of Earth's medicine in the story "The Legend of Hackberry Hill." Stories such as the Seneca tale "The Little Water Medicine" teach us to respect Earth and its animals. They show us how we are all connected. These are lessons we still need today—perhaps more than ever.

A beautiful story of healing, interconnectedness, and interaction between
people and the creatures of the earth.
Animal helpers and the healing power
of water are just two of the themes to
explore in this tale.

## The Little Water Medicine
## (Seneca)

**L**ong ago there was a man named Red Hand, who
was a good hunter. Not only was he usually successful when
he went to hunt, he also showed great respect for the animals
and birds. Before he hunted he would always throw tobacco
and ask permission to hunt for game. He never shot a
mother animal with young. He did not take unfair advantage
by shooting animals when they were swimming or asleep,
and he never hunted unless he and the other people of his
village were in need. Whenever he was successful, he would
share part of his kill with the birds of the air and the animals
such as the wolf and the fox. When he harvested his fields he
always left some of the ears of corn on the ground and called
to the crows and other birds to come and take their part.
Because of this, all of the animals and birds loved him.

One day, he went south with a party of men to trade.
As they traveled through the forest, they were ambushed by
a group of men from another nation with whom they had
been at war. In the fight, Red Hand was struck down, and as
he lay there, the enemies cut his scalp from his head and
took it back to their village as a trophy.

After a time, night fell and the owl, seeing the man
lying there, came and hovered above his body. A wolf caught
the scent of the man's blood and came close, recognizing
him as the great friend of the animals. He sat beside the
man's body and howled in sorrow. Before long, all of the
birds and animals who had been treated with respect and fed
by Red Hand had gathered around.

The great eagle perched on a stump above the man's body. "This is our friend," said the eagle. "What shall we do?"

"He is the one who feeds us," said the wolf. "We must not let him die."

"If he grows too cold, he cannot return to life again. I will keep the warmth in him," said the bear. Then she lifted up Red Hand's body and held it close.

"A human being cannot live without his scalp," said the owl. "It must be restored to him."

Then the crow flew through the forest to the village where the enemy people lived. The crow saw the scalp hanging from a pole near the smoke-hole of the lodge, but when he flew too close, the people threw rocks to chase him away. When the crow returned to the other animals, he told what he had seen.

"I will go and bring back our brother's scalp," said the heron, and flew to the village of the enemy people, but she, too, was driven away.

Next to try was the falcon. Swifter than the others, he swooped in to grasp the scalp, but the enemy people saw him and fired arrows so close that he barely escaped.

Then the little hummingbird flew off. So small and swift she could hardly be seen, she dove down and speared the scalp with her sharp beak and flew swiftly back to where the animals waited in the clearing.

The great eagle took the dry scalp and shook the dew from his wings onto it, moistening it again.

"Now we must make a powerful medicine," the eagle said.

Then each of the birds and animals gathered there gave a part of his or her own flesh and, with herbs and clear water from a nearby spring, mixed it into a powerful medicine. They poured the medicine into Red Hand's mouth and pressed the moist scalp onto his head. As soon as they did so, Red Hand began to breathe deeply. He heard the sounds of the animals around him and he could understand their voices. He opened his eyes and there, all around him in the moonlight, he saw the animals who had healed him.

Then, as he sat there, the animals explained what they had done. They told him how to make the healing medicine that would be the most powerful medicine the Seneca people would ever know.

"You have been our greatest friend. So we give you this medicine," they told him. "Take it back to your people."

So, from that day on, Red Hand was a great healer. With the medicine the animals had given him, he was able to heal all wounds. It became known as the *niga'ni'ga'a,* the Little Water Medicine, and it was passed down within the Medicine Lodge from generation to generation. Those who were to be entrusted with it always had to show their gratitude through songs and dances to the medicine animals. That way the people would always remember to be thankful to the birds and animals who had saved the life of their greatest friend.

∾ Retold by Joseph Bruchac, *Parabola,* Volume XVIII, No. 1. February 1993, pp. 37–38.

Greed destroys in this story. The medicine spear is responsible for overkill that ruins the lives of everyone around. A timely message in the age of consumerism and unprecedented wealth for some.

## The Medicine Spear
## (Zambia)

Deep in the bush of Africa, lived a hunter and his family. The hunter's work was to bring home enough food to feed his family. He traveled to distant places to hunt. He hunted where he had found success previously. He hunted on the edge of the bush. He hunted every day and every place he thought he might find some game.

Sometimes his hunt was successful and he would bring home a bush rat. Another time he might take joy in getting an undersized antelope. But no matter how hard and how far he went to hunt, he was not able to bring home enough meat to feed his family.

He sought advice from his father-in-law. He traveled to his village, and after greetings they conferred. "All of my days, every day, I go hunting. I travel everywhere in search of game. It always seems to elude me and I return home empty-handed. I work very hard to feed your daughter and our family, but the game has always just left every place I go."

He continued, "My wife scorns me saying, 'You are lazy. All of our neighbors seem to find food when they go out hunting. But not you! You scarcely bring home enough food to feed us.' "

The hunter, looked his father-in-law in his eyes and begged, "Father of my wife, do you have any advice? What can I do?"

"I know that you are sincere and earnest about hunting," replied his father-in-law. "I myself cannot help you. You must seek out the wise old man named Sabatu, who lives in the village north of here. He is the only one I can think of that might help you. One piece of advice: take something as payment to him."

All the hunter had of any value were some pelts. So he gathered them up and traded them for a goat. Then he led this goat to the village of the wise old man in the north. He was in luck, for when he arrived at the home of Sabatu, he found him sitting in front of it. Sabatu was indeed old, but more that that he was blind and his body was withered.

The hunter respectfully asked to sit with him and seek his wise advice. He explained why he had come. "I hunt endlessly and widely but cannot find any game to kill and bring home to feed my family. Always I find clues that game had recently been there but I never find any. Every day I go to the bush, and if I am lucky I come home with birds or bush rats that do not make a satisfying meal for my dear family. My wife tells me I have no ambition or skill. There must be some evil spirit driving the game away from me. I went to my father-in-law for advice and he told me to come to you. That is why I am here. I have brought a goat for payment for any help you can give me."

The wizened old man, with skin like parchment, just sat there and threw cowry shells in the dust. He felt them with his fingers and threw them again. He did this over and over again. After a lengthy time, he said, "Even though I am blind, I see it clearly. There is a bush spirit hiding the game from you." As he said this, Sabatu put some red powder and feathers in a small cloth and tied them into a medicine packet. "Attach this packet to your spear. It will enable you to overcome the bush spirit who is hiding the game."

After giving the old man the goat and many respectful thanks, the hunter returned to his hut along the edge of the bush. His wife didn't say anything to him at all.

He fastened the medicine packet to the shaft of his spear. He then left his hut and went hunting. He didn't go very far until he saw a large antelope before him. He joyfully killed it and brought the meat home. The next day, he hunted and came across another large antelope that he killed and cleaned and then brought the meat home to his family. Day after day, he hunted and found rich game.

"There is too much meat. It will rot," his wife complained.

The hunter looked at her and said, "Never again will you say I am too lazy. I will hunt. I will bring home meat." So he did. Every day he hunted and every day there was more meat.

"The meat is rotting. It is stacking up everywhere and rotting. The smell of it fills the whole village," complained his wife.

"Every day I hunt. I never rest. Why are you complaining? I am not lazy," the hunter told his wife.

The next morning he decided that he would let his medicine spear do the hunting so he sent the medicine spear out to hunt by itself. It went and quickly returned home, bringing more meat. The next day the hunter again sent the spear out by itself. Just as had happened the day before, it returned with more meat. More and more meat accumulated in the hunter's home. It rotted and began to stink. The smell of decay was everywhere.

The hunter was stubborn and thought that life had never before been so good to him. So things continued on until the day his family could no longer stand the stench. It was at this point that the hunter told his medicine spear, "Stop the hunting. It is now finished. Hunt no more."

There was only one problem, the spear was more stubborn than he. It ignored his requests. It went on hunting day after day. Soon the stink of rotting meat became unbearable.

"Let us take what things we can carry and move away from here," the hunter told his family. They built a new home but even that didn't work. The stench of the rotting meat followed them on the wind. Again and again they moved. Farther and farther from their old home they moved but the stink of the meat followed them wherever they went.

They had reached a distant country and none of their relatives knew where to find them. For a while people said to each other, "Where can the hunter and his family have gone?" Years passed and people forgot them and eventually no one mentioned their names any longer. Somewhere, out in the bush, the medicine spear still hunts.

Trees have always held magic and symbolism for people. Some cultures worship trees, and many superstitions involve them. An example is knocking on wood for good luck, which comes from the time of the Druids. People knocked on trees to let the tree spirit know they had a request.

## The Legend of Hackberry Hill (Colorado, United States)

On a hill located in a place called Arvada, Colorado, there stands a hackberry tree. Naturally the hill is now called Hackberry Hill. However, the tree that grows there now is not the original tree.

When pioneers traveling west came to the Denver area, they saw a tree growing on a hill as they headed toward the foothills. One of the earliest records of the sighting of the hackberry tree by white men was made by John Torrey, the naturalist with the 1843 Fremont Expedition.

Colorado plains were generally devoid of trees except for cottonwoods growing in the stream areas, so this hackberry tree was used as a landmark for the travelers. What was also unusual about this tree was that it was a hackberry tree, whose natural territory stopped more than six hundred miles to the east, near St. Louis. The tree was fourteen inches in diameter at its base and was sixteen feet high. It had grown in such a manner that its trunk was twisted to form a seat that travelers used to sit on to rest. The tree bore a reddish cherry-like fruit every year as far back as it was known to the white man. How did this tree get where it was?

Some people say that this tree growing all alone on its rocky, barren hill might have been planted by early explorers. Others suggest that wild birds from the Missouri River Valley may have carried the seeds. The Indians of the area had a different legend that explained how the tree got there.

Long ago, they said, a great chief killed in battle was buried on the bluff. The Indians considered this hill sacred. Mountain and plains tribes came to the hill to worship the Great Spirit, hold pow wows, and smoke peace pipes.

The old-time burial custom of the Plains Indians was to put the body upon a scaffold of poles or a platform among the boughs of a tree. This was their only means of placing the body out of reach of wild beasts, and they had no tools with which to dig a suitable grave. The corpse was prepared by dressing it in the finest clothes, together with some personal possessions and ornaments, wrapped in several robes, and finally in a secure covering of rawhide. Then the whole community would break camp and depart to a distance, leaving the dead alone in an honorable solitude.

The great chief, the Indians said, was dressed in his chief's robes with his favorite war bonnet and healing objects beside him. Around his neck was his medicine bag, which held those things that were his own charms against bad luck. In the bag were hackberry seeds that were the gift of the medicine man. Over time, one of these seeds started to grow within the breast of the chief, sending its branches to the sun and its roots to the water far below.

In 1936, the state highway department of Colorado planned a new road over Hackberry Hill where the old hackberry tree stood. The engineers decided the tree would have to be cut down. Many people insisted that the ancient tree should be saved. After much discussion and argument, the officials finally agreed to transplant the tree. They dug a ditch around the tree leaving a large mass of soil clinging to the roots but the day before the tree was to be removed it was mysteriously cut down.

Some people of the time had a theory that the Great Indian Father brought revenge on the white man for building a road that would destroy an Indian altar, but others were more suspicious of the telltale marks of a rusty hand-saw on the stump.

In 1974, a man named Ford Fox confessed to cutting down the hackberry tree because he thought too much fuss was being made over the old tree. Bits of the original hackberry tree remain as mementos. The gavel used by the Arvada Garden Club, a group formed in opposition to the destruction of the tree, was made from the old tree.

In 1966, the Arvada Garden Club planted a commemorative hackberry tree in a small park donated by the Colorado Division of Highways. The plaque reads "This young hackberry tree was planted here in memory of an old hackberry tree which stood on the top of this hill as a landmark for pioneers coming west. It was the only hackberry tree anywhere around this region for 600 miles." This original tree had stood proudly atop the hill with Indians, buffalo, and a few white settlers for companions. Its replacement tree is hidden in a tiny roadside park beside a heavily traveled, crowded highway. What would the Great Chief have said if he knew what happened to the original tree that had grown from the hackberry seed in his medicine bag from his very own heart?

Traditions such as honoring certain creatures are part of ancient appreciation and recognition of people's interaction with inhabitants of the natural world. In this story, a young hunter makes a promise to the forces of nature, then makes a serious mistake.

## The Ptarmigan
## (Japan)

A long time ago when monsters and giants still lived in the mountains of Japan, a group of hunters came upon some ptarmigan, the "thunderbird," which is sacred to the thunder god. That same night, all but one of the hunters mysteriously disappeared. The young hunter who was left went to search for the others.

He found them in the home of Snow Woman, who slaughters everyone who strays into her domain in the high mountains. Her house was made of smooth rocks from the surrounding fields, and the stones were covered with lichen. Moss was stuffed between the rocks. The young hunter saw a picture of a ptarmigan hanging in the doorway. He knew that it was there to keep the lightning away.

The young hunter called to Snow Woman just as she whacked the last of the lost hunters over his head. "Why do you kill all who stray into your territory?" he demanded.

Snow Woman turned to seize him but was instantly struck by something special about this man. "I kill those who come here and stay too long because they threaten me and the mountains," she replied. As Snow Woman and the hunter talked, she softened and even started to care about this brave, earnest young man.

She decided not to kill him as she had always done with others. "You must go now," she told him. "You have stayed too long in the mountains. I will spare your life but only if you promise not to tell anyone about me and what you have seen here. If you tell anyone, I will slay you."

197

The young hunter made the promise and left her home and the mountains. As he passed through the doorway of Snow Woman's home, he noticed that the eyes of the ptarmigan in the picture appeared to watch him. Then he climbed down the mountains.

Because he was above tree line, there were only rocks in the fields where he walked; but as he looked closer, one of the rocks moved. The moving rock was a camouflaged ptarmigan, who blended right into the surroundings. The ptarmigan in his mottled colors showed no fear of the hunter.

Years went by and the young man told no one of his adventures while hunting in the mountains, but friends noticed that he was somehow different. He seemed detached. Everyone was pleased for him when he met a beautiful young raven-haired maiden at a local festival and fell immediately in love with her.

The raven-haired girl returned his love, so they married. She hung a picture of a ptarmigan in the doorway of their home to protect them from lightning. Happy years passed and they were blessed with beautiful children who looked like their mother.

One beautiful moonlit evening as they sat in their cozy kitchen and talked, the moonlight lit up the ptarmigan picture; the picture reminded the husband of the Snow Woman and how she had spared his life. He felt secure and safe with the woman he loved. "I want to share a very important time of my life with you," he said. He told her of the hunting trip, the mysterious disappearance of his hunting friends, and how he had found them all killed by the Snow Woman of the mountains. "The ptarmigan picture in the moonlight reminded me of that time. I'll never know why she spared my life."

His wife looked at him with a dreadful sadness. "You have broken the promise you made to the Snow Woman never to tell anyone about her," she said with a hoarse whisper. "And now it is done! I am the Snow Woman. Even today I cannot kill you but with great sadness for all I leave behind, I must now leave you and go back to the mountains."

Before his startled eyes, his beautiful raven-haired wife, the mother of his children, turned into Snow Woman. As Snow Woman left their home, the husband heard her wailing as she disappeared into the shimmering moonlight.

For the rest of his life the man was constantly reminded of what he had lost when he looked at his children or at the picture of the ptarmigan.

Rainbows have always held a fascination for people. Some peoples in Africa believe the rainbow is a giant snake that comes out to graze after a rainfall. African tribes, and of course the Irish, have stories about the rainbow's end and treasures to be found there. Many Native Americans connect flower petals to the rainbow. The Finns see it as the sickle or bow of the thunder god. And the Japanese believe that the rainbow is the floating bridge to heaven. All of these meanings for the rainbow help us develop appreciation for the natural world around us and possible relationships with objects. In this tale our rainbow is created from a monstrosity but comes to symbolize the balance between forces of creation and those of destruction.

## The Rainbow
## (Iroquois)

**B**ack when the Earth was created on Turtle's back, Sky Woman gave birth to twin sons, Good-Minded and Bad-Minded. With their birth, good and evil came to the world. The two brothers were in continual battle because Good-Minded worked to create things that were beautiful and Bad-Minded was only interested in disfiguring and destroying.

199

Good-Minded made the rivers, and he placed high hills on the sides of the rivers to guard the flow of the water through the valleys. This infuriated Bad-Minded, and he created a sea monster to travel the rivers and destroy them. Because the sea monster was used to the freedom of the wide seas, he was furious with the hills and the way they restricted him. He writhed through the waters, ripped and tore at the sides of the hills, and threw great boulders into the rivers.

When Good-Minded saw this, he worried that the rivers would be clogged and engulfed in deep seas and that the mountains and valleys would become dry and arid. Good-Minded rushed to rescue the rivers. The sea monster tried to escape when he saw Good-Minded because he knew and feared his powers. But the monster was unable to return through the destroyed rivers, so he fled to the sky.

Meanwhile, the Sun was peacefully making his colorful trail across the heavens. When the Sun learned what the sea monster had done, he found the monster and threw him across the sky, pinning him down to the east and west. The monster's scales flashed beautiful colors in the light. The Sun was satisfied that the sea monster would never return to the Earth to ruin Good-Minded's creations.

At that same time, Thunderer was passing on his way through a storm and saw the monster stretched across the sky. Thunderer admired the beautiful colors of the monster as it arched across the sky, so he picked him up and carried the monster to his lodge. "This will be perfect for the bow of my Lightning Hunter," thought Thunderer.

To this day the sea monster is in the heavens, constantly trying to escape from Thunderer when Thunderer is away directing the storms. But the ever watchful Sun always sees the sea monster and bends him across the sky. Sun paints the monster with the brightest colors so that Thunderer will discover the monster. And so, each time Thunderer finds the monster in the sky, he carries it back to his lodge.

During summer showers, when you look at the sky and see the resplendent hues that arch the sky, notice how they fade away when the Sun comes forth. That is only Thunderer taking the monster back to his lodge.

*Ecosystem* is a relatively new word, but the ancients understood the concept. Here is a vivid story of our connectedness of to the world and a lesson about speaking out against what's wrong.

## The Fallibility of Chiefs (Zaire)

**B**ack a long time ago, before people used common sense, there was a chief in a village. He had many slaves. Whatever he wanted to be done, he just ordered others to do it. If it was a wise thing he wanted, his various counselors said to him, "Yes, of course it is good," because if they disagreed with him, he only got angry.

"Yes, it is good," he would say. But if they they did disagree with him, his face got red, and he became agitated and roared, "What! Do you say that your chief doesn't know what he is doing is good?"

None of the counselors from the highest to the lowest ever said yes or no to him.

In fact, if the chief asked the lowest counselor about a particular thing, the counselor would just think for a while and then reply, "All things are linked."

Near where the chief lived were some marshes. The marshes were filled with frogs. These frogs were healthy and croaked loudly. One night, the chief could not sleep because of the croaking of the frogs. After that, night after night he could not sleep.

"The frogs must be exterminated," he commanded his counselors. One by one they all agreed with him, "Yes, it is good." That is all of the counselors except the lowest of them who did not speak.

"You must not have a tongue in your mouth, counselor," remarked the chief. "You have not given an answer."

The man thought for a while and then replied slowly, "O chief, all things are linked."

201

The chief had heard this so many times from this man he thought, "This man knows nothing else to say. All he can say is 'all things are linked.'"

Shortly after this, the chief sent his slaves out to exterminate all of the frogs in the marsh. They chased frogs, killed frogs, and searched for more frogs to kill until there were no more frogs left. When they returned to the chief they told him, "Sir, there are no more frogs. They are all gone. We have done as you asked."

That night for the first time in a long time the chief slept peacefully. And so, he slept quite well for many nights after that. He was pleased with life.

Meanwhile, in the marshes, the mosquitoes began to rise in buzzing storms because, of course, there were no frogs to eat their larvae.

The mosquitoes buzzed into the village. They buzzed into the chief's house and bit him on his ears, his arms, and his nose—they bit him everywhere! They made his life a misery. The whole village suffered.

The chief did as he usually did. He gave orders. He ordered the slaves to go out and kill the mosquitoes. The slaves went out, they tried, but there were too many mosquitoes. The mosquitoes zipped and whizzed everywhere and escaped all the efforts of the slaves. The flying hoard continued to plague the village.

The chief gathered his counselors. "When I asked you about killing the frogs, you answered, 'It is good.' Why did you not say, 'If the frogs are killed, the mosquitoes will multiply'?" he scolded them. "Only one of you said something that made me think. He said, 'All things are linked,' but I did not understand the value of his words."

The mosquito hordes made life so unbearable that the villagers left their houses and fields and went away. They traveled to distant places, cleared new fields, and began their lives in a new place. The old village became deserted except for the chief and his family. Finally, the chief could stand it no longer. He took his family and also fled.

Because of what happened there are people who say, "Yes, it is good" caused a village to become deserted, and "All things are linked" was a message they never forgot.

This story combines the universal
themes of floods and creation. It depicts
a world where all of Earth's creatures
are part of the same family.

## Creation, Flood, Naming Story
## (Hmong)

A very long time ago, the universe turned upside
down and the whole world was flooded with water. All living
beings were killed except one boy and his sister, who had
taken refuge in an unusually large wooden funeral drum.

The flood waters had risen higher and higher until
they reached the sky. Then this drum bumped against the
land of the sky and made a sound like NDOO NDONG!
NDOO NDONG! Sky people heard the sound and asked,
"Why is the earthly world making this noise? What could be
happening?"

Some sky people were sent down to find out what
was happening, and they saw that the water had already
covered the Earth and reached up as high as the sky. The
sky people said, "Let us use copper lances and iron spears to
puncture holes in the earth so that the water can flow away."

So the sky people hurled the lances and spears into
the Earth, and the water flowed down and away. Finally, the
big drum came back down to the surface of the Earth.

The brother and sister heard the noise when the
drum came back to the Earth, and they knew they had
reached land. They broke open the drum and climbed out.

"Where are all the people?" the girl asked.

"Dead," answered the boy.

"Are all the animals dead too?"

"Yes, there are only you and I."

Then they were both full of despair. "Marry me," said
the boy. "We can have a baby. We can make more people."

"I cannot marry you. You are my brother," said the
girl.

The next day the boy asked again, "Marry me."

The sister would not listen to him. But after many days of her brother asking her to marry him, she finally said, "If you really want to marry me, we must each bring a stone and climb up on that mountain. When we get to the top, we will roll your stone down one side of the mountain and roll mine down the other side. The next morning, if both stones have gone back up the mountain and we find them lying together on the mountaintop, then I will agree to marry you. But if the stones do not go back up the mountain, you will stop asking me to marry you."

So they took two stones that were used for grinding and fit together smoothly, and each carried one stone up to the top of the mountain. The sister rolled her stone down one side and the brother rolled his stone down the other.

The boy wanted to marry his sister very much, so that night he went to the mountain. He carried his stone back up the mountain and put it on the grass. Then he went down the mountain again and carried his sister's stone back up.

In the morning the sister said it was too bad there was no one to come along as a witness. The two of them went to the top of the mountain. "Look at the stones," said the brother. "They have come back up the mountain and are together in the same place. Now we can be married."

So the sister finally agreed. After all, hadn't the stones come back up the mountain as a sign that it would be all right?

The sister and brother married and lived together as husband and wife. After a while, they had a baby, but it did not look like an ordinary baby. It was round like a big soft egg, and it had no arms and no legs. "What kind of a baby is this?" they said to each other. "Maybe it is a baby seed. Let's cut it into pieces."

So they cut the baby seed into little pieces and scattered the pieces in all directions. Some pieces fell into the garden and made people. Their name was Vang,* because Vang sounds like the Hmong word for garden.

Some pieces fell in the weeds and grass and made more people. Their name was Thao, because Thao sounds like the Hmong word for weeds and grass.

---

*Vang, Thao, Li, and Moua are some of the Hmong clan names.

Some pieces fell in the goat house, and the people from those pieces were called Li. Other pieces fell in the pig house, and those people were named Moua, for the Hmong word for pig.

Three days later, the village was full of houses for every family. People were making fires and smoke was curling above every roof.

But this wonderful baby seed not only created people. Pieces of it also made chickens, pigs, oxen, buffaloes, horses, all sorts of insects, rodents, and birds. This is how the world was once more filled with living beings.

The brother and sister said, "Now we aren't sad because we are not alone any more."

What goes around, comes around. This fox story demonstrates the connectedness of Earth's creatures to each other and to the world around us. In the end, compassion toward animals is rewarded.

## The Grateful Foxes
## (Japan)

On one of those fine spring days when there is a heavy dew on the ground and the sun is shyly peeking from behind fluffy clouds, two friends went out to gather fern. With them they had a youngster who carried a bottle of wine and a box filled with things that would help them enjoy the day.

They saw at the foot of a hill two foxes that had brought out their cub to play. Three children from a neighboring village with baskets in their hands came up and they, too, saw the foxes.

"They must be collecting ferns like us," one of the men said.

While they watched, one of the children picked up a bamboo stick and crept up behind the foxes. When the old foxes fled, the boys surrounded the fox family and beat them with the stick. The two older foxes got away but the boys held down the cub and carrying it by the scruff of its neck, they went off in high glee.

One of the fellows looking on shouted out, "Hello! You boys! What are you doing with that fox?"

The oldest of the boys replied, "We're going to take him home and sell him to a young man in our village. He'll buy him, and then he'll boil him in a pot and eat him."

"Well," replied the man after thinking about it for a while, "I suppose it's all the same to you as to whom you sell the fox. You'd better let me have him."

"Oh," answered the boy, "that may be true but the fellow in our village promised us a good sum if we could find a fox. In fact, it was he who got us to come out to the hills and catch one. No, we can't sell him to you."

"Be that as it may, how much would the young man give you for the cub?" asked the man.

"Oh, he will give us enough to make it worth our while," said the boy.

"I will give you double the amount you think your village fellow would give you," insisted the man.

"Oh, for that amount, we will sell him to you, sir," said the boy as he tied the cub up.

The man made a string of the napkin from the luncheon box and tied that to the string the boy had put around the cub's neck. He gave the money to the three boys. They were delighted with the money and ran away laughing and talking.

The man's friend grumbled, "You have queer tastes. What on Earth are you going to keep the fox for?"

"That is a rude question," bristled the man. "If we had not interfered, the cub would have lost its life. If we hadn't seen what happened, there would have been no help for it. But how could I stand by and see life taken? It was only a little bit of money to save the cub, but even if it had cost a fortune I should not have begrudged it. I thought you knew my heart. I see how mistaken I have been with you. From this day, our friendship ends!"

He said this with such firmness that his friend bowed to him with his hands on his knees. "Indeed, indeed. I am filled with admiration at your goodness of heart. I mistakenly thought that you might want to use the cub as a sort of decoy to lead the old ones to you. I am truly ashamed of myself."

The man who had the fox on a string said, "Really! Was that what you thought? Please forgive me for my violent words."

The two friends then examined the cub and saw that it had a slight wound in its foot. It could not walk. While they were pondering what to do, they saw the herb called Doctor's Nakase, which was just sprouting. They rolled up a little of it in their fingers and applied it to the cub's foot.

Then they took out some boiled rice from their lunch box and offered it to the cub, but it refused their offer. They petted and stroked it gently on the back. It seemed that the cub was in less pain now, so the friends were commenting on the healing power of the herb. Then they saw the two old foxes sitting by the side of some stacks of rice straw opposite them.

"Look there! The old foxes have come back. They are worried for the safety of their cub. Let's set it free." And with these words they untied the string around the cub's neck and headed it toward the spot where the old foxes sat. With one bound it dashed to its parents' side and licked them all over for joy. And strangely, it seemed as if the old foxes bowed to give their thanks to the friends.

Feeling tenderhearted, the two friends went off to a pretty place, took out the wine bottle and food and ate and drank. After the pleasant day they had together, they were firmer friends than ever.

The one who saved the fox cub's life was a successful businessman and lived a life that did not have the trials of the average person. He was married and had a son. But then, some time after saving the cub, a strange disease attacked the man's son in his tenth year. The disease defied all the physicians' skill and drugs. At last a famous physician prescribed the liver taken from a live fox which would effect a cure. The physician told the father, "If the liver taken from a live fox does not cure the boy, the most expensive medicine in the world will not be able to do it."

When the parents heard this, they were at their wits' end. They sought the advice of a wise old man who lived high in the mountains. They explained the situation with their son. "Even though our child should die for it," they told the wise man, "we will not ourselves deprive other creatures of their lives. Possibly you, who live among the mountains, might hear when people go out fox hunting. We don't care what price we have to pay for a fox's liver. We will buy one for any expense." The wise old man promised to help them.

In fact, the night of the following day, there came a messenger from the wise old man. "I have come from the wise old man of the mountains. Last night the fox's liver that you required fell into his hands. He sent me here to bring it to you." The messenger held out a small jar, adding, "In a few days he will let you know the price."

"Tell your man of the mountains that I am greatly pleased and grateful to him. This kindness is all that can save my son's life," the father told the messenger.

His wife came out and received the jar with every mark of respect and politeness. "We must make a present to the messenger," she told her husband.

"Indeed sir, that is not necessary. I have already been paid for my trouble," said the messenger as he bowed.

"Well, at least, you must stay the night here and rest," said the father.

"Thank you sir, but I have a relation in the next village whom I have not seen for a long while, and I will stay the night with him," and so he took his leave and went away.

The parents lost no time in sending word to the physician that they had received the fox's liver. The very next day the doctor came and compounded a medicine for the boy that at once produced a positive effect. There was great joy in the household.

Three days after this, the wise old mountain man came to the house. The wife rushed out to greet and welcome him. "How quickly you fulfilled our wishes. How kind you are to send at once the cure. The doctor prepared the medicine and now our boy can get up and walk about the house. It is all owing to your great goodness."

"Wait!" cried the guest, who did not know what to make of the joy of the two parents. "What you asked me to do turned out to be an impossibility. I have come to commiserate with you. I don't understand why you are so grateful to me."

"We are thanking you, sir," replied the master of the house, bowing with his hands on the ground, "for the fox's liver which we asked you to obtain for us."

"I do not know anything about the fox's liver. There must be some mistake here," advised the old man.

"Well, this is very strange indeed. Four nights ago, a man of about thirty-six years of age came with a verbal message from you. He gave us the liver that you had obtained for us," the father explained. "When we asked the price, he said he would come and tell us the price in the future. When we invited him to spend the night with us, he answered that he planned to stay with a relative in the next village. Then he left."

The visitor was more and more amazed. Leaning his head on one side in deep thought he confessed that he knew absolutely nothing about any of this. After a bit more discussion, the old man left.

That night there appeared at the pillow of the master of the house, a woman of about thirty-two years of age. She said, "I am the fox that lives in the mountain. Last spring, when I was taking my cub out to play, it was carried off by some boys and only saved by your goodness. When calamity struck your house, I thought I might be of use to you. I killed my cub and took out its liver. I then took up the disguise of the messenger and brought the liver to you."

As she said this, the fox began to cry. The husband sat up in bed and his wife awoke. "Why are you weeping?" she asked her tearful husband.

"Last spring, when I was out for a pleasant day I saved the life of a fox's cub. I told you about it at the time," her husband told her as he wiped away at his tears. "When I talked with the old man of the mountain, I told him that I would not be the means of killing a fox on purpose even to save my son. Then I asked him to buy the liver of a fox from any hunter he might come across. How the foxes came to hear of this I do not know. However, the foxes to whom I had shown kindness killed their own cub and took out the liver. The old fox disguised as a messenger brought the liver to us. That is why I cannot stop crying!"

Upon hearing this, the wife likewise was overcome by tears. They got up and lighted the lamp on the shelf on which the family altar stood. They spent the rest of the night in prayers and praises.

The next day they told everyone in their household and all of their relatives and friends what had happened. The story became the talk of the whole country. The now healthy boy selected the prettiest spot on their grounds and erected a shrine to the Fox God or *Inari Sama*. There it stands to this day, to remind us of the kindly man and the grateful foxes.

Following is another story that explains how our world came to be. It shows an appreciation of the Earth and everything on it.

## Tibetan Creation
## (Tibet)

Empty. Great void. That was all there was in the beginning until gentle winds stirred, thickened, and formed the thunderbolt scepter. It created the clouds and began the cycle of clouds and rain. Over the years the rain became a primeval ocean. The winds churned the ocean and the Earth rose.

The center of the world was the great, four-sided mountain made of precious stones and endless other beautiful things. This center of the world was surrounded by seven lakes within seven golden mountains. Four worlds took shape with distinct inhabitants. The East World was shaped like the half moon, and their peoples lived for five hundred years with bodies like giants and half-moon-shaped faces. The Western World was like the sun in shape. The people of the Western World were also large and lived for five hundred years. Their faces were shaped like the sun. They kept many kinds of cattle.

The Land of the North was square and inhabited by people with square faces who lived for a thousand years or more. Everything was abundant there. They lived an effortless life until the last seven days of their life when pain and mental torture attacked. They were doomed to die and suffer monstrously.

The World of the South had no pain or sickness, and everyone lived in contentment and contemplation. Each being emitted a pure light. This peaceful life ended when they noticed a cream-like substance on the surface of the Earth and tasted it. Thereafter they ate nothing else. Their powers diminished and were lost. Darkness came and the inhabitants became human beings.

There were other changes in the World of the South. People became greedy and wicked. Women were created, and soon children were born. People became so nasty, real suffering became common. The people gathered together and selected a king who taught the people to live peacefully.

In this story, you can easily see how the rock could represent the Earth or the world. Native Americans believe that everything has life. The gifts in the story could be symbols of the work we do in the world—our treasures, the very best that we can leave behind when we are gone.

The Earth's gifts are many. In this Native American tale, the Earth has even given us the gift of story.

## Where Stories Come From (Seneca, Huron, and Wyandot)

In another time long before this one, there was a boy who hunted daily in the woods for food. While on these trips he used to sit down beside a great rock to fix his bows or work on new arrow points. One day while sitting beside the rock, he heard a voice. "Let me tell you a story," it said.

The boy looked carefully around him and then circled the rock looking for the owner of the voice. He decided that it must be a magic rock that had the ability to talk. Even though he was afraid, he asked the rock, "What story do you want to tell me?"

"Before I start, you must give me a gift. Then I will tell you an ancient story that will explain many things to you," said the voice.

"This morning I killed this pheasant. Will this do as a present?" asked the boy as he carefully placed the bird on top of the boulder.

"Yes, it will do nicely. Come back in the twilight, and I will tell you about another time and the way of the world during that time," came the answer from the stone.

Just as the sun was ready to set below the far distant hillside, the boy returned to the rock. He settled down on the moss beside the stone, and the voice began:

"Since there was no Earth, the first people lived beyond the sky. The people had a great chief who had a beautiful daughter whom he loved dearly. But the girl became sick, and nothing could be found to cure her.

"The great chief consulted the wise old man who knew many things. The wise old man told the chief to dig up a large tree and lay the sick girl beside the hole. So the chief ordered his son to dig up an especially fine tree. Because there were many strong young men and they cared deeply for both their chief and his daughter, they dug a huge hole. Suddenly, before they could lift the tree out, the tree fell right down through the bottom of the hole. Worst of all, the girl fell along with it.

"Below there was a vast sea of water that had two swans floating on it. The swans became alarmed at a sudden thunderclap and looked up. Just as they did, they saw the sky fall apart, and they watched the huge tree fall into the water. The waves made by the gigantic tree hadn't calmed down before the swans saw a girl also falling from the sky. The swans could see that she was quite beautiful and didn't want her to drown or get hurt, so they swam to her. They knew they needed help to support her, though, so they swam to the Great Turtle, who was the master of all the animals. The great Turtle announced to all the assembled animals that this beautiful girl falling from the sky was a sign of future good fortune. He explained that they needed to find where the tree had sunk because it had earth entwined in its roots. He told them to bring back some of the earth to put on his back and make an island for the girl to live on.

"One of the animals asked the great Turtle how they would know where to look, and the answer was that the swans would lead them because they had seen where the tree had fallen.

"The swans did indeed remember where the tree had splashed into the water. Three of the animals were chosen to dive for the earth. First Otter, then Muskrat, and then Beaver. One after the other each dived to the depths, and one after the other, when each animal came back from the dive, it rolled over so exhausted that it died. After them, many other animals tried to bring up some earth, but each met the same fate. The last animal to volunteer was the old lady Toad. She made the dive and was below for a long time. All of the animals thought that she, too, was lost.

"At last she surfaced with a splash and a gasp and spit a mouthful of earth onto the back of the Great Turtle. Then she gave another gasp and died.

"The earth old lady Toad had brought up was magical and started to grow. It grew until it was as big as an island, and then the maiden was set down on it by the two white swans. They continued to swim around the island, and it grew and grew until it became the world island we know today."

When the voice had finished, it told the boy that his eyelids were drooping, his head was nodding, and that he was about to fall asleep. "It will be better if you come back tomorrow evening, and I will tell you more of the story. Remember to bring my present," said the boulder.

The next evening as dusk was falling, the boy returned to the rock with a string of rabbits. He put them carefully on top of the stone and sat down to hear the next story.

The voice began, "This new world, wonderful as it was, had a big problem. It was dark. Everywhere it was dark. There was no light anywhere. Great Turtle called all the animals together again to find a solution to the darkness. They decided to put a great light high in the sky. The next problem was that there was no one who could do this. Great Turtle turned to Little Turtle and asked her if she could do this great task. Little Turtle thought and then shyly offered that she might be able to climb the dangerous unknown path to the sky. Everyone invoked their own magical powers to help Little Turtle. Their magic formed a great black cloud that was full of clashing rocks that made lightening whenever they smashed together.

"Brave Little Turtle climbed into this cloud and was carried around the sky. She collected all the lightning she could find as she went. She made a big bright ball out of it, and then she threw this ball as far as she could into the sky. She looked at it all and decided that more light was needed, so she gathered more lightning for a smaller ball. She again threw it as far into the sky as she could. The first big ball became the sun, and the second smaller ball became the moon.

"Great Turtle studied the sky and then ordered the burrowing animals to make holes in the corners of the sky so that the sun and moon could go down through one and climb up again through the other as they circled the sky. Great Turtle bent his neck to look at the sky and smiled. Now there was day and night."

The boy returned to the rock each evening with a gift and heard more stories. His friend became curious about where he went each night. The boy told him that he went to listen to stories. The friend wondered what stories were, but the boy couldn't explain them. So he told his friend to go with him that night to find out for himself. As the sun glowed red over the horizon, the boy and his friend placed gifts on top of the storytelling stone. They heard more amazing stories and then went home to their beds.

The news of the stone and the stories swept through the village, and the boys were asked to lead their people to the place where the stone rested in the Earth. The people took the meat of deer with them that they left respectfully on the top of the rock. They all marveled over the stories they heard that night. They learned things that even the wisest among them had never known. And so the stone continued to tell the stories for four years. Then, all the tales had been told.

That last evening after all the others had gone, the boulder told the boy to stay. "When you are old and not able to hunt, tell these stories to others. But make sure that the people give you something in return for them," said the stone. After the voice of the rock had told the boy this, it became silent and never spoke again.

And so it was that as an old man he told stories to everyone who would come to him to listen. Listeners gladly gave him tobacco, furs, meats, and feathers. This is the way stories came to be and why there are many stories in the world today. The people from the world before ours gave us the strong, wonderful stories that we tell one another even today.

# APPENDIX I:
# HEALING BELIEFS AND LORE

## Beliefs and Practices
## Throughout the World

Many lands throughout the world have places of healing and faith, such as the Shrine of Lourdes, where the faithful have reported miracle cures. The folklore of Scotland is rich with healing practices. On the Isle of Skye, for instance, there is a well with water reputed to cure all diseases instantly. In the southwestern United States, there are numerous hot springs that Native Americans used to aid in healing. Today current residents of the Southwest continue to use these springs. In Yellowstone Park, even the bison "take the hot baths" to ease aches and pains.

Beliefs about the utensils that are used in healing are also legendary. One such belief from Scotland was that water (from beneath the bridge over which the dead and the living pass, meaning funerals went over the bridge) was given to sick children with a wooden ladle to avoid using utensils made of metal.

Finns, Scandinavians, Russians, and Native Americans, as well as people of many other cultures, maintain that sweating cures from saunas, steam baths, and sweathouses, often accompanied by traditional rituals, are possible.

In a chapter on the importance of highland folklore, Donald A. MacKenzie, a Scottish folklorist, says that when an individual became seriously ill, the women baked cakes. They left them on an ancient standing stone. If the cakes were "taken" before the next morning, it was believed that the patient would recover. These are just a few healing folk traditions.

For the Native Americans, Celts, and many other world groups, the symbol of the circle is important in healing and in life. Native Americans built their homes (tepees or wigwams) in circles. The sweat bath is also circular. Their drums are round. They danced in circles. Life, from birth to death, is circular. Seasons pass as the circle of life. The medicine wheel (such as the one in the Bighorn Mountains in Wyoming) is a sacred circle for rituals of healing. During ceremonies at a medicine wheel, people are asked to share what is in their hearts. As they do this, a talking stick is passed around the circle in a sunwise direction.

Thirty-five rocks are used in the construction of a medicine wheel, and a special rock, or horns or antlers, are placed in the center. Sometimes ceremonies at the medicine wheel are used for healing circles, connecting people with the Earth Mother. Stone Henge and other archeological remains of ancient cultures also incorporate the symbol of circle.

Some trees (such as the oak) have been considered to be the dwelling places of the gods. The world tree of Scandinavian myth is an ash or rowan. It was believed that if you passed a child through a cleft in an ash tree, he or she would be cured of ruptures or rickets. The astringent sap of the ash was given to children in Scotland as a protection against witchcraft. If you had warts, it was said that you could lose them by rubbing them with a piece of bacon, then sticking the bacon under the bark of an ash tree. So trees were not only considered sacred but also held healing powers.

The Pennsylvania Dutch people have maintained many beliefs that originated in the cultures of the old countries from which they came. To *brauche* is "to heal," usually through prayers, blessings, herbs, and other plants. My own grandmother cut herself while working out in the fields with a sickle. The healer, who also was out there working, applied some fresh cow dung to the wound. It worked but left her with permanent ghostly white skin where the wound had been. For further information on the beliefs of the Pennsylvania Dutch, cures, and plant legends, refer to *In Days Gone By* (folklore and traditions of the Pennsylvania Dutch) by Audrey Burie Kirchner and Margaret R. Tassia (Libraries Unlimited, 1996).

## Navajo Health Care System

For centuries, the Navajos believed they needed only wind, water, earth, and sacred traditions to effectively prevent illness and heal themselves spiritually and physically. Traditional Navajos feel the survival of the medicine man is vital to their survival. Medicine men are, for the most part, responsible for all the teaching and spiritual aspects of the community. The Navajos still rely on their ceremonies for their health care and their mental care as well.

"We must give the medicine men respect equivalent to doctors," said Arizona Senator Jack Jackson,* a Navajo. He argues that spirituality is based on the teaching that you exist within the universe with Mother Earth and Father Sky. He has also stated that "Many of our older people live to be one hundred years old and never went to a hospital. They live by the laws of the universe."

---

*Interview March 26, 1999.

# Foods That Are Taken When Ill
# (Hmong)

When you are ill, is there a particular dish you eat, such as the popular remedy of chicken soup and rice? This common cure is so well known that it is referred to as "Jewish penicillin." Other cultures have developed variations of such cures for a variety of needs. The following recipe is from the Hmong people from South East Asia.

## *New Mother's Menu for the First Thirty Days After Giving Birth*

2 quarts water
1 stalk lemongrass
1 chicken, or a turkey or a Cornish hen
Cilantro
Green onions
Salt and black pepper to taste

Directions: Add all of the ingredients to a large pot. Cover. Bring to a boil. Reduce the heat and simmer until cooked. Skim off the chicken scum. Remove the chicken and cut it into small pieces. Serve the chicken with steamed rice. The broth can be drunk either hot in winter or cool in the summer.

Hmong traditions also dictate that someone who is sick should not eat garlic, onion, cucumber, hot pepper, or any vegetables or fruits that are sour. Furthermore, sick people should eat only boiled and steamed food, no stir-fried, malodorous, or oily food.

Reprinted with special permission of North American Syndicate.

# Folk Medicine

### Earth's Bounty—Healing with Herbs

The world of plants and critters is a virtual gold mine of new chemical compounds. Today we are learning the scientific basis of some of these traditional folk remedies are based on. In fact, many of them have potential for future benefits to humanity. This is one of the reasons for concern over the rapid disappearance of rain forests—plants may be eliminated before they are ever discovered and analyzed for their medicinal potential.

*Caution:* The following comments and list of folk remedies are in no way meant to be prescriptive. Not all herbal remedies are effective and, in fact, nature can be a dangerous drugstore. Some herbs have harmful side effects, and even the beneficial herbs can be toxic if abused. People taking prescription medications should consult their pharmacist before using herbal remedies to be sure that there are no interactions.

Some interesting facts: Ancient healers dried plants to make medicines. Our word *"drug"* comes from an old German word meaning "to dry." For centuries, the ancient Arabs had a monopoly on the spice market. To protect their interests, traders would invent frightening stories of how and where the spices were grown. Cassia, a type of cinnamon, was said to grow in shallow lakes guarded by winged animals, while true cinnamon was rumored to grow only in deep glens infested with poisonous snakes.

Folklorists and researchers agree that cod liver oil is good for arthritis. Folklorists have long believed that cod liver oil works by "oiling" the joints. Now researchers concur that fatty fish (such as salmon, mackerel, and herring), as well as cod and shark-liver oils, contain beneficial fatty acids that appear to slow the body's production of inflammatory agents linked to arthritis. There is also evidence that these fatty acids help protect against heart disease and psoriasis. Aunt Minnie's instructions to take one tablespoon of cod liver oil along with two tablespoons of vinegar each morning may not be so foolish after all!

In the meantime, a Scottish mixture of rhubarb, ginger, and magnesia was until quite recently the world's most frequently prescribed medication.

Today researchers indicate that we can "flea-proof" ourselves with brewer's yeast. Humans produce a flea-repelling odor when yeast is metabolized through the sweat glands. (Because dogs' sweat glands are limited to their noses and pads, yeast unfortunately does not work for them.)

Folk tradition holds that for heartburn, you should use something alkaline (e.g., seltzer or club soda) to neutralize the acid and wash it back down into the stomach. Scientists today confirm the effectiveness of this practice.

These are a few examples of the concurrence of modern medicinal practice and traditional, folkloric remedies and beliefs. The uses of plants and flowers may be common to cultures worldwide, part of specific cultural lore, or known only to a culture's healers. All peoples have used natural remedies for health disorders; sometimes these beliefs and practices are part of religion. In some cultures, healers learn their practices through special initiations, dreams, ordeals, or through their experiences as an apprentice to an older healer. Some healers use symbolic objects that strengthen their powers, such as rattles, drums, masks, and fetishes. In the American southwest, Hispanic folk seek the advice of a *curandero* (healer). Believing that all healing derives from God, the *curanderos* rely heavily on religious paraphernalia such as crosses, pictures of saints, and holy water.

However, *curanderos* also are adept at herbal healing. What are some of the items you would find in their little black bags? Some of the herbs the *curanderos* use in their healing include the following:

> ❧ *Ajo* (garlic) is used to lessen toothaches by pressing one crushed clove against the gum. Garlic is also said to be good for stomach trouble and, after being thoroughly chewed and swallowed with cold water, can reduce gas.

∾ *Alhucema* (lavender) used to help eliminate phlegm, colic, headaches, and stomach trouble.

∾ *Anis* (anise), when made into a tea, is prescribed as a stomach remedy to overcome gas, nausea, and colic. Anis is also said to help soothe coughs. The seeds are ground up, toasted, mixed with whiskey, and rubbed on painful muscles to dispel discomfort.

∾ *Chamiso* (sage) is a well-known seasoning for meats, but this herb has also been used as a remedy for stomach ailments, nervous troubles, and fever. It is believed that sage can stop bleeding wounds and a wash with sage tea can help wounds of any kind heal more rapidly.

∾ *Manzanilla* (chamomile) is said to be beneficial for a weak stomach, colds, fever, bronchitis, and kidneys when used in a tea. Chamomile tea is also used as a rinse for hair, for earaches, and as a soothing way to calm oneself before bedtime.

∾ *Oregano* is used as a tea to ease cold symptoms. Ground powder is rubbed on the head for headache or on the body for fever. For sore throats, curanderos suggest it can be drunk as a tea, while also wearing some around the neck in a bag. (Refer to information about medicine bags in the introduction of "The Legend of Hackberry Hill.")

∾ *Poleo* (peppermint) makes a tea said to help reduce fever, chills, colic, dizziness, and stomach ailments. It is said to strengthen the heart muscle. Some people take peppermint in place of aspirin. It is also a refreshing body bath.

∾ *Raiz de osha del monte* (root of osha of the mountain) sheepherders used this plant to draw out poison from snakebites and to ward off reptiles. It was ground and used for stomach trouble (gas) and made as a tea for colds, pneumonia, and headaches.

∾ *Romero* (rosemary) was recommended as a remedy to reduce symptoms of colds, colic, and nervous conditions and also said to strengthen the eyes. Rosemary tea was used as a mouthwash to cleanse the mouth and gums, improve halitosis, or ease a sore throat. The oil is often used as perfume in ointments, liniments, and shampoos.

∾ *Yerba buena* (spearmint) was used to improve symptoms of indigestion, hangovers, and diarrhea. It was also used as a wash for wounds and sores.

For centuries general herbal and folk remedies have been collected and prescribed around the world. And herbal remedies are commonly shared between cultures. For example, in the West there is currently great interest in the remedies of Asian cultures. The following list contains only a small sample of the plant and herbal lore connected with healing and remedies. Nevertheless, herbal healing, plant magic and superstitions are recurrent themes and artifacts in stories throughout the world, and the storyteller's knowledge of this background enriches and verifies the story details.

## Herbal Lore from Around the World

∾ *Aloe vera.* A leaf or stalk from the plant was broken off and the gel used to help heal burns. It is said that the quicker you apply the gel, the better the effect. Today aloe is also used in many cosmetic products and skin creams.

∾ *Apples.* Two apples a day contain a day's dose of boron, which some believe can affect the electrical activity of your brain and help keep you mentally alert.

∾ *Beets.* These vegetables are said to help prevent kidney stones.

∾ *Bitterroot.* Pioneers and Indians considered the bitterroot a great delicacy. After peeling off the bark, they boiled, baked, or grated it. They added the root to flour or meal.

∾ *Blackberry juice.* Traditional healers administered half a glassful of blackberry juice, boiled with four tablespoons of honey and a pinch of clove or allspice, every one or two hours for diarrhea. (I have a personal story concerning blackberry wine to endorse this remedy.)

∾ *Bluebell.* American Indians boiled bluebell and made a tea to cure intestinal worms.

∾ *Boxwood juice.* This juice is said to stop nosebleeds.

∾ *Burdock.* At one time, the seed pods of the burdock plant were eaten to improve memory. Pioneers made tea from the roots to help purify the blood. A poultice made from boiling the leaves in salt water was said to be good for bruises and swelling.

∾ *Carrots.* These vegetables have long been considered good for one's eyesight, but they have also been used to lower the risk of strokes and relieve the aches and pains of arthritis.

∾ *Cattail.* The root of the cattail was often given to women and animals in labor. When boiled in milk, it was said to be effective against diarrhea. Cattail tea was drunk to help stop hemorrhaging.

∾ *Celery.* A stalk a day was recommended for treating high blood pressure.

∾ *Chicken soup.* A study in England confirmed that chicken soup's effect on flu and colds won out against Tylenol, which verifies this well-established Jewish folk tradition.

∾ *Chicory.* Chicory "coffee" is said to be good for liver and gall bladder ailments.

∾ *Cinquefoil.* A tea made from the leaves of this plant was used as a gargle and mouthwash and was said to cure inflammation of the mouth and gums. Witches supposedly used cinquefoil as a drug, rubbing it over their bodies to produce a trance-like state. Ironically, cinquefoil was also used as protection against witches.

∾ *Clove.* This spice is an ancient remedy for toothache pain.

∾ *Clover.* The blossoms of this plant were used to prepare a cough medicine. It was also brewed as a tea, to improve the texture of finger and toenails. The tea also purportedly thinned and purified the blood.

∾ *Columbine.* The juice of a fresh plant was used to cure jaundice or abdominal pains or to reduce swelling of the liver. This plant also was said to be a cure for measles and smallpox.

ꙮ *Corn (parched, cracked), brown corn meal.* Corn mixed with skim milk was used to treat diarrhea. Corn meal was also used for sties.

ꙮ *Cowpeas.* People once threw cowpeas onto the road to ensure fertility.

ꙮ *Cranberries.* These berries and their juice were used for bladder and urinary tract problems.

ꙮ *Daisy fleabane.* An old superstition said that if a pregnant woman wanted to know the gender of her baby, she should plant a seed of fleabane. If the flowers were tinged with pink, she would have a girl; if blue, she would have a boy.

ꙮ *Dandelion.* This "weed" contains high amounts of vitamins A and C and is used as a general antidote. An old mountain superstition says if you drink a cup of dandelion tea every morning and every evening, you will never have rheumatism. A Dutch legend says if you eat dandelion salad on Monday and Thursday, you will always be healthy.

ꙮ *Dwarf crested iris.* American Indians used this iris to treat sores on legs. The roots were cleaned and boiled and mashed into a poultice that was applied to the affected area. The Indians also used it as a cartharctic, a substance believed to purify one of negative emotions and tension.

ꙮ *Elderberry.* The juice of the black elderberry has been used to treat flu, coughs, and colds for more than two thousand years. In a recent scientific study, people who took elderberry extract experienced a significant improvement of flu symptoms within two days.

ꙮ *Field mustard.* A powder made from mustard seeds was eaten to improve the appetite and promote digestion.

ꙮ *Fireweed.* To relieve symptoms of asthma and whooping cough, young shoots of the fireweed were boiled and eaten like asparagus.

ꙮ *Flax seed.* Ground flax seed (or bread) was made into poultices for abscesses, burns, and sprains.

∾ *Forget-me-not.* Boiled in wine, forget-me-nots were said to be effective antidotes for the bite of an adder. Egyptians believed if you put the leaves over your eyes during the month of Thoth, you would have visions.

∾ *Foxglove.* Digitalis, used for heart conditions, is derived from this plant.

∾ *Garlic.* Superstition says that if you wear garlic around your neck it will protect you from vampires. In fact, raw garlic has antibacterial and antiviral properties and has been shown to help fight blood clots. The Chinese used garlic to treat high blood pressure and other cardiovascular ailments.

∾ *Gentian.* North American Indians used it to ease back pain. Pioneers added a little bit of gentian to gin or brandy to stimulate the appetite and aid in digestion.

∾ *Geranium.* A boiled root concoction of this plant was used to treat sore throats and mouth ulcers. Native Americans used it as a tonic and as an astringent. Northern tribes also used the powdered root when they were wounded to help coagulate the blood.

∾ *Ginger.* Powdered ginger was dissolved in water and taken to relieve the inflammation of arthritis. It was also believed to ease stomach upset and help circulation.

∾ *Ginseng.* In China, ginseng has been used as a heart stimulant as well as an aphrodisiac. Native Americans used it to treat coughs, headaches, and fevers.

∾ *Goldenrod.* American Indians used the goldenrod as a component in steam baths to steam pain out of an ailing person.

∾ *Hepatica.* This plant was thought to cure lung diseases.

∾ *Horseradish.* To get rid of warts, oldtimers rubbed them daily with horseradish. It was said that a spoonful of crushed horseradish and honey, taken three times per day, promoted kidney action.

❧ *Indian paintbrush.* Native Americans once used this plant to soothe burned skin and to ease the burning sting of the centipede. Indian women drank a concoction made from its roots to dry up menstrual flow.

❧ *Jack-in-the-pulpit.* American Indians used the powdered root to make flour. The pulp was applied to the forehead in an attempt to cure headaches.

❧ *Jimsonweed.* Native Americans would heat the leaves of the jimsonweed and apply them directly to burned skin to soothe it. American pioneers smoked the leaves like tobacco to relieve labored breathing.

❧ *Marsh mallow.* Old time herbalists said that one tablespoon of the mallows daily would keep one free of disease. It was said to be especially good for cramps and convulsions, bee stings, dandruff, and hair loss.

❧ *Mayapple.* The Shawnee tribe used the boiled root as a very strong laxative.

❧ *Milkweed.* The Quebec Indians used milkweed roots as a contraceptive. The Shawnee tribe used the white sap to remove warts.

❧ *Morning glory.* Leaves boiled in water and taken before breakfast were promoted as a gentle laxative.

❧ *Moss.* In the Okefenokee swamp in Georgia, a love potion was produced from the white moss from the skull of a murdered man. This practice came from the belief that the body of one whose life was prematurely terminated retained an unexhausted quantity of life force that can be drawn upon for therapeutic purposes or for love magic.

❧ *Mustard flour, crushed mustard seed.* Mixed with cold water or vinegar to make a paste, mustard was said to help with arthritic and gout conditions. Also used in mustard plasters chest colds, coughing, bronchitis and sore muscles.

❧ *Parsley and linden flowers* The Czechs treated sluggishness with tea brewed from these plants.

❧ *Phlox.* An extract made from phlox leaves was used as a laxative.

❧ *Pickle.* An extract made from pickle leaves was used as a laxative.

❧ *Pine rosin and sugar.* A mixture of these applied daily was used to treat abscesses.

❧ *Pokeweed.* An old mountain recipe says to wash and cook the stems and leaves of the pokeweed together and then boil and drain them several times. Eaten in the spring, it is said to revive the blood. The Algonquin tribe called the plant *puccoon,* which means "plant used for staining or dyeing."

❧ *Pumpkin, crushed pumpkin seed tea.* This plant said to be an effective treatment for kidney and bladder ailments.

❧ *Queen Anne's lace.* This flowering plant had a reputation for curing internal parasites such as worms. Eating the center purple floret was once thought to cure epilepsy.

❧ *Rose.* A wash made from two or three flowers steeped in four ounces of warm water was said to assuage eye irritations of all kinds.

❧ *Sage.* For generations American Indians have burned wild sage in purifying ceremonies. It has also been used as a remedy for stomach upset, nervous troubles, and fever. It is said it will stop bleeding wounds, and when made into a tea and used as a wash will help them heal rapidly. An old time remedy for a stuffed nose says to place two handfuls of sage leaves in boiling water and breathe in the vapors. Leaves rubbed on the skin are said to repel insects.

❧ *Sassafras.* The roots of the sassafras tree were boiled into a tea and believed to calm queasy stomachs. This plant is very aromatic.

❧ *Sheep Sorrel.* Chopped leaves were eaten with a cup of wine to soothe queasy stomachs.

❧ *Skunk cabbage.* Once sought after as a contraceptive, skunk cabbage was thought to cause permanent sterility in men or women who took one tablespoon three times a day for three weeks. Native Americans smelled the crushed leaves for headaches. Boiled root was used as a cough syrup.

∾ *Snakeroot (powdered).* This plant was often prescribed for headaches.

∾ *Snapdragon.* Choctaws applied them directly to the head to relieve a headache. The smoked leaves were used for respiratory ailments. Native Americans also boiled the leaves and applied them to body joints to relieve the aches of rheumatism.

∾ *Soapwort.* This plant has been used to clean and lightly bleach fabric. It is also quite effective in restoring the color and sheen to old china and glass.

∾ *Tabasco sauce.* Ten to twenty drops of Tabasco sauce dissolved in a glass of water and then gargled or sipped were said to relieve congestion better than cough drops.

∾ *Tansy.* It was believed that a leaf on the navel of a pregnant woman would induce childbirth. A powder made from the leaves was used to kill fleas and lice.

∾ *Tobacco (chewing).* Pioneers applied fresh chewed tobacco to wounds to sterilize them. After the wound healed, the skin was much whiter than surrounding tissue.

∾ *Turpentine and sweet oil.* A mixture of one part turpentine and two parts sweet oil was rubbed into the skin to relieve sore backs.

∾ *Vinegar and brown paper bandage.* Brown paper soaked in vinegar was applied to sprains and strains.

∾ *Violet.* The leaves are high in vitamins A and C and can be eaten raw in salads or cooked like greens. Made into a tea, violets are said to help get rid of a headache. Violet poultices were used in treating ulcers and bedsores.

∾ *Watercress.* Today this leafy vegetable is used in salads and as garnish. In ancient Rome watercress was used to quiet deranged minds.

∾ *White oak bark, calcium, myrrh.* The Amish use these for circulation problems.

∾ *Wild lupine.* In the thirteenth century, lupine was used in healing the spot left after an infant's umbilical cord was cut.

ॐ *Wild onion.* The Winnebago and Dakota tribes used the onion for treating bee and wasp stings. The eastern tribes would slice an onion, wrap it in cloth, and tie it around their wrists when they were ill. They believed it drew out fever from the body. If worn around the neck, it would prevent disease from entering the body.

ॐ *Yams, beans.* The Yoruba people of western Nigeria have the highest rate of fraternal twinning in the world. This is attributed to their diet of yams and beans. Twins are said to be a blessing reserved only for the poor and kind-hearted. They say twins bring luck and are given to the poor to make them rich.

ॐ *Yarrow.* The most frequent use of yarrow was to staunch the flow of blood from a wound. Settlers of the West called yarrow "nosebleed plant" because they found it effective in stopping nose bleeding. The leaves were ground up, boiled, and made into a salve that was applied to wounds. According to legend, Achilles always carried the plant with him to treat wounded soldiers during the Trojan Wars. American Indians soothed bruises and burns with it.

ॐ *Yew trees.* Scientists have discovered the bark of the yew tree is another miracle drug targeting cancer, and the drug that has been developed is taxol. Contact a druggist for further information.

Recently scientists have been prospecting for medicines in remote areas throughout the world, as well as North American woodlands. In North America, the woodlands have given us taxol, a weapon against ovarian cancer, as well as ivermectin, which kills livestock parasites. Today's researchers are learning important information of cures from remote populations where these medicines have been used over the ages. For more information on herb lore and the medicinal uses of herbs, consult the following sources:

Brodin, Michael B. *The Over-the-Counter Drug Book.* New York: Pocket Books.

Griffith, H. Winter. *Vitamins, Herbs, Minerals & Supplements.* Tucson, AZ: Fisher Books.

McCaleb, Rob. *Encyclopedia of Popular Herbs*. Boulder, CO: Herb Research Foundation, 2000.

    This is a collection of the latest scientific research and information about the most popular herbal medicines. The foundation has a library of scientific articles on clinical trials, safety records, and history of medicinal herbs that includes more than 250,000 documents. The Foundation also publishes a newsletter and magazine called *Herbal-Gram*.

Schuster, Angela M. H. "On the Healer's Path, a Journey through the Maya Rain Forest." *Archaeology* 54, Number 4 (July/August, 2001): 34–38.

Travis, John. "Building Better Bandages." *Science News* 155, No. 25 (July 19, 1999): 396–397.

# Proverbs and Quotes

Take the proverb to thy heart, take and hold it fast.
People live Now and Tomorrow, learning, always,
from the past.

*Anonymous*

    Proverbs are defined as the "wisdom of many, and the wit of one." These lean, didactic, aphoristic statements are nuggets of truth. The universal message is expressed in concrete, poetic language, but the meaning is deeper and more abstract. Proverbs are subtle symbols and guides through the thicket of social life. Plain people making everyday observations, philosophers, and writers of literature have contributed to this pool of proverbs. What are some of the proverbs about health and healing? Let's take a look.

❧ Patients with the same disease sympathize with each other. (Japanese)

❧ When a Jewish farmer eats a chicken, one of them is sick. (Jewish)

❧ When the Czar has a cold all Russia coughs. (Russian)

❧ Prevention is better than cure.

❧ Good men must die but death cannot kill their names.

✺ An apple a day keeps the doctor away.

✺ Illness brings fame to the wealthy but the poor never attain fame, not even in death. (Finnish)

✺ Laughter prolongs life. (Finnish)

✺ A good story fills the belly. (Irish)

✺ Sleep is medicine to a child. (Finnish)

✺ Sing and cares disappear. (Polish)

✺ Eat to live, not live to eat. (Greece)

✺ Joy, moderation, and rest shut out the doctors. (Germany)

✺ No one dies twice. (Finnish)

✺ Don't burn your candle at both ends.

✺ Life is not a problem to be solved, but a gift to be enjoyed.

✺ Physician, heal thyself.

✺ The burned child fears the fire.

✺ Early to bed, early to rise, makes a man healthy, wealthy and wise. (Benjamin Franklin)

✺ Sauna is the poor man's drugstore. (Finnish)

✺ If a sauna, whiskey and tar do not help, the disease is fatal. (Finnish)

✺ Time heals all wounds.

✺ People are the home. (African)

✺ There is nothing in the world you don't need. (Chinese)

Here are some other interesting comments about sickness and health.

> I have never been anywhere but sick. In a sense sickness is a place more instructive than a long trip to Europe, and it's always a place where there's no company, where nobody can follow. Sickness before death is a very appropriate thing and I think those who don't have it miss one of God's mercies.
>
> *Flannery O'Connor in* The Habit of Being
> (New York: Farrar, Straus & Giroux, 1979).

> News was brought to Rabbi Moshe Leib that his friend the rabbi of Berditchev had fallen ill. On the Sabbath he said his name over and over and prayed for his recovery. Then he put on new shoes made of morocco leather, laced them up tight and danced.
>
> A zaddik who was present said: "Power flowed forth from his dancing. Every step was a powerful mystery. An unfamiliar light suffused the house, and everyone watching saw the heavenly hosts join in his dance."
>
> *Martin Buber,* Tales of the Hasidim:
> The Later Masters
> (New York: Schocken Books, 1964, p. 30).

> When you have a terminal illness, you either have hope or freedom. I've chosen freedom. I try to live for the day.
>
> *From Joe Katka,*
> *"AIDS victim reflects on life and death,"*
> Indian Country News, *October 22, 1992.*

> Health is the state about which medicine has nothing to say. Sanctity is the state about which theology has nothing to say.
>
> *W. H. Auden,*
> The Atlantic, *May, 1970. p. 185.*

When the earth is sick and polluted, human health is impossible. . . . To heal ourselves we must heal our planet and to heal the planet we must heal ourselves.

*Bobby McLeod from*
Voices of the First Day
*by Robert Lawlor*
(Rochester, VT: Inner Traditions Intl., 1991, p. 90).

# APPENDIX II:
# ROOTS OF WESTERN MEDICINE

## Hippocratic Oath

Hippocrates, a Greek who lived in the fifth century B.C., founded the most successful medical "school" of antiquity. His followers developed an oath embodying a code of ethics that is usually taken by those about to begin medical practice. Interestingly, Hippocrates himself did not write the oath. Today this oath continues to inform the practice of medicine in the Western world, providing an important message for all times.

### *Hippocratic Oath*

I swear by Apollo Physician and Asclepius and Hygieia and Panaceia and all the gods and goddesses, making them my witnesses, that I will fulfill according to my ability and judgment this oath and this covenant:

To hold him who has taught me this art as equal to my parents and to live my life in partnership with him, and if he is in need of money to give him a share of mine, and to regard his offspring as equal to my brothers in male lineage and to teach them this art—if they desire to learn it—without fee and covenant; to give a share of precepts and oral instruction and all the other learning to my sons and to the sons of him who has instructed me and to pupils who have signed the covenant and have taken an oath according to the medical law, but to no one else.

I will apply dietetic measures for the benefit of the sick according to my ability and judgment; I will keep them from harm and injustice.

I will neither give a deadly drug to anybody if asked for it, nor will I make a suggestion to this effect. Similarly I will not give to a woman an abortive remedy. In purity and holiness I will guard my life and my art.

I will not use the knife, not even on sufferers from stone, but will withdraw in favor of such men as are engaged in this work.

Whatever houses I may visit, I will come for the benefit of the sick, remaining free of all intentional injustice, of all mischief and in particular of sexual relations with both female and male persons, be they free or slaves.

What I may see or hear in the course of the treatment or even outside of the treatment in regard to the life of men, which on no account one must spread abroad, I will keep to myself holding such things shameful to be spoken about.

If I fulfill this oath and do not violate it, may it be granted to me to enjoy life and art, being honored with fame among all men for all time to come; if I transgress it and swear falsely, may the opposite of all this be my lot.

# The Caduceus

In the Western world, the *caduceus* is the symbol of the medical profession. Here is some background information on this emblem of medicine and the healing arts.

### *The Caduceus*

In Greek mythology, Hermes was a god of music, travel, and communication. Hermes obtained his golden herald's rod from his brother Apollo. Hermes spoke magical words, and his rod was an instrument of enchantment. The caduceus is charged with magic and power.

Hermes was traveling through Arcadia when he came upon two snakes that were fighting. The serpents were intertwined with one another and locked in deadly combat when Hermes put down his staff between them. At that moment they climbed up its shaft in a perpetual dance.

In the *Iliad*, Hermes used the wand to charm people asleep and elsewhere he used it to conduct the souls of the dead. Because of its magical powers, the rod made dreams come true. It became the symbol of a golden age of peace and plenty.

In a metaphysical sense, the staff represents the World Axis at the center of the universe, around which all things revolve. The coils of the serpent represent the veils of time and space that are wrapped around the timeless center. The cosmic axis links together the heavens, the human world, and the underworld; it is a place of power, divine creativity, and prophecy.

Because snakes shed their skins, they are a symbol of life and rejuvenation. The travels of the snakes up the World Axis signifies the growth of shoots of plants reaching for the sun. Life can be said to be a dance of opposites that involves destruction, rebirth, pain, and joy. What a noble symbol for the world of healing!

Is there some relationship between the Cadeceus and the Old Testament? Consider the following passage (Num. 21:4-9):

4. And they journeyed from mount Hor by the way of the Red Sea, to compass the land of Edom: and the soul of the people was much discouraged because of the way.

5. And the people spake against God and against Moses, Wherefore have ye brought us up out of Egypt to die in the wilderness? For there is no bread neither is there any water; and our soul loatheth this light bread.

6. And the Lord sent fiery serpents among the people, and they bit the people; and much people of Israel died.

7. Therefore the people came to Moses, and said, We have sinned, for we have spoken against the Lord, and against thee; pray unto the Lord, that he take away the serpents from us. And Moses prayed for the people.

8. And the Lord said unto Moses, Make thee a fiery serpent, and set it upon a pole: and it shall come to pass, that every one that is bitten, when he looketh upon it, shall live.

9. And Moses made a serpent of brass, and put it upon a pole: and it came to pass, that if a serpent had bitten any man, when he beheld the serpent of brass, he lived.

# BIBLIOGRAPHY

Allen, Barbara. *Guide to Bibliotherapy*. Chicago: American Library Association Editions, 1982.

Applebaum, David, Editor. *Parabola: Threshold* 25, no. 1 (February 2000).

Bear, Sun and Wabun. *The Medicine Wheel*. New York, NY: Prentice Hall, 1980.

Beith, Mary. *Healing Threads* (traditional medicines of the Highlands and Islands). Edinburgh, Scotland: Polygon, 1995.

Brun, Birgitte, Ernst W. Pedersen, and Marianne Runberg. *Symbols of the Soul: Therapy and Guidance Through Fairy Tales*. United Kingdom: Jessica Kingsley, 1993.

Campbell, Laura Ann, and Laura K. Campbell. *Storybooks for Tough Times*. Golden, CO: Fulcrum, 1999.

Cha, Dia, and Norma J. Livo. *Teaching with Folk Stories of the Hmong*. Englewood, CO: Libraries Unlimited, 2000.

Chinen, Allan. *Beyond the Hero: Classic Stories of Men in Search of Soul*. New York: Tarcher/Putnam, 1993.

——. *In the Ever After*. Wilmette, IL: Chiron Publications, 1992.

——. *Once upon a Midlife: Classic Stories and Mythic Tales to Illuminate the Middle Years*. New York: Tarcher, 1992.

Collodi, Carlo. *Adventures of Pinocchio*. New York: Macmillan, 1925.

Curry, Lindy Soon. *A Tiger by the Tail and Other Stories from the Heart of Korea*. Englewood, CO: Libraries Unlimited, 1999.

Draper, Ellen Dooling. *Parabola: Issue on Healing* XVIII, no. 1 (February 1993).

——. *Parabola: Hospitality* XV, no. 4. New York, NY: 1990.

Estes, Clarissa Pinkola. *Women Who Run with the Wolves*. New York: Ballantine Books, 1992.

——. *The Gift of Story*. New York: Ballantine Books, 1993.

Fitzhugh, Louise. *Harriet the Spy*. New York: Harper, 1964.

Heide, Florence Parry. *The Shrinking of Treehorn*. Illustrations by Edward Gorey. New York: Holiday House, 1971.

Hillman, James. *Healing Fiction*. Barrytown, NY: Station Hill, 1983.

Jacobs, Joseph. *English Fairy Tales*. New York: Dover, 1967.

Janos, Elisabeth, and Elizabeth Janos. *Country Folk Medicine: Tales of Skunk Oil, Sassafras Tea, and Other Old-Time Remedies*. New York: Budget Book Service, 1995.

Jones, Blackwolf, and Gina Jones. *Listen to the Drum*. Salt Lake City, UT: Commune-A-Key, 1995.

Kirchner, Audrey Burie, and Margaret R. Tassia. *In Days Gone By, Folklore and Traditions of the Pennsylvania Dutch*. Englewood, CO: Libraries Unlimited, 1996.

Kuskin, Karla. *Just Like Everyone Else*. New York: Harper & Row, 1959.

Livo, Norma J. *Celebrating the Earth: Stories, Experiences and Activities*. Englewood, CO: Libraries Unlimited, 2000.

——. *From Moon Cakes to Maize: Delicious World Folktales*. Golden, CO: Fulcrum, 1999.

——. *Troubadour's Storybag*. Golden, CO: Fulcrum, 1996.

——. *Who's Afraid...? Facing Children's Fears with Folktales*. Englewood, CO: Libraries Unlimited, 1994.

Livo, Norma J., and Dia Cha. *Folk Stories of the Hmong*. Englewood, CO: Libraries Unlimited, 1991.

Livo, Norma J., and George O. Livo. *The Enchanted Wood and Other Tales from Finland*. Englewood, CO: Libraries Unlimited, 1999.

Louis, Liliane Nerette. *When Night Falls, Kric! Krac!: Haitian Folktales*. Englewood, CO: Libraries Unlimited, 1999.

Lopez, Barry. *Crow and Weasel*. San Francisco: North Point Press, 1990.

MacKenzie, Donald A. *Scottish Folk-lore and Folk Life*. Glasgow, Scotland: Blackie and Son Limited, 1935.

Martin, Bill, Jr., and John Archambault. Illustrations by Ted Rand. *Knots on a Counting Rope*. New York: Henry Holt, 1987.

Mohr, Carolyn, Dorothy Nixon, and Shirley Vickers. Illustrated by Linda East. *Books That Heal: A Whole Language Approach*. Englewood, CO: Libraries Unlimited, 1991.

Pardeck, John T., and Jean A. Pardeck. *Bibliotherapy: A Clinical Approach for Helping Children*. Vol. 16 of *Special Aspects of Education*. The Netherlands: Gordon & Breach Science, 1993.

Pearl, Patricia. *Helping Children Through Books*. Portland, OR: Church and Synagogue, 1990.

———. *Helping Children Through Books: A Selected Booklist*. Portland, OR: Church and Synagogue, 1990.

Remen, Rachael Naomi. *Kitchen Table Wisdom: Stories That Heal*. New York: Berkeley Publishing, 1996.

———. *My Grandfather's Blessings: Stories of Strength, Refuge and Belonging*. New York: Riverhead Books, 2000.

Norman, Robert A., and Brenda Fewox, Editors. *Mother Nature, Father Time (Tales of Medicine)*. New Zealand: North Shore, 1998.

Roberts, Glenn, and Jeremy Holmes, Editors. *Healing Stories: Narrative in Psychiatry and Psychotherapy*. Oxford, England: Oxford University Press, 1999.

Rushworth, Stan. *American Healing: The Teaching Tales of Sam Woods*. Barrytown, NY: Station Hill, 1998.

Seik, Keigo. *Folktales of Japan*. Chicago: University of Chicago Press, 1963.

Simpkinson, Charles, and Anne Simpkinson, Editors. *Sacred Stories: A Celebration of the Power of Stories to Transform and Heal*. New York: HarperCollins, 1993.

Spagnoli, Cathy, and Paramasivam Samanna. *Jasmine and Coconuts: South Indian Tales*. Englewood, CO: Libraries Unlimited, 1999.

Stanley, Jacqueline D. *Reading to Heal: How to Use Bibliotherapy to Improve Your Life*. Boston: Element, 1999.

Steptoe, John. *The Story of Jumping Mouse*. New York: Lothrop, Lee & Shepard, 1984.

Stone, Richard. *The Healing Art of Storytelling: A Sacred Journey of Personal Discovery*. New York: Hyperion, 1996.

Storm, Hyemeyohsts. *Seven Arrows*. New York: Ballantine, 1972.

Suwyn, Barbara J. *The Magic Egg and Other Tales from Ukraine*. Englewood, CO: Libraries Unlimited, 1997.

Taylor, Eric K. *Using Folktales*. New York: Cambridge University Press, 2000.

Walsh, Edward L. *Unbound Spirit: Personal Stories of Transformation.* Long Beach, CA: Open Wings, 2000.

Yolen, Jane. *The Seeing Stick.* Illustrations by Remy Charlip and Demetra Maraslis. New York: Thomas Y. Crowell, 1977.

Zolotow, Charlotte. *William's Doll.* Illustrations by William Pene Du Bois. New York: Harper & Row, 1972.

## Internet

**Aging and Death in Folklore**
http://www.pitt.edu/~dash/aging.html

**American Association for Therapeutic Humor**
http://www.aath.org

**Resources and Products**
http://www.humorproject.com

## Organizations

National Storytelling Network, Special Interest Group, Healing Arts. Contact: Gail Rosen, 410-486-3551; e-mail: gailstory@aol.com

# Index